MUSE IN THE MACHINE

MUSE IN THE MACHINE

American Fiction and Mass Publicity

Mark Conroy

The Ohio State University Press
Columbus

Library of Congress Cataloging-in-Publication Data

Conroy, Mark.
  Muse in the machine : American fiction and mass publicity/Mark Conroy.
     p. cm.
  Includes bibliographical references and index.
  ISBN 0-8142-0962-9 (alk. paper)—ISBN 0-8142-9028-0 (cd-rom)
  1. American fiction—20th century—History and criticism. 2. Mass
media in literature. 3. American fiction—19th century—History and
criticism. 4. Authors and publishers—United States—History. 5. Literature publishing—United States—History. 6. Fiction—Marketing—
United States—History. 7. Authors and readers—United States—History. 8. Mass media—United States—History. I. Title.
  PS374.M38C66 2004
  813'.509—dc22

                            2004002172

Type set in Adobe Garamond.
Printed by Thomson-Shore, Inc.

9 8 7 6 5 4 3 2 1

contents

acknowledgments

T here are so many people to thank, I not only do not know where to begin; I am tempted not to begin at all. But some organizations and a few individuals must be mentioned by name. *The University of Windsor Review, Pynchon Notes,* and *Critique* have all published chapters of this book in earlier versions as articles. My home institution once provided me with a sabbatical year, during which this book project started to take its shape. Discussions with both students and colleagues have helped to refine some of my ideas. Henry Sussman, Allan Stoekl, and Walter A. Davis stand out for providing strategic advice and encouragement at critical moments. Bainard Cowan's commentary improved my project enormously, though any surviving weaknesses are my own fault. Heather Lee Miller, Karie Kirkpatrick, and Eugene O'Connor all shepherded the manuscript through press with great good humor and efficiency. Finally and above all, I thank the person to whom this book, flaws and all, is dedicated: Mary, the true and only muse.

Part One

Theoretical and Historical Prologue

chapter one

Introduction: Literature, Inc.

The history of literature has been the history of mass publicity. To adapt Walter Benjamin, almost every document of literary art has also been the artifact of an essentially commercial process of publication and distribution. Certainly the modern form taken by the literary as an institution since the late eighteenth century would have been impossible had not the publishing apparatus of the West generated it. This state of affairs is not in every way negative or crass, especially in view of the way publishing houses typically acknowledged competing pulls and tugs and were never thought to be merely pecuniary entities. In some ways, in fact, the impersonality of the market permitted an autonomy, and an anonymity, previously unavailable to writers. (The anonymity almost perished when electronic media placed new urgency on the book tour, though many nineteenth-century authors were also platform performers.) The helping hand of patronage could also be a dead hand weighing on its recipients, and much of the independence the romantic literary artist was able to declare resulted from the fact that literature was taken out of that circle of patronage and thrust into the great world.

Of course, surrendering the claustrophobia of patronage meant taking on the agoraphobia ("fear of the marketplace") attendant on the emerging arrangements. As the texts in this book attest, the partnership between author and publicity machine has always been necessary, above all since the rise of mass literacy. But like so many close partnerships, it has also been fraught with tension, subject to resentments and pique. This is especially inevitable with the collaboration between literary authors and the machinery of marketplace distribution, because part of the way a writer defines him- or herself as literary is by not being *too* good a partner to the mechanism of commerce. In their various ways, all the writers I treat dramatize the flaws and contradictions in the commercial cultural apparatus of their day; and in looking outward, they also look inward—to their own complicity in the process they critique and their own need to be outside it, or to seem to be.

It is by now a critical commonplace to sketch forth all the ways literary writers were responding to the welter of mass-cultural messages. Time and again we are informed that T. S. Eliot knew of and eulogized Marie Lloyd, that James Joyce loved and used techniques from the cinema, that Marianne Moore was really excited by advertising. True and useful as this emphasis is, it threatens to make our literary figures too cuddly and populist sounding. In truth, the greater awareness of mass culture on the part of modern writers is not really a mitigation of their suspicion of it. If anything, it may have aggravated those suspicions. What it did do is to increase their nostalgia for the kind of deep mythic resonance that the more successful mass-cultural products seem to attain with people. What should be added to an already raised awareness of how much influence the products of mass publicity have had on serious literature is a sense of how much dismay and fear literature has had of them: fear of being beaten by them and fear of joining them (at least on terms other than its own). The machine insists, in the end, on (its perception of) the audience, the muse on itself. But the muse still wants an audience and needs the machine to provide it. And this machine was a printing press long before it was supplemented by sight and sound.

Although the novelists I treat are late-nineteenth- and twentieth-century Americans, the riven nature of the modern literary enterprise goes back at least to romanticism. This may be the place to acknowledge that even if much of this study's material concerns the electronic media and their famed capacity for simulation—an issue for Nathanael West's *Day of the Locust*, Thomas Pynchon's *Crying of Lot 49* and Don DeLillo's *White Noise*—it is nonetheless the burden of my argument that the particular anxiety in these reflections on the media originates not merely from the evident competition between word and image (a competition where image seems destined to have the last word), but more from a long-standing condition of modern letters, one that implicates the very source of the literary as a category. I contend that the commercial configuration and the imperatives of the publicity apparatus are more disturbing to literary people than any later electronic technology could ever be, precisely because that apparatus was so vital to creating the conditions of their own emergence in their modern form. (In fact, there may be a sense in which the iconic form of electronic media production is actually reassuring to authors: there seems, after all, a natural divide between writing books and manipulating sight and sound. One is consigned to irrelevance, at worst, and this is a familiar condition for literature; but at least one is not seduced into complicity with the commercial apparatus.) This is why I do not consider this a study of the media primarily; it is more a glimpse at a much older and more persistent phenomenon of Western society: the commercial publicity apparatus. If the authors in this study seem suspicious, even disapproving, of this process, this ingratitude is understandable. The only possibility of being heard, since the era of patronage, is through this megaphone, and the people who own it determine what gets said by its means. Many changes have been brought about in this process with the advent of electronic media, and these will be taken into account. But the process itself has changed surprisingly little, and the same could well be said of the queasiness about the process on the part of the authors confronting it and caught up within it.

Pandora's Press: The Whored Muse

The growing post–Renaissance interest in fame as a possible route to life after death gives rise to the ideology of authorship. So goes the oft-told story, and for a reason. But a material ingredient of the concept of authorship, even if not the only begetter of the "onlie Begetter," is the development of commercial publishing and its replacement of gentlemanly patronage. Under that regime, the role of the poet or musician was primarily to solemnize certain occasions and to praise his patrons the rest of the time. This process often yielded very good results (J. S. Bach and Wolfgang Mozart come to mind). But the stance that grew up by the turn of the nineteenth century, the rebellious artist with whom we associate romanticism both English and continental, was inconceivable under such tutelage.[1]

The artistic sensibility, chief if not sole guarantor of the work of art according to Pierre Bourdieu, was far from the priority before the growth of publishing that it became afterward. For the personal "take" of artist on world to be the central fact of literary endeavor, it had to be possible for writers to confront a readership without the requirement of pleasing some specific set of people.[2] There is much said about the nostalgia of writers for patrons—and there have been twentieth-century writers (James Joyce and Robert Musil, for instance) who had much patronage—but the defenestration of the patron can be liberating as well as disquieting. Furthermore, the anonymous marketplace of letters almost necessitated at least the attempt at a personal style, if for no other reason then as a means of differentiating one's own writing from that of other people. In many instances, at first almost all, anonymity was itself a blessing of Grub Street economics, although that rapidly became less of an option. In any case, the fact that the author, named or not, was relatively unknown personally to the reader allowed an artful arrangement of self, a dramaturgy of the personality, to develop.[3] The essay form was just such a use of style to present personality.

Even though we can see that, by the time of Henry James's artist tales at least, personality and prose style have already been primly separated into their respective functions (the former iconic and promotional, the latter textual and literary), it is my impression that this was less if at all the case during the era of the English romantics. The tendency of romantic poets such as William Wordsworth to inscribe when the poem was "composed" constitutes itself as an open invitation to read the poem without any persona, as legitimately reflecting the author's sentiments. Furthermore, much as people like to exile the publicity-hungry Lord Byron from other, nobler souls, the reality is that the romantic poets saw the opportunity in the new modes of distribution for using the process of mass circulation itself against the mass culture of their day. More than that, their strategy revolved around the very populist idea of giving pleasure.[4] Even the inevitable twin to artistic sensibility—alienation—was more available as a stance to unaffiliated authors than it would have been to their patronized predecessors. After all, one had better not be alienated from the hand that feeds one.[5]

For all of these reasons, then, the anonymous and distant marketplace actually worked to foster the attitudes that seemed to spring up in opposition to it. This is true not only in the trivial sense that were it not for the marketplace there would be nothing to react against, but also in the strong sense that the preconditions for presenting the figure of an autonomous artist bravely breasting society's waves were met by moving from recipient of patronage to free agent. At the same time, this very freedom was underwritten by a different sort of bondage, and a harder one to fathom: to the public.[6] Michael McKeon is describing this soft indenture when he insists that "publication . . . participates in a system of commodity exchange in which the rewards of production and the release from paternalistic patronage are inseparable from an obligation to be consumed with some regularity."[7]

When they saw the formless and void chaos into which they had been thrust, literary people reacted by seeking smaller publics within the larger. (Just how determinate this "smaller public" often was helps account for how it could be thought that John Keats had been killed by a review.) The rejection of society, in this regard, could be read as the signal to a smaller, more select society to gather round the story tree—and so it was taken by various coterie audiences as the nineteenth century progressed.[8] It is not without reason that the growth of that very middle-class counterweight to the middle class known as bohemia comes along soon after the romantic era.[9] Regardless of their disdain for the mechanisms of civilization, though, authors romantic or bohemian never objected to being published, the usual prerequisite to being read. Add to that the fact that the individual sensibility so prized by literary people could only be highlighted properly when placed outside the circle of any obvious enfolding protection. Since the orphanage that gives birth to this autonomous sensibility is only sustainable by the modern mechanism of publishing and distribution, it is fair to say that in this sense the machine itself produces the muse.[10]

Why is the muse necessary to the very viability of the machine itself? Arguably it is not, but it acquires the illusion of centrality in part by the peculiar avenue of copyright law. Martha Woodmansee has shown that in some sense the very concept of authorial intention, now a commonplace of literary criticism and rightly so, has its origins in the industrialization of print, the desire of the authors to show that a "work transcends its physical foundation" and the consequent need to show that it "is an emanation of [an author's] intellect—an intentional, as opposed to a merely physical object."[11] Woodmansee points out that earlier, in the eighteenth century, writing was "considered a mere vehicle of received ideas that were already in the public domain," and so was "by extension . . . considered part of the public domain" itself.[12] In a way, the development of copyright law in this regard shows how the growing pride of authorship of the writer post–Renaissance comes to clash with the newly installed industrial process of mass printing and distribution.[13] Yet the very fixity of the written result and the clear demarcation drawn by mechanical reproduction between the type and the token both produce a paradoxically easier case for declaring a text utterly unique to its author.[14] Oral pronouncements are fleeting and fall back readily into the oral tradition from which they come; writing remains irreducibly itself and not something else.

The sort of originality obsession with which the English romantics are associated springs naturally from this state of affairs. Starting with Alexander Pope (not coincidentally the first English author to get rich from the publication of his writings) on through William Wordsworth, the inspired moment becomes ever more central, and in the process becomes less the property of God, more the flower of genius: "And as they [the writings] are increasingly credited to the writer's own genius, they transform the writer into a unique individual responsible for a unique product. [Note how uniqueness seems to move from product backward to source, for some reason.] That is, from a (mere) vehicle of preordained truths—truths as ordained either by universal human agreement or by some higher agency— the *writer* becomes an *author*."[15]

Woodmansee allies the growing nineteenth-century concern for originality, the horror of being a mere scribe, to writers' desire to lay a secure claim to their province of the written and published word. But I would add that the constant fear of the scribal, of regression to the taking of dictation that writing once usually implied, gets displaced from technology (since printing presses now copy things, and with increased efficiency as the century proceeds) and even from piracy (since copyright regulations help as they are introduced) onto the literary marketplace itself.[16] But what is remarkable is how fast a society of "individuals" has to form to promote free-spirited expression and nonconformity. Literary culture, a lonely endeavor in the throes of creation itself, is quickly fortified by houses of its own: cenacles, salons, publications that announced the favored works and authors, eventually imprints for individual literary editors within publishing houses.[17] I would suggest that such bulwarks are essential against the loneliness of the misunderstood individual writer confronting the marketplace alone, a confrontation only Ayn Rand could really have loved.

Culture of any sort, high or folk, seems always to need a house, and coteries and their institutions have traditionally supplied a house for writing. Without enough such shelter, the danger is that the unaided writer will prove unequal to the greater force of mass taste and its imperatives. That such a force may be indirect, working as it were from the inside of the author, makes it possibly even more disturbing. The inkling that the inspiration, or muse, is itself already whored—that it is the ventriloquism of public taste—troubles the sleep of many a writer.

America, Ink: The Republic and Letters

But, at least in the American context, the answer may be more complex, and more melancholy, than that. After all, there never was a system of patronage in the United States, or a very rickety one in any case.[18] Hence the marketplace, always in place and never congenial, could not prompt any feeling of manumission. In addition was the problem that the public had little use for serious literature, in the nineteenth century or the 1990s. For figures such as Melville and Hawthorne, the variegated American public is already the same sort of threat a living patron's rejection would have been.[19] Above all, in the American discourse a proponent of serious literature has no easy recourse to the assumption that cultural refinement is a civic good, in the way a European nation tended to have. The storied American restlessness with all forms of authority, particularly those smacking of Europe, seems to have been in play here, even bedeviling Ralph Waldo Emerson.[20]

The publicity apparatus that has become so hypertrophied in the current electronic mass culture was already a strong and unavoidable determinant of American literary life by the time antebellum had turned to postbellum.[21] It has always been a part of the widened national marketplace for written work brought gradually into being throughout the nineteenth century.[22] Indeed, this early version of the literary marketplace was so powerful that William Charvat makes the case for changing our classic dyadic relationship between author and reader into a triangle, with one of the three sides of the dynamic representing the "book and magazine trade."[23] The fact is that in many ways serious writers in the United States have always had this tug-of-war with their distribution apparatus. The change in publishing from a gentleman's pastime to a professional's trade took several decades to accomplish. Arguably it was not until the conglomerates came to the large publishing firms in the seventies that the process of commercialization became essentially complete. But by the Gilded Age it had already commenced.[24]

Little noticed but equally important to the growing commercialization of the literary life was the shift toward more popular magazine journalism, which began in earnest somewhat later than the comparable process in book publishing itself had. Such venerable old journals of New England as the *Atlantic* were being jostled by inferior but racier product such as *McClure's* and the *Saturday Evening Post,* an especially significant trend because serialization had provided for authors what Christopher Wilson has called "a vocational springboard."[25] The nationalization of the readership for magazines and books prompted this rationalization, and what some close observers of publishing would view as degradation, within the literary market.[26]

By common consent, though, it takes the aftermath of World War I—with its combination of pent-up hedonistic demand, proliferation of photographic and radio technology, and improved transportation owing to the automobile and better roads—to institutionalize publicity culture in a serious way. The claim has been made that American advertising revenue went from $682 million in 1914 to almost $3 billion in 1929.[27] Ann Douglas has made the interesting point that many of the writers and artists of the twenties in America were actually very well disposed toward the advertising system that was developing at that time. Part of the reason for this was sheer novelty and the delight in it, but Douglas also suspects that the evident psychic harm and exploitation of the advertising system was not yet as blatant.[28] The advent of the Great Depression reminded writers of the deadly seriousness that underlies the playful consumerism of the interwar economy. Nathanael West's more jaded response to the media carnival of his day could be partially put down to his position as a writer primarily of the thirties, not the twenties.[29]

It is really in the thirties that the fragile partnership between literati and mass culture is most dramatically frayed, despite the fact that more writers than ever—more serious writers—were employed in Hollywood and mass journalism. In fact, the very well-defined nature of electronic media in particular made it easier psychologically for the serious writer to imagine he or she was engaged in an entirely different enterprise from that of entertainment: when the model was primarily print journalism, the distinction was somewhat harder to maintain since it was all writing and only writing. As the example of Tod Hackett in West's *Day of the Locust* would suggest, however, the seeming divide between entertainment and art could be overwhelmed by entertainment even then. In West's allegory of mass culture and high art, it is not so much the former's diabolical similitude that causes it to triumph over the latter: it is sheer *force majeure*. Size really did matter in this regard after all—and essentially nothing else.

One reason why American writers seem more aware of their alienation from the public than do comparably serious writers in France or England is that for the latter authors there really is an alternative, however unrewarding, to popularity—and that is very palpable prestige. In the United States, by contrast, there is scarcely even prestige awaiting the impecunious author. The aristocratic stance of a Gustave Flaubert or Charles Baudelaire, so definitive of the modern artist and writer, is less available to Americans, who do not have the same assurance that in the extreme future generations will "catch up" with their productions.[30] In addition, there is no competing discourse to the bourgeois language of democracy and the "common man" to fall back on. (The only possible alternative, the pseudo-aristocratic language of social Darwinism, is in practice only ready to hand for defenders of the propertied.) Often, even self-styled avant-gardists in the United States have a sentimental vestige of democratic ideology and cannot finally bring themselves to acknowledge the ineluctable dissonance between their work and the public appetites.[31] Between the individual writer and the national readership falls a shadow too deep and dark to be overcome. Another way of saying this is to note that although there has always been in America, from the Civil War on, a *kind* of coterie audience for serious art, it was never large or concentrated enough, in either numbers or geography, to produce its own institutional counterweight to the great, undifferentiated reading public.[32] And even *this* seemingly vast "public" is such a small fraction of the population at large that little can be retrieved for high seriousness by its means.[33]

The culture bearers in the fiction I have chosen to treat are disparate, sharing only their isolation. But the isolation of their creators has an additional source: the lack of that strong and deep support from "minority" culture that is the defining feature of countries where literature and art are vibrant and thriving.[34]

The impersonality and wide reach of commercial distribution are what allowed a new sort of literary person to flourish, unaided by direct patronage, first in England from the time of Samuel Johnson onward, then in France after the Revolution and in America after the Civil War. This new machinery really did help birth a new muse, even bringing about the independence and creative freedom of artists and writers who then sometimes felt free to turn against it. The not very hidden weapon in the arsenals of most of those who did strike out seemingly on their own, except for a few with very strong wills like Nietzsche's or an inheritance like Flaubert's, was a second, substitute "patron" in the form of a smaller but reliable knot of interested and discerning critics and consumers. These coterie audiences have been the salvation of high seriousness elsewhere in the industrial world. And they do exist also in the United States. But they are largely left to their own devices here, our minimal public arts aid sustained chiefly to incite public fury and be routinely punished with budget cuts. Our creative writing departments are possibly the closest thing we have to a patron for serious authors. But aspiring writers are a poor substitute for enthusiastic readers.[35] The actual numbers of this serious audience, especially by comparison to the titanic proportions of the overall population, are ludicrously tiny and, owing to the distribution of urban areas, widely scattered. The fabled rigors of that rite of American authorial passage known as the book tour take on a special color when the sheer vastness of the country is factored in.[36]

The reader may think that the contemporary situation I evoke goes too far ahead. It may, but it does not go far afield. The famously marginal status of *gens de lettres* today in America has been prepared for by a process that really got going by the latter nineteenth century. Small wonder that authors who first saw this process beginning, and not only in the United States, wondered whether they would be returned, by the circuitous route of public taste without serious tastemakers to guide it, to the sort of activity they had only recently been freed from having to perform, ironically as a result of the rise of commercial presses. That activity is figured as above all scribal. The very mechanism that once allowed authors to claim absolute originality and pride of ownership seemed increasingly to herald a return to the whoredom of copying. It is not for nothing that the banally reproduced image, the hackneyed turn of phrase or piece of received wisdom, comes to be called "stereotype." It does not take long for the creative author, the genius newly minted from the machine of marketplace publishing, to become haunted by the opposite number: the copyist.

Refusing Dictation: Authenticity and Authorship

Gustave Flaubert anticipated this obsession with originality and uniqueness—as usual in the form of fearing their opposite—in his late work *Bouvard et Pécuchet,* whose heroes are two copyists who try to become original thinkers and writers and who, in one version of the ending, hit upon the solution to the problems that result from their quest: "Copier comme autrefois."[37] An offshoot of his work on this volume was his "Dictionary of Received Ideas," which gives a good idea of what literary people construed as the enemy. (Of course, it is the fatal ambiguity of a project such as the dictionary that it is undecidable whether, by defining banality at length, one has confined it as well or merely succumbed to it. We know how often parody becomes earnest.)

But Flaubert was not the first or the last to see the uncanny closeness of quirky writer to impersonal, repetitive mechanism—and to reject it, or try to. The resistance to banality was to become, for the literary craftsman, something like what resistance to common wisdom would be for the scientist or the Enlightenment philosopher. What is striking about the literary, in contrast to visual art or music, for instance, is that when all is said and done, there are many fewer markers by which to set apart serious endeavor from frivolous or meretricious product than in those other fields.[38] But if the things of culture in modernity usually have a house—if classical music is performed generally in a concert hall by a chamber ensemble or orchestra, and painting and sculpture of value are found in museums and galleries—then an odd thing about prose literature (one of many) is the way it sits in the bookstore cheek by jowl, seemingly unfazed, among the banal best sellers. Some of them, wonderfully, are even themselves best sellers.

Assuming that Flaubert's concern about reduction to the scribal is shared by other writers (and a reading of George Gissing, Henry James, or Nathanael West would suggest that it is), the obvious reply is: Why do they care? The literary merit and seriousness of a work of art is proven in the reading, like pudding in the tasting. If it's there, the right people will know it. But again, who are the right people? What does knowing it mean? The forms of recognition in the literary life are few, uncertain, and usually late in coming—if they come at all. There are myriad informal ways of seeking membership in the confraternity of serious writing; but uniquely, I think, membership is never conferred. First of all, the novel's very marketplace origin assures that any particular specimen is suspect. (At least poetry's pedigree antedates publicity culture and its apparatus.) Beyond that, in order to be published in the first place, a work has to be assumed to be of some commercial potential, a fact of which the novelist is aware in advance and which must order at least some of his or her thinking. To seek publication at all, in a situation where the delivery system is in essence not cultural but commercial, is to offer oneself as of commercial potential. This means one very important, insufficiently remarked thing: that literature, from at least the time of romanticism, was no realm set apart from the commercial arena, but rather a *contesting of the ground of the "Publick"* that had been seized first by meretricious product without aspirational intent. In a real sense, the so-called art novel is the latecomer, the potboiler the legitimate contender.

The inescapable conclusion is that the field of mass distribution itself formed the conditions for serious prose literature in two contradictory ways: it made novels and prose fiction generally possible—that is, commercially viable—and the run of its products provided something for serious writers to undermine with their own elitist example. The problem is that in the absence of the sort of strong barriers separating other forms of artistic endeavor from their mass-cultural counterparts, the serious writer could never be sure just how different he or she was from the low-minded doppelgänger on Grub Street. To contest the site of mass distribution was to some extent to play on its terms to begin with; and of course even the purest of writers (except those such as Flaubert who had an inheritance) were not untempted by the prospect of actually earning a living, which could be done under the reign of the printing houses as never before.[39]

The overwhelming structural fact is that modern publishing, though it takes place in "houses," cannot truly be a house for culture but is ineluctably a quasi-industrial process that uses cultural materials to make profit. Possibilities open to the writer involving freedom from previous constraint and sycophancy, but the price is the homelessness of the traveling salesman and a similar worry about authenticity and "the genuine." By placing oneself on the other side of the divide from the Philistine best seller or maker of potboilers, one can distinguish one's own making of myth from that of one's opposite number—and, into the bargain, create a countermyth of one's own heroism and purity. One may not create more effective public myths than those who write for the masses, but at least one can create a myth for oneself. Since the terms are set by commercial enterprise, however, the battle (less a public one than an interior one) has ever to be rejoined, the myth ever forged anew. The *gens de lettres* try to separate themselves utterly from their pedestrian commercial counterparts but at the same time turn back to them constantly to reassure themselves that they are different. They need the publicity apparatus they despise in order to be read, and they need the humbler servants of that apparatus to remind themselves that others have stooped far lower than they.[40]

There may be a particular appeal to this countermyth for male writers, who are inclined to a heroic view of their own endeavors anyway, and even more so in America. This is partially the legacy of Herman Melville and Walt Whitman, no doubt, but also connected to the rise of mass literacy and the journalism that grew up after the Civil War to supply it. Rightly or wrongly, the high-end constituency for the advertising machinery has long been thought to be female, as for the fiction that has arisen since the Civil War. Nathaniel Hawthorne's infamous comments about the "damn'd mob of scribbling women" have been echoed by many other male authors since his time.[41] Beyond that, the heroics implied in battling the market-place can conceal the more mundane reality of cooperating with it, a real-ity that to some male artists looks too much like emasculation. Does a male author prefer indeed to be thought of as one lone man fighting the world even when he is benefited by networks and coteries? One suspects that Ralph Waldo Emerson himself could be the ghost harbored within the myth of the muse in the machine.

Such speculations lead me beyond the scope of my study, though it inevitably prompts them. To see more directly how the emergent world of publicity affected a serious American writer, one could do far worse than to examine some of the literary responses of Henry James. In the nineties James made a dramatic and fateful decision: in effect, *not* to take dictation from the marketplace as it existed. Although our inclination now in looking back is to assume that this decision was inevitable—and given the market-place's near total neglect of him from the 1880s onward, it does seem so—it was a palpable wrench to the author at the time. In making it, James has given critics a pregnant exemplum, a tale in miniature of the larger move-ment so many writers in the next two decades would make from realism to symbolism, from late Victorian to modernist fiction, from middlebrow to highbrow. What is especially interesting for my purposes, which are to trace how serious writers' tortured relationship to the publicity marketplace affects their fiction, is that the first one to create an allegory of this sort for James's career was James himself. His artist tales, from before but particu-larly during the nineties, constitute a kind of declaration of independence from the Publick, and not coincidentally come as close to propaganda as the author would permit himself to venture. In the next chapter, I examine some of the things that impel this declaration and how it is fashioned.

chapter two

Ghosts and Muses: Henry James

H enry James's long career spanned the period from shortly after the
Civil War to the eve of World War I. Although we now associate
him chiefly with the late novels and the mandarin rigor they seem to
embody, he spent much of his earlier life trying to achieve popular as well
as critical success. But his career was undertaken during a time when the
economics of book publishing had started to change, to the detriment of
his kind of dual marketing to both a larger reading public and to connois-
seurs.[1] Added to this burden were the failures of the dramatic pieces he had
mounted at the turn of the nineties, culminating in his public booing by a
disgruntled opening night audience for his play *Guy Domville*. It is thought
that the irritation sprang from the unsexy ending where the hero renounces
his love.[2] Regardless of the reason, the hostility was real and astonishing to
James. In response to it he renounced the dream of popular success, perhaps offstage as well as on. The bulk of his artist tales come from this era
of his life or shortly after, and their apparent cynicism about the audience
for serious literature can be attributed in part to their author's crashing
blunder in having attempted the stage.

Attributed, but not reduced, I think. For the *Guy Domville* incident was
only the culmination for James of a series of humiliations at the hands of
a new and harsher publishing market, with a new and harsher readership
to serve. Although the postbellum market was in some ways a boon to
James, particularly in view of his ability to publish editions on both sides
of the Atlantic, he began to wonder if the market was squeezing out talents
of his sort.[3] Also, even in the debacle of *Guy Domville* itself, James is complicit in his own humiliation, not only for having produced a play that was
either bad or merely too high-minded, but also for having gone onstage in
the first place.

To be fair, though, even those ventures onto the stage, both figurative
and literal, had been prompted by a crisis that already shadowed James's
career. His big novels of the latter 1880s, *The Princess Cassamassima* and

15

The Tragic Muse, had both failed commercially. The chill wind of market change had already contributed to his decision to turn to the stage, even if it was only a "half turn," as Fred Kaplan calls it.[4] He was suitably disabused of any idealism in confronting the new, less patient public of the era, having already given a fair accounting of the new world of publicity in the short novel *The Reverberator* (1888). He was fully prepared to write down to the public, but maybe the bad faith of the enterprise was sensed in the result.[5] Who knows?

What is easier to assess is that James took the early failures of his big novels and the later debacles of his stage plays as proof that the artist in him would never survive contact with mercenary necessities. Most Jamesians have noted how many tales of the literary life James published in the late 1880s through the late 1890s and have attributed much of their energy to mere self-pity. This is hard to dispute, but is surely the least interesting aspect of the better tales of this type. Or rather, the inevitable self-pity becomes interesting only as a means through which a shrewder, more acute understanding of the new psychology of the aesthete could emerge: an aesthete who also had to survive and wanted to prosper.[6] The push and pull of financial and artistic ambition, the feeling that they were increasingly contradictory and not synergistic impulses, provides much of the impetus for the artist tales of this period.

It is certainly true that in some ways Henry James, in this as in so much else, is a special case. It is not surprising that an author who has left his native land for another and then has fallen out of favor with his adoptive audience as well would feel doubly alienated: from the audience he abandoned and also from the audience that abandoned him. Still, both his feeling of dispossession and his use of fiction to examine that feeling were actually becoming more commonplace among serious writers in this period.[7] In the brave new publicity world of the turn of the century, James appears to have had considerable company in his misery, which suggests that the pity of these tales, for his characters and for himself, comes from a more pervasive state of affairs than one play, however spectacular a failure, could account for.[8] For one thing, the changed circumstances of letters as the century waned were much of the impetus in the first place for his unwise decision to try for a splashy popular success, the very thing he would be least likely to achieve. The embarrassments and terminations James recounts in his artist tales represent just such unwise decisions, but in doing so describe a market wherein refraining from those decisions is often just as unwise.

In Search of Lost Texts

From the welter of James's artist tales we focus on three stories: "The Lesson of the Master" (1888), "The Death of the Lion" (1894), and "The Next Time" (1895). All of them feature in some symbolically telling capacity a missing, suppressed, or otherwise absent piece of writing. The first two tales take as their symbolic center a physical piece of writing that is destroyed or neglected. The last evokes a virtual or desired text that is powerless to be born. But in each case the absent text becomes the center of a resonating symbolic field, stand-in for possibilities forgone and authenticity forgotten. Although I plan to look at more aspects of these stories than just this and aspects of more stories than these, the lost texts of these artist tales will serve as the place where the larger relation of serious writers to publicity culture is played out or given over.

"The Lesson of the Master," as the title implies, focuses on the dyad of ephebe and covering cherub, with Paul Overt as the first and Henry St. George as the second. There is also a love interest, Miss Marian Fancourt, but even she arguably ends up as part of the master's object lesson to the pupil. Not just here but elsewhere in the artist tales it becomes typical for James to inscribe an older man and younger disciple, one of the more famous instances being "The Middle Years" (1894). But in this case his central idea seems to suspend master and pupil in some midpoint between mutual regard and competition. His notebooks record his initial setup: "a very interesting situation would be that of an elder artist or writer, who has been ruined (in his own sight) by his marriage and its forcing him to produce promiscuously and cheaply—his position in regard to a younger *confrère* whom he sees on the brink of the same disaster and whom he endeavours to save, to rescue, by some act of bold interference—breaking off the marriage, annihilating the wife, making trouble between the parties."[9] In the final event, James has Paul Overt take a long sabbatical in Switzerland, there to ruminate on and perfect his art, thus allowing St. George to pursue an engagement to Miss Fancourt, whom Overt had thought was his. St. George's own wife is only "annihilated" by natural means, thus paving the way for this union.

The reason St. George gives is indeed the one credited in James's notebooks, and to judge by the notebooks he must be sincere. But readers a century on have doubted his sincerity, just as Paul does. For all that, the elder writer's obvious disappointment with his lot as a productive but mediocre storyteller suggests the possibility that he at least *thinks* his coup is the best thing for Overt's career, as he clearly believes it to be for his own life. Overt is skeptical of St. George's generosity:

> "You ought to be ashamed," said Paul. . . .
>
> "Ah, never, never! I wanted to save you, rare and precious as you are."
> "Are you marrying Miss Fancourt to save me?"
> "Not absolutely, but it adds to the pleasure. I shall be the making of
> you," said St. George, smiling.[10]

Paul clearly feels that St. George has been his destruction rather than his making, but St. George assures him that not marrying will save him as a writer. To boot, St. George says he has stopped writing and "for the rest of my life . . . shall only read" (283). The key to this maneuver, or at least St. George's rationale for it, comes earlier in the story, when Paul is visiting Henry St. George at his home. He first sees the place where St. George writes the many books required by his luxury-loving wife and the "living, thriving, consuming organisms" that are for him their boys (264). Then Paul mentions the early work that Mrs. St. George burned, "the one she didn't like," as Overt puts it. After making a visible effort to remember what it was about, St. George brings it out: "Oh, yes, it was about myself" (267). This mysterious burnt offering becomes the occasion for the older man's reflections on the role a woman can play in the creative process: positive for the first year, but a "millstone" round the writer's neck thereafter (268). He also notes at that time that Paul Overt's ideal of perfection will have to be forsworn if his already avowed intentions toward Miss Fancourt proceed.

James's tale makes it hard to avoid the economy that what profits marriage will harm art and vice versa. Paul condemns this view—understandably, since he wants to have a life. It is not surprising that he comes to condemn St. George as well for depriving him of that life. The fact, though, that the narrator ends the story averring that St George is "essentially right" in the belief that "Nature had dedicated [Paul] to intellectual, not to personal passion" suggests that this monkish existence is in the end affirmed (284). Coming from the lifelong bachelor, this has a logic to it. But equally interesting is that Miss Fancourt's role in the story is a strange amalgam. On the one hand, she is a true supporter of literature, the "fan" in "Fancourt" quite genuine. On the other hand, St. George at least implies that as a woman she will ultimately choose life and its needs over art: that in some fundamental way she will just not "get it" about being an artist. Readers can be forgiven being reminded of Mrs. Ambient in James's earlier tale "The Author of Beltraffio" (1884), though in fairness Miss Fancourt is a far less malevolent presence. Yet for James it seems that even women well disposed to art are not completely "on the team." At the same time, St. George's insistence that women cannot "take part" in the sacrifice of art since "[t]hey themselves are the sacrifice . . . the idol and the altar and the flame" also has its resonance for James's own method, as we shall later see (268). But ultimately, the only sacrifice Mrs. St. George is known to have conducted was the one performed on her husband's early text, the one "about myself." The clear implication is that St. George's art was somehow severed from its roots in deep personal expression by his wife's interest in practical efficiency and success. Instead of expressing deep wellsprings of sensibility, St. George's writing springs in fact from subjection and represents "a kind of hell," he says (262). Symbolic of this confinement is his writing room, which his "wife invented" and in which "she locks me up . . . every morning" (258). By allowing that a wife can inspire a man for at least the first year of a marriage, though, St. George has introduced the other—for James even more troubling—side of the equation for the male artist: woman as muse or inspiration. It will not surprise that eventually James's solution to this dilemma will be to worship only at the altar of women already dead. But for the St. Georges of the world, living women "think they understand, they think they sympathize. Then it is that they are most dangerous" (264).

The manuscript, in its absence, is intended to stand in for the perfection and truth to inner light that Henry St. George is not able or willing, or perhaps just not allowed, to bring to bear on the art he has since produced, published, and become famous for writing. He sees Paul Overt as his lieutenant, deputized to produce the miracle of self-expression his elder had forgotten to write. In fact, in a weird transfer from his own lost text to someone else's possible future project, St. George proposes that Paul's next book be about him: "Oh, but *you* should write it—*you* should do me. There's a subject, my boy; no end of stuff in it!" (267–68). The implicit division of labor—Henry St. George to live the life, with Paul Overt to write about it—would be insulting were it not so obvious St. George would rather the roles could have been reversed at this moment. This late-eighties tale is James's clearest statement, albeit expressed with light comedy, of his growing belief that being a success and writing your best were incompatible. That he seems to have ignored his own advice in going into the theater probably only made the ignominious upshot seem all the more like the thundering voice of conscience to him.[11] Like St. George, James sacrificed his artistic self, burned his truest writing on the altar of theater. Did the gods sense that his was an impure offering?

If the lost text is a burnt offering on the sacrifice of fame, the manuscript that gets lost in "The Death of the Lion" (1894) is an unintended sacrifice—along with its author, as it happens. Indeed, the society feeding frenzy surrounding author Neil Paraday in "Lion" recalls nothing so much as the myth in which Orpheus is torn limb from limb by the Maenads, except that at least it is Orpheus's song that prompts the *sparagmos;* in Paraday's case it is only the manuscript, read in pieces and neglected, that is dismembered.

Neil Paraday carries the sort of dilemma Henry St. George worried about to another level. For him, it is not a question of marriage, his wife having died; it is, however, a question of society (or at least Society). The ambiguous nature of the great world in "Lesson," representing at once material and impressions for the artist and also temptation to materialism and betrayal of high artistic mission, here seems more uniformly negative. In part, I suspect, that is signaled by the extent to which that realm is identified with the female. James's *Notebooks* sketch out "the party at the country-house, and the ultra-modern hostess [Mrs. Weeks Wimbush], and the autograph hunters and interviewers—and the collapse, the extinction of the [writer] hero."[12] Along with the Orpheus imagery goes that of Artemis, as Wimbush is described as hunting down the lion, getting the trophy. Interestingly, Paraday's presence is required chiefly to bring out her wit, not so that she can bring out his. Even the cult of personality turns out to be about hers, not his.

Meanwhile, the manuscript, honored as a cult object in its own right but not as something to actually read, becomes ever more forgotten as it is passed from hand to hand. The fate of the manuscript prefigures the author's, as Paraday himself falls ill and dies. The *sparagmos* here comes about not through any attack on his person, or even on the manuscript; it rather comes about through neglect and indifference. The author is passed indifferently from hostess to hostess, just as his manuscript is read idly and only in bits and pieces. As with Henry St. George's famous manuscript, there is a strangely intimate identification of Paraday's work with his person.[13]

Yet if it is impersonality that James ultimately has in mind for the product of the writing process, then in what sense does the fate of the manuscript implicate the author? Part of the answer may lie in the dual nature of the manuscript: at once objective, an outward sign of the author's interpretation of the world, and also secret, because not understood. The delicate question concerns in what respect this secrecy is the inevitable result of incomprehension by the public, and in what respect deliberately hidden, intended only for a few. If on the one hand the public will inevitably neglect the hard work of interpreting the deeper meaning of the artist, on the other the artist may positively encourage such miscomprehension, the better to limit his followers to those capable of making the journey with him.

Such esotericism tells us a great deal about the cult of text that James would later come to substitute for the cult of person. But this lonely labor of secrecy does not occur in isolation; rather, a community is implied for those labors. (Otherwise, surely, there would be no reason to publish.) Whereas Miss Fancourt embodies the readership in "Lesson," the more discerning inner circle is represented in "Death," "Figure in the Carpet," and "The Middle Years" by younger men. Leon Edel points out that this to some degree mirrors nature.[14] But it also figures an ideal community of readers: a small coterie to counterpose to the unfeeling multitude.

For James, incomprehensibility was the price and proof of literary eminence: to be great is indeed to be misunderstood for the James of this era. It is significant that the greatest proof that the "Lion" is one is in fact the neglect to which his books are subjected. Is the mere fact of going unread sufficient reason to praise a writer? One could be forgiven for concluding that in James's world, it is. The temptation to frequent Society, then, yields the paradoxical proof that the author is "too good" for Society, in the form of demonstrating its lack of interest in his art. He has become the sacrificial lamb for their profane rites, in the case of Paraday literally, since the same houseguests who pass around his book without reading it neglect its (as it happens) dying author as well. The wrong sort of attention—to the person rather than the work—is in James's tale worse than no attention at all.[15] The narrator, by contrast, is part of the smaller circle of acolytes who wish to preserve the author's memory by preserving his books.

The condemnation of the social world, not too strong a term for the mordancy of James's satire here, thus depends on the motif we have seen from "The Aspern Papers" (1887): the aggressivity of fandom and its cult of celebrity. The "publishing scoundrel" of a critic who connived to get Jeffrey Aspern's (possibly incriminating) papers from the Bordereaus had at least some genuine interest in Aspern's poetry. But the crowd at the Wimbush estate is even worse than its "Aspern" counterpart, being interested almost solely in the personality rather than the work.

In "Death" Neil Paraday (whose name means either "parody" or, more likely, "for-a-day") is the male writer sacrificed by his female admirers; the only male admirers in the tale are very positive figures. (Although "Dora Forbes," another male writer, is not, he has also assumed a woman's name.) We arrive hereby closer to the sacrificial economy operated by the Jamesian cult as his artist tales adumbrate it. In the wake of romanticism, after all, mere observation and recording is not enough to define the novelist's task.

Imagination, that transformative power, is also to be his portion. For that power to operate it needs material, of course; and James's fondness for detailing exactly where he got the anecdotal *donnée* for his fiction illustrates his understanding of this. In the repressive structure of James's sublimating vision, women play an especially major role as muses. Susanne Kappeler is right to make that goddess figure central to James's "tribe," but as Sigmund Freud reminds us, totemic figures are often primal victims as well. The instance of Minnie Temple seems to have taught James that the only living muse is a dead woman.[16]

The living women, on the other hand, are death to the author's work—and apparently to the author himself as well. Instead of the suppressed text of "The Lesson of the Master," this tale offers the completed but unread text. Like its counterpart, Paraday's manuscript is the emblem of a connection not made, a work whose meaning has been overshadowed by the person, or persona, of the author. As the figure of the author waxes, that of the work wanes. Publicity culture has here enacted an obvious revenge, and to drive the point home James has the author actually die. This may be a self-pitying excess, but it also tells us just how James felt the emerging world of publicity would prove to be to a writer. When one is shown rather than read, one dies twice, which is why, oddly, the tale can be said to have a happy ending.[17]

But the masculinist cult of art sketched out by James in the nineties, undermined though it is by women as it searches for discerning (i.e., male) readers in the marketplace, actively needs the female principle in order to fuel the writer's imagination. If the mass-market reality has for James a female face, so does the source of inspiration; and squaring the former with the latter is not easy. The incompatibility of domestic charms and female admirers with the purity of artistic vocation is presented not only through Neil Paraday's fate but also, and more comically, through Ray Limbert's in "The Next Time." In this tale, a writer constantly on the lookout for ways and means of prostituting his talent for money ends up writing marvelous books that nobody buys. On the surface, the tale actually appears to have the opposing moral from that of "Death" and to an even greater extent "Lesson of the Master": here, that is, a man with a wife and family, who must write trash in order to survive, cannot betray his gift even if he wants to. This is, however, only an apparent contradiction, since he never manages to make a proper living as a writer in the end, which is his goal. (His opposite number, by the way, a writer who desires a *succès d'estime* and ineluctably winds up with a runaway trashy best seller, is a woman, Jane Highmore.) Limbert's predicament is a slightly lighter version of Paraday's.

Where Paraday perishes from the fraudulent appearance of interest and fundamental disinterest in his work, Limbert's work is received in undisguised apathy, about which he is never in doubt. Still, like Paraday, Limbert is sacrificed. The manuscript Limbert "loses" is the best-selling book he tries and fails time and again to write.

It begins to emerge from all of these burned, unread, and unrealized texts that the needs of self-expression, that romantic sine qua non for the artist, are in various ways undermined by the exigencies, and the *force majeure,* of the distribution apparatus into which literature had to be introduced. To this one could add the quasi-romantic conception of the perfect—because unachieved or occluded—masterwork, a Balzacian chef d'oeuvre *inconnu* of the sort invoked by his dying author Dencombe, from another tale of this era called "The Middle Years," who says, "The pearl is the unwritten—the pearl, the unalloyed, the *rest,* the lost!"[18]

It may also be relevant that in the first two instances women are the agents of destroying or neglecting the literary work: Henry St. George's wife burns her husband's manuscript, which in good romantic fashion was of course "about myself" (though "myself" as a writer was, for James, not necessarily "myself" as a man: the whole story is about the danger of conflating the two, no doubt, since St. George's fulfillment as a man is bought by the suppression of himself as a writer); and Mrs. Weeks Wimbush's guests at Prestidge collaborate in handing the work from one to the other, threatening to lose it in the process (here writer and work seem in eerie tandem, for passing Neil Paraday among the guests at Prestidge, it is implied, has a similar deleterious effect on him that passing along his text has on it). Even for Ray Limbert in "The Next Time," who desires a cheap popular success and always achieves a perfectly realized literary failure, there is a kind of evil-twin sibling rival in Jane Highmore, a woman who effortlessly achieves mass acceptance each time she sets forth—and desires to be thought literary. It is hard to escape an implication in these tales of the literary life that something about women is just not healthy for James's notion of literature.[19] In a pattern we shall find also in Nathanael West, with different emphasis, James's fear of the marketplace seems doubled by a fear of the feminine.

Altering the Figure: "A Woman Will Never Find Out"

Few, even his staunchest defenders, have ever attempted to claim for Henry James the title of champion of womanhood. Even a possible exception such as Ross Posnock, whose mission seems to be to make James safe for all things postmodern, does not finally make that sort of case.[20] There are readers who never forgive him *The Bostonians* and its satirical treatment of feminist concerns; and although his Isabel Archer in *Portrait of a Lady* and Maggie Verver in *The Golden Bowl,* to name no others, are usually hailed as sympathetic and finely drawn glimpses into female psychology, he never extended this sympathy to the generality of the gender. And he certainly never extended it to novelists with whom he was in competition. He probably knew that most of the new readers of novels that had become such a force in the publishing world he knew were alleged to be women, and that therefore some of the most successful novelists also were. As "The Lesson of the Master" shows, James also attributed much of the impetus to compromise one's artistic principles for salability to the kind of breadwinning pressure that marriage and children subject one to and had reason to suspect women of (in this case largely innocent) designs on the artist as well.

In James's case, there was an additional fear. It is clear that while women provide much of the inspiration for the artistic process of men for James, they have to be taken in a certain way in order to be of use. Minnie Temple, James's cousin who died in her twenties, is the most famous example: James was able to use her memory decades later as the original of Milly Theale in *The Wings of the Dove* (1902). He was quite honest to say that he found her more useful in the "crystal walls of the past," the better to serve as inspiration to his imagination "by all the bright intensity of [her] example," than he had during her life.[21] In his personal mythology, then, the death of a beautiful woman may not always have been the subject of his best art, *pace* Edgar Allan Poe, but it could be the precondition for some of it. By contrast, women were not generally fortuitous readers of the resulting art: Mrs. Ambient in "The Author of Beltraffio" is an early attempt to map female misreading. In real life, James's vexed relationship with Constance Fenimore Woolson suggests that he seems to have misread her as well, which her suicide had the effect of bearing in upon him. The decade of the nineties, rightly termed "treacherous" by Leon Edel, saw not only James's fatal failure in the theatrical arena but also Fenimore's death, and his straightforward spite toward the marketplace that had no use for him is confounded by a subtler guilt and bitterness over this death, which was very unlike Minnie Temple's and would not rest easy in the crystal cave.

With this in mind, we turn from tales of lost texts (with their simple equation of writing with expression) to "The Altar of the Dead" (1895) and "The Figure in the Carpet" (1896), both of which celebrate obscurity and secrecy in a way for which the earlier mourning of lost chances at communication would not have prepared us. If in the previous tales the women were seemingly out to get the authorial text, either to extirpate the deepest forms of expression or to kill them with kindness, in these next tales it is not open expression (i.e., publication) that is sought so much as secret ritual or esoteric meaning. George Stransom in "Altar," not an artist but bearing some striking similarities, flees the realm of publicity as such, though a woman disrupts his plans for escape; and Hugh Vereker in "Figure" prides himself on his ability to secrete a meaning within his texts that will escape readers regardless of their attempts to find it out.[22]

If the artist tales before Fenimore's death imply that to be great is to be misunderstood, then at least "Figure," which comes after it, seems to suggest that to be misunderstood is not so dire a fate anyway and has its advantages. The loss of texts, and of the self-expression for which they are a figure, is a great tragedy (or at best a grim comedy, as in "Death of the Lion"), but by the time of "Figure" meanings are not only misconceived by the public but also concealed by the author himself. We are in addition invited to be amused by the endless search of the narrator for the hidden meaning that, as of the story's ending, he still has not found, and to feel as if the author has thus somehow "won." Is there some way to suggest how it might be that James has gone, in the space of a couple of years, from lamenting the loss of personal expression to hoping that not too much meaning is conveyed after all?

Of course there is no simple line to be drawn between any two aspects of an author's life, even between the suicide of one of his closest friends whose executor he then became and the obvious shift in how he assesses those guises an author dons when entering the public arena. But one way of charting the alteration is to examine in some depth a story he wrote shortly after Feminore's death called "The Altar of the Dead," a tale that, on the surface, has little if anything to do with making literary art in the first place. What about it concerns this process—and *doesn't* concern it—is what will detain us as we read it.

The case for interpreting "The Altar of the Dead" in artistic terms comes from several facets of the tale. First of all, the inspiration for George Stansom's preservation project is similar to that for art: the death of a woman whose memory Stransom guards because he has not taken possession of the actual person. She provides, in other words, the muse that incites Stransom to pursue his project of honoring the Dead, the more for dying without having married him; so that their union's very lack of formal recognition contributes to Stransom's desire to embody his memory of her, and of "his" other Dead, in a concrete form: "They [the Dead] had no organized service, no reserved place, no honour, no shelter, no safety."[23]

The term *safety* seems especially odd as applied to dead people, but in Stransom's terms it means the safety of assured dignity. The grave and the cemetery do not, apparently, supply this—which is, above all else, the clue that Stransom's project is in many ways parallel to that of artistic creation for James.

There are also divergences. Stransom sees his project as not so much as artistic as in essence an extension of religious worship: "the religion instilled by his earliest consciousness had been simply the religion of the Dead" (233). Even though in sketch form James's story called for Stransom to build his altar solely in his own mind, in finished form it makes such an altar quite literal, perhaps because he realized that plot complications would be hard to pull off if the altar was purely mental but also having the effect of strengthening the parallel to artistic creativity by stressing the need to grant memory material form.[24] This form, which consists of candles placed on a disused altar in an actually existing church, has the effect of underlining the scandalous relation this supplementary religion has to conventional forms of faith; but a form of faith, more than art strictly considered, is how Stransom himself views it.[25]

The project takes its further inspiration from Stransom's chance encounter with Paul Creston and his new American wife, with whom he has hastily supplanted the first, late Mrs. Creston, who "had been more living for him [Stransom] than any woman but one" (235). This incident's venue is a "shop-front which lighted the dull brown air with its mercenary grin. . . . several persons were gathered" before a jewelry window "whose diamonds and sapphires seemed to laugh . . . with the mere joy of knowing how much more they were 'worth' than most of the dingy pedestrians staring at them" (233–34). Stransom, among the dingy pedestrians, suspends, "in a vision, a string of pearls about the white neck of Mary Antrim" at the point when he encounters Creston *en famille*. Thus does the dead woman become the point of intersection for a dual inspiration: the spiritual desire to possess those who have died along with the need for Stransom to "find his real comfort in some material act, some outward worship" (239). The circulation of commodities in secular flux is represented here by both sides of the shop window: by the jewels themselves and by Creston's hot new American number, "that hired performer" despised by the pious Stransom (235).

The institutional space granted to Stransom's activities figures a tense relation not only to religion, then, but also to commerce. With regard to religion, even if Stransom does figure his memories as so many lights on an actually existing altar, this is still a private service, in effect a rite for one.

Outwardly manifested, his devotion is still secret, expressing itself in "rites more public, yet certainly esoteric" (240). Moreover, what inspires his vision of the blazing candles is the shop-window jewels he has witnessed when he encounters the new Crestons. In effect he has mimicked the blazing lights of commodity culture, which also secularizes his own sacred memories, but removed them from view and from sale. Stransom's gesture of mentally buying a string of pearls for his dead woman rather than entering the store to buy one for a living woman, as Creston may have been at the point of doing, becomes the sign of his larger attitude.[26]

Yet the tone taken by the tale toward its hero—James's attitude toward Stransom's attitude, so to speak—is complicated. Stransom goes home and decides: "*He* could spend an evening with Kate Creston [the first wife], if the man to whom she had given everything couldn't" (236). This tribute has its charm but also its self-regarding aspect: "he [Stransom] had that evening a rich, almost happy sense that he alone, in a world without delicacy, had a right to hold up his head." Such a suspicion of vanity, of excessive pride of authorship, is confirmed upon realizing that the death of Acton Hague is also an inducement to building his altar, precisely because he can omit a candle for his hated betrayer. In fact, such is the power of hatred for Hague that one can be forgiven skepticism about the profusion of other candles, each numbering supposedly beloved dead, that Stransom lights. After all, such was the friendship enjoyed by Stransom and Hague that "after that catastrophe," whose specifics go uncited, Hague's "deposition from this eminence [of friendship with Stransom] had practically left it without an occupant" (237). The omitted candle, thus, looks like almost as much the point of Stransom's enterprise as the lighted candles for Mary Antrim or Kate Creston.

There is another intriguing facet to this betrayal by Hague: its public nature. Their quarrel was "tainted at the time . . . with a horrible publicity," which was so severe that "he [Stransom] had never spoken of it to a human creature, . . . he had completely overlooked it" (237). This extreme expression of the public quarrel goes far toward explaining the intense privacy with which Stransom's life is attended when we come upon him, and it also prepares the logic for the unlit candle. Stransom "has no comment" on Hague, even to himself; and he constructs an altar to his lack of comment. Like any cultic artist, Stransom withdraws from the world of publicity, which I suspect as much as any specific insult is what he really flees when he banishes Acton Hague from his secret realm. By being the one dead person to whom Stransom will not burn a candle, Hague threatens to become the Freudian absent cause for the entire would-be pious project.

Instead of the missing manuscript, for Stransom is not a writer, here the missing link is a candle. Another difference is that here the reader knows what has been omitted and why, altering the attitude toward what is dramatized in James's tale, I think. One instinctively exalts what is unstated; this is almost the definition of mystique. Yet here, the founding wound is as baldly announced as James can manage to do: Philoctetes' tale was scarcely more direct. Not only that, the nature of the wound is inescapably a blow to vanity (what James describes as "insult" attended by "horrible publicity"), so that there is little to which to credit the reaction other than base self-protection. When James describes Stransom's "life, round its central hollow," as "packed close enough," this resonant absence is probably Mary Antrim but could be the candle not present on the altar (249). In fact, James directly maintains this ambiguity in presenting Stransom's thought when the woman who frequents his altar assures him she can "perfectly imagine some of the echoes with which his silences were peopled." He decides she cannot imagine this because "one's relations to what one had loved and hated had been a relation too distinct from the relations of others." The operative words here are "and hated," indicating as they do the at least double purpose to which Stransom's altar is bound.

This woman who comes to frequent George Stransom's private altar is, not incidentally, also its most direct occasion. She is the other person attending the church Stransom enters the day after Hague's death is announced in the papers, a sequence that provides the reader with a clue to their later misunderstanding. It is she who provides the example he follows with a vengeance: "while, at a distance, the black-robed lady continued prostrate," Stransom formulates a "conception" that prompts in him "the sudden excitement of a plan"—the plan for his altar of the dead (239). Doubly inspired, the altar honors the memory of Mary Antrim as well as the example of his fellow mourner. The analogy to artistic creation makes this tale unusually generous to women's role in prompting the imagination, providing as they do both the memories and the sensibility's attention to memory, which is after all part of what grief signifies.

The irony is that her grief is the hollow of his: not its reversal exactly, it inhabits precisely a space his cannot fill, honoring a memory he refuses to honor. Yet she is his muse all the same, and possibly for this very reason.[27] Like Marcher in halfhearted mourning at the close of "Beast in the Jungle" (1903), Stransom recognizes the real thing when he sees it. But unlike Marcher, Stransom decides not to be shamed by it, nor even to try to match her in grief. Instead, he chooses to see her as pointing his way toward celebrating his own capacity to grieve. He even mistakes the qualitative nature of her desolation for the quantitative, seemingly forgetting his own devotion to Mary Antrim: "She was always black-robed, as if she had had a succession of sorrows. People were not poor, after all, whom so many losses could overtake; they were positively rich when they had so much to give up" (244). Only later does he find out that her wealth springs from only one source, one he cannot acknowledge. Her riches, then, come from the very source of which he has deprived himself, so that when revealed it only calls Stransom's attention to his own impoverishment.

If such fearful symmetry gives their relationship the aspect of sibling rivalry, this feature is strangely enhanced by her profession of letters, as she earns "money by her pen, writing under a designation that she never told him in magazines that he never saw" (250). Stransom, predictably, takes comfort in the obscurity and anonymity of her writings since that frees him to think of her as solely "the priestess of his altar . . . he felt his fidelity pale and faint in comparison with hers." He plans, in fact, to commend the altar to her care upon his death, "and if the spirit should move her she might kindle a taper even for him." When she asks who will kindle one for her, however, his reply is not given.

The central revelation of the tale, of course, is the fact that her own inner sanctum of the bedroom has been "a museum in his honour, . . . that the shrine he himself had reared had been passionately converted to this use," and that it was "all for Acton Hague that she had kneeled every day at his altar" (254). This shock causes a profound rift between the two, since his refusal to "give him his candle" makes it impossible for her to see the altar as expressing her intention as well as his (258). Paradoxically, the fact that she assumed her counterpart had never known Hague had made it simpler to appropriate the shrine for her purposes. The threat she never posed to Stransom as a successful writer she now poses as a failed reader. Her fatal misreading of the sacred text compromises his own relationship to it as well. Like him, she has not discussed with a soul Hague's effect on her (apparently disastrous). She even postponed inviting Stransom to her house as long as the aunt who knew about her secret was alive. So the secret shared by Stransom and the woman provokes the gap between them—and the reader is even given to wonder if the secret may not be of the same sort somehow.[28]

James's point about the secrecy that inevitably attends all public matters is hard to miss here. Acton Hague, whose very name suggests a purposeful man of affairs, is the urtext for both Stransom and his lady friend; and the vastly different way they regard him, despite their similar treatment at his hands, is a tribute to his protean abilities. The woman is even compared to

Hague's work of art: "Moulded indeed she had been by powerful hands, to have converted her injury into an exaltation so sublime" (260). The public sphere, in the person of Hague, assumes in this story a predatory aspect, fashioning lives such as that of Stransom's woman friend, but by deceit and treachery, part of "that plasticity Stransom had supreme reason to know so great a master could have been trusted to produce." (The word *trusted*, in this context, is especially pungent.) As against the exploitation of others enacted by public men such as Hague, his victims chose instead to fashion their works in semiprivacy: Stransom in the bizarre form of his public yet esoteric altar, his lady friend through anonymous writing.

Especially disquieting is that her appropriation of his shrine for honoring the man Stransom most hates is so coincidental it has the air less of misreading than of reading far too well; in a reverse way the altar really *is* "about" Hague. Even the vanity project it represents hints at the need to retrieve lost recognition. Stransom, for instance, plans on his candle being "the tallest . . . of all"—a facet of his conception that accounts in good part for his interest in having a priestess for his shrine (250). It is rather as if he wishes to recuperate in semiprivate form the honor he lost at the hands of Hague—the word *honour,* by the way, making almost as regular an appearance in this tale as it does in *Tom Jones.* Unlike the other candles, his will be unmistakable, and his woman friend is to light it in his name.[29] But George Stransom's prospects for immortality seem almost as faint as those for his ritual's decipherability. In this his private cult only follows the public career of his old enemy, who more actively defrauds his interpreters.

Failing as he does in his attempt to mold his fellow cultist into his Galatea, it falls to Stransom to mold himself as the sacrificial offering for his altar. This is why their abrupt severance brings about his descent into death: "The church had become a void; it was his presence, her presence, their common presence, that had made the indispensable medium. If anything was wrong everything was—her silence spoiled the tune" (266). This absence of a successor priestess molded to his specifications is why "all his Dead had died again," and why it is only logical that he soon join them himself.

In the end, the Dead are the only Galatea he has, which is why he revisits them even after the break with his counterpart. His creation, now distinctly divorced from any "dim theological rescue," is not religious in any sense but aesthetic. As the fetish value of the altar increases, so does its likeness to an artwork. Of Stransom James says, "He took, in fancy, his composition to pieces, redistributing it into other lines, making other juxtapositions and contrasts. He shifted this and that candle, he made the spaces different, he effaced the disfigurement of a possible gap" (268). At this point he has become little different from an artist fussing with a painting's final touches, a writer forming the last stylistic arrangements of his "composition."

At the last moment, Stransom begins to succumb to death himself and haunts his old altar to join his Dead, particularly "the far-off face of Mary Antrim," who is "the glowing heart of the brightness" of the candles (269–70). The eroticism of this *unio mystica* is hard to overlook, and as before, the inspirational ghost is rhymed with the present-day woman. In a final reversal, the "reader" of Stransom's text has intervened in his private revision of it. It is, however, the inner logic of the composition itself—its formalist teleology, as it were—that impels him to this crowning revision, with its different intention. The temptation of the cynical is to ascribe his "change of heart" to a weak-willed desire that his monument to self continue after his imminent death, but James insists on his independent arrival at the decision to honor his betrayer. His "very rapture" before the memory of his lost love causes him to "contrast [it] with the bliss he had refused to another. . . . [T]he descent of Mary Antrim opened his spirit with a great compunctious throb for the descent of Acton Hague" (270).

This visitation, comparable in strange ways to the "miracle" or sign so often sought in Christian services, ministers to Stransom's own guilt over his stubborn hatred of Hague, causing that hatred to be replaced by honor. It also erases the "difference" between the woman and Stransom, which she announces in her coincidental appearance at the church just in time for Stransom to breathe his last. This Paraclete-like descent of Acton Hague can be figured as a homosocial reunion between two men, for which the woman has been at most a kind of facilitator, and the fact that Stransom is now himself in the identical position to the woman earlier—that he is now in some sense feminized—is an important detail we return to later. But queering Henry James, requisite as it sometimes is, is here only part of the story. For equally important is the fact that the same woman whose example proved inspiring to Stransom at the start of his project has now inspired him to alter the altar itself to reflect her meaning as well as his own. Uniting with Hague means accepting her vision. Once the repressed has returned to his project, a woman has been instrumental in bearing it even if its content may be male.[30]

Acton Hague, who in addition to carrying the name of the Catholic Lord Acton also has a name that puns on "action," has hitherto been excluded not just because Stransom was wronged by him but also, and crucially, because he was wronged in public—and in banishing Hague from his altar, he keeps out the spirit of publicity itself. What the woman's anguish at Hague's exclusion teaches Stransom is the limit of such exclusionary zeal. To reject the public sphere may be acceptable in itself, even laudable; but as soon as one's creation, however secret its venue, is open to reading by another it becomes at least potentially public. The egotism of the creator at first brings her in, assuming that the terms will be his; but the exigencies of the work itself, for James surely the crucial detail, come to demand that he include exactly the condemned part of his own past.

Leon Edel has argued that there is a struggle to the death between Stransom and the woman for control of the meaning of the altar, and that the woman (i.e. the reader) triumphs.[31] Although this overstates things, there is some truth to it. Stransom cannot continue his loathing of Hague, which also requires him to shut out the woman who honors his memory. He is unable to continue living because banishing the public from his creation was part of a desire to construe his life in a cruelly limiting fashion. The woman's ability to forgive a man who wronged her, the same who wronged Stransom, prepares the way for him to follow her lead at the end as at the beginning, and to read his project now fully in the light of her intention. Whereas the women of James's earlier stories had been misreaders, even actively hostile to writing, here the female reading of George Stransom's intention at first frightens him precisely because it is *too* perceptive—and indeed, he ends up accepting her reading as the deeper meaning of his own intention, as perfecting it. Letting a stranger into his project results not in alienating it from him, but rather in better ascertaining its authentic meaning, regardless of his initial desires. Whether this is completely welcome by Stransom is not a small matter, and it is well to keep it in mind as we turn to James's famous celebratory tale of the esoteric, "The Figure in the Carpet."

One could say that for James at this point, recovering from the death of Constance Fenimore Woolson, women are now a sort of triple threat. We have already seen that they are competition for him as fellow novelists, as Jane Highmore is to poor Ray Limbert; and we have seen that they can also harm a novelist as readers, fans, or partners, as witness Mrs. Ambient, Mrs. St. George, the ladies of Prestidge, and even Miss Fancourt. As Fenimore's suicide and the story analyzed above both indicate, there are also dangers to the artist even in their roles as muses or inspirations: the female character in "Altar" combines all three facets. But the nature of the danger has subtly shifted. Whereas the prior tendency is to see the women in James's artist tales as embodiments of the denseness of the age, an active power to misread, in "Altar" that very misreading changes: it is strangely intuitive, and its power overwhelms the project's inventor to the point where its meaning alters. The woman may misread on the surface, but she actually sees into and transforms Stransom's cult and its function after all. Without herself knowing it, she ferrets out the most abysmal secret of his project—the one unlit candle on the altar—and ultimately makes him reposition the project around that central meaning in her way rather than his. Also, as we noted, the fact that both were wronged by Hague means that Stransom puts himself in an implicitly female position at the end, as he prepares for his ecstatic visitation in a mode eerily like St. Theresa's.

Admittedly, the implied thematic of the story would be that he has been "saved," or at least purged of a disfiguring grudge, by the female example. But it is exactly here that the *distinctions* between Stransom's project and that of the literary artist have to be kept in mind, for though an imaginative idea, his is nevertheless one that honors real people. There is no fictional element: each candle stands in for people whose "endless histories" he reads in the chapel. He doesn't write them, so that the interpretation all has to do with his attitude toward these actually existing people, one of whom was also known to the woman. Reconciliation with a specific person can be on the agenda of a project such as this, whereas with fiction it is a different matter. And James may have thought that a good thing.

As a historical note, it was just during this period that literary criticism, then more high journalistic than scholastic in origin, was beginning to traffic in more explicitly psychological and biographical explanations for "artistic genius." English speakers were being introduced to Max Nordau and Cesare Lombroso, among others, who were looking closely at the connection between aesthetic products and the creator's psychic torments and shortcomings.[32] As the public became less inclined to sit still for long and involved literary fiction, its reviewers and critics became ever more inclined to slake its appetite for prurient or striking tidbits of knowledge about the lives and presumably flawed mentalities of its writers. With this for context, it is surely small wonder that one finds an especially pregnant observation in James's notebooks, to the effect that "The Figure in the Carpet" with its critic narrator will provide "a "lovely chance for fine irony on the subject of that fraternity."[33]

In some ways "Figure" replays the contest between writer and reader that forms the structure of "The Death of the Lion." But here, despite dying, the writer triumphs. The critic, though he outlives the writer, endures defeat. The central idea of the story is that a critic meets the author Hugh Vereker and is told by him that of all the articles devoted to his works, and presumably to teasing out some or another hidden truth thereof, nobody has been able to find the deepest intention that runs throughout the oeuvre itself, from beginning to end. Few have gotten even close. The disciple has just published an appreciation of the author, which the latter blandly pronounces "the usual twaddle." When the critic takes offense the author, out of guilt and possibly pity, explains that like everybody else he has missed the deep, inner essence of his work. This kindness proves killing to the critic as he sets off to learn, by frantic rereading and aggressive quizzing of the author's acquaintances, just what this mysterious message could be. Preparing to find out this "Author's Secret," as James calls it in his notes, the narrator seems to be embarking for the North Pole.[34]

He never does find out the "Author's Secret," naturally. Its MacGuffin of a secret is in a way the most obvious thing about it. But, in an almost too neat illustration of life (and critique) imitating art, critics since then have often put candidates forward. Frank Kermode, for instance, argues for a kind of sexual double entendre, and to be sure James implies such a reading in many ways.[35] (The detail that Gwendolen Erme, prior to this point a comfortable writer of second-rate books, becomes after marriage privy to "the secret," suggests to Kermode a parallel between marital and literary cults.)[36]

This analogy of James's is the source of much of the tale's sardonic humor. The critic's innocence in procreativity is rhymed in many respects with his innocence of creativity as well. Tzvetan Todorov's famous analysis of James's short story—that its point is its lack of point, as with Vereker's "secret"—has merit.[37] But Kermode's linking of sexual with artistic truth gives an unmistakable torque to this secret: one that, to use the old song, "some cats know" and others do not. The further significance of this linkage is that this sexual knowledge appears to be coded "male." When the critic approaches Vereker with the disturbing news that someone else is in on the secret ("It's a woman, into the bargain'"), Vereker reassures him and himself: "A woman will never find out.'"[38]

Why not? one has to ask. It is hard to avoid the conclusion that whatever it is that Vereker "has," apart from "faint wandering notes of a hidden music," it is a principle not available, at least not directly, to a female writer.[39] Such a secret is not a hermeneutical mystery, to be unraveled by astute detective work. Rather, it is a facet of sensibility in action. The figure in a Persian carpet is not the depiction of any object, overt or hidden, since the art is not representational. Therefore, what the figure figures, finally, is the active creative force of the artist. The activity is coded male because it is activity, perhaps, but also because it reserves to the male principle the province of art.

Kermode shrewdly notes the way Corvick's quandary about whether to "marry Mrs. Corvick to get what I wanted" after her enlightened husband dies echoes the narrator's similar dilemma in "The Aspern Papers."[40] This relay points out the vicarious relation of the critic both to sexuality and to productivity. Like the narrator in "Aspern," the critic remains permanently removed from sexual as from creative understanding; excluded from both inner realms, he can know their importance (and those finer points that, in James's world, are the only points there are) only by hearsay.

Kermode makes the passage between artistic and sexual initiation evident in his introduction to the Penguin edition of James's artist tales: "the bright young man's misapprehensions concerning the secrets of marriage—of the growing point of one kind of life—are matched by his ignorance—accompanied by an excessive, impotent interest—in another kind of creative secret."[41] But it is also likely that by making the narrator a man equally excluded from the realms of both sexuality and art, James discreetly shades the differences between the two realms. The economies of romantic love and of artistic creation are not finally compatible here, even though the same figure may be mystified by both. By allowing women admission only as muses, the artistic sensibility can reserve a male vector of force for itself.

The altar prepared the muses, then, is also an altar of sacrifice; living women must die in order to assume the muse role for James. Like Minnie Temple, they had to be locked away in the "crystal walls of the past," the better to serve as inspiration to his imagination "by all the bright intensity of [their] example."[42]

All of which leads the reader inevitably back to the other enduring peculiarity of "Figure," and that is all of those deaths that occur in it. The artistic secret, the wonderful mystery of James's, and Vereker's, art cult, is connected not only to life but also to death in some form. The reason for that may well be this vampiric artistic energy, taking its cue and its inspiration from living examples of sensibility and of lively moral judgment: examples that, owing to the essential innocence necessary to such qualities for James, cannot live too long.

Fenimore's suicide confused this economy whereby once-living girls become posthumous inspirations. For one thing, she lived too long to be convincingly virginal; and for another, Henry James himself suspected that his own neglect of her played its role in bringing about her death. All forms of totemism, including that required of muse worship, combine reverence with aggression, or with the memory of aggression. But here was a case where aggression could not be disguised as mere ill fortune. James had here, rather directly, sacrificed somebody else to his own art. The vigorous celebration of the mysteries of style characteristic of "Figure," as a result, conceals a rather more specific hermeneutic. All of those deaths that accumulate imply more than the impervious monomania of the narrator, although they abundantly do that. They are also the excessive index of a sacrificial economy. But just what, or who, is being sacrificed?

To answer that, we return to the crucial reason why what Stransom made in "The Altar of the Dead" was not, for all its similarities, in the end a work of art. It was not fiction. On the one hand, actually existing people had to die in order to be included on the altar; but George Stransom's own identity was secure until his candle joined theirs. The memory of each person was very much Stransom's memory, which was why the remembered person he didn't honor was so central to the significance for him of those he did. But because it is completely private, but for one other mourner, his concealment is simple. The lives are symbolized, but simply, and they are not transformed. But in fiction, of course, they are, which means they become material in a new creation that adds imagination to memory and eclipses it. Hence, while its creative aspect begs comparison with sexuality, its relation to reality is closer to sacrifice and homage, or totemism.[43]

Central to this strategy is the fact of publication itself. To write fiction is to present one's story as neither true nor false, and the critics would have nothing to hate after if all stories were not based in some way on actuality. But if the deepest secret lies in the transformation, then that can by definition only be known to the artist, and perhaps to a very few on that particular wavelength, who somehow catch the music as it wanders. Such a secret will also evade those analysts, increasing in number and noise in James's day, who see fiction as the merest palimpsest for the author's life. In a way, this joke of James's is salutary. But it was probably also reassuring to the author. After all, if the deepest secret was the art itself, the process of transformation, then discovering ugly personal realities behind the work would not tell people very much. And if the motive force of this transformation is at root a male endowment, then no amount of female intuition of the sort that invades George Stransom's space will trespass on the secret either.

The new marketplace of the end of the nineteenth century was a space Henry James feared at least as much as he sought it, not only because fewer people than ever seemed interested in literature but also because more people than ever seemed inquisitive and prying about literati. Such a worry may have been particularly acute after Fenimore's suicide, when James was careful to destroy any correspondence between them that would provide clues to whatever happened, or didn't, between them. In this light he began to inscribe obscurity in more positive ways, not as the stifling of self-expression but as the persistence of a more private self, pursuing its discreet life underneath the surface of story, hidden in plain sight. What it conceals may be art or life, or more likely some never-ending strife between them; but regardless, it becomes James's sense that the public square, properly entered, can be a very good place to go undetected. Best of all, those critics who may be interested in where the bodies are buried will always lose, because they will lose the insight to be gleaned from experiencing the work. This is the aspect of James's joke that strikes us as wish fulfillment: we know now that critics are not so easily gotten rid of. And the notion that the secret consists in its absence is somehow too familiar to postmoderns to be persuasive. The rise of "symptomatic reading" probably did come about from the sort of alienation of authors from publics that Allon White describes, but that does not mean critics do not continue to this day to find it useful.[44] I have used a bit of it here, for example. The last artist tale we look at expresses the belief that the fruits of the marketplace could somehow foster the interests of authorial anonymity rather than ruin them as it does for Neil Paraday. Being misunderstood has its advantages, and writing in disguise confers them.

But Don DeLillo's Bill Gray discovers how hard it is to be well and truly anonymous, and his *Mao II,* the very last book I treat (in chapter 9), is also the next to have a literary figure for its protagonist. In the novels that follow James in examining the perils of publicity, we see set designers and lovelorn columnists, translators and former English majors, history professors and screenwriters: no authors of high seriousness to speak of. But it will not take much "symptomatic reading" to discern how the concerns of these characters' creators, writers of high seriousness all, shine through their stories all the same. Those concerns also conveniently track the development of the publicity apparatus that James confronted only in its infancy, and to these twentieth-century works we now turn.

part two

The Twentieth Century

chapter three

Machine Age and Beyond: From West to DeLillo

Henry James wrote at a time when the engines of publicity were large-ly verbal. The telegraph was still a more important force than the then emerging technique of photography that eventually made the Hearst papers possible. James certainly does address the fetishism that visual imagery can augment, for instance in the hilarious short story "The Real Thing," which makes fun of the still common superstition about the cam-era as truth ray. But the overwhelming realities of the symbolic market-place of James's era were still pulp fiction and the lower journalism. Even if some of his nineties artist tales can be dismissed as partly therapeutic, bitter balm for a wounded dramatist, still the clear divide he makes between the better and lesser angels of the written word, between St. George and Overt, let us say, comes within a structure common to both. The finer writers and the coarser writers are, after all, both writers, and cannot be distinguished for the purposes of a brief story except by nega-tional qualities. It is by not "getting the girl," for Overt, or by not getting the best-selling payoff, for Limbert, that the finer sensibilities mark them-selves off. It is very close to the artist's ideological economy Pierre Bourdieu succinctly defines as "loser take all."[1] While it is probably true that the English setting alone, with its country house weekends and titled aristoc-racy, makes some of James's specifics hard to translate even across the Atlantic of his own day, nevertheless there is enough testimony from cor-respondents of his such as William Dean Howells that popular journalism and its assumptions were already working their rigors in similar ways on both sides of the pond.

Still, even if some of the moral clarity of James's artist tales was facti-tious, as "The Altar of the Dead" for one instance demonstrates, it was all the same a world wherein it was possible to discern what the publicity apparatus was (a world of pushy individual reporters and "publishing scoundrels") and what the literary individual ideally should be (dedicated only to the highest and the best, possessed of lordly indifference to getting and spending). Considering James's much heralded ambiguity, the universe of these literary stories, for all their intrigues and subterfuge, turns out to have been fairly straightforward both epistemologically and morally. In other words, we are left in little doubt what, finally, is going on; which side is virtuous; and what the virtuous are obligated to do to combat the wicked, whether or not they win. (Actually, a surprising number of James's novels also have, at root, this sort of moral simplicity.) That so many of James's literary figures are innocents and new to the world only confirms their goodness for him and the reader, as befits the author of *What Maisie Knew, The Wings of the Dove,* and *The Awkward Age.* But that world, evil as it is, is not particularly bewildering after first encounters with it. By the thirties, things have changed.

The journalistic world Nathanael West describes in *Miss Lonelyhearts,* the motion picture industry whose demimonde he depicts in *Day of the Locust,* are no less commercial entities than the publishing world of the 1890s; indeed, they are arguably far more so. The transactional imperative that was already shaping James's literary world was still in place, more determinative than ever. To the basic motive force of commerce, though, had been added a new national marketplace, made possible by mail order, department store chains, parcel post, the smoothing of America's roads, and numerous other innovations of the turn of the twentieth century.[2] And to this in turn had been added another important element: iconic representation. When James was writing his stories, only the photograph and the telegraph were of any moment in mass culture, but by the thirties radio and the cinema had been invented, and photography had begun to assume a far more prominent place in the repertoire of mass publicity.

With all the changes that occur, can we enunciate anything that endures? In a way, this entire study is an implicit answer to that question. In brief, the underlying tension of the literary figure who both disdains and fears the marketplace yet must rely on it for access to readers continues to subtend what is written in serious fiction in the twentieth century, just as it did in the late Victorian new Grub Street James depicts. We can also say that the novels, few and far between in modern American letters, that try to describe the workings of the marketplace inevitably fall under a similar paradox. However, the great difference is that, at least until Bill Gray in Don DeLillo's *Mao II,* the contradictions this predicament implies are best termed displaced. They enter the peripheral vision at times but seldom assume a more central location on the stage.

The obvious point here is also the essential one: that the protagonists of these novels, though most of them are recognizably bearers (or anyway recipients) of culture, are not themselves literary people. Though the title character of *Miss Lonelyhearts* writes, it is not literature but rather a column for the lovelorn; when he conjures higher aspirations for his lowly practice, they are (perhaps symptomatically) not artistic, really, so much as religious. Vladimir Nabokov's *Lolita* narrator, Humbert Humbert, is probably the closest thing to a literary figure, and even he has been an academic and translator whose only foray into creative writing turns out to be the very book we are reading. Certainly, his concerns are not on the surface all that aesthetic either, focusing more on Priapus than Parnassus. *Day of the Locust*'s Tod Hackett is a visual artist, appropriately for a Hollywood novel no doubt; Oedipa Maas in Pynchon's *Crying of Lot 49* is the surviving mistress of a business tycoon, though she is also a onetime English major whose skills stand her in good stead as the novel progresses; and J. A. K. (Jack) Gladney is a historian who openly admits that the discipline he founds, Hitler Studies, is faintly disreputable and who cannot speak or read German.

If none of these people, strictly speaking, qualifies as a writer in classic *Künstlerroman* terms, then what are they? The briefest answer would be readers, of their own situations and then by extension of the larger publicity landscape that so situates them. It is as readers, critics, and amateur anthropologists—most generally one could say detectives—that these central characters embody literary traits and carry out their roles as bearers of culture and analysis. But what is the object of their scrutiny? What particular various anxieties or hopes prompt their quests? What larger ends does their detective work serve in any given case? And above all, is there a way in which they are themselves implicated in the world whose workings they attempt to uncover?

The Facsimiles of Life, the Truths of Fiction

To answer the first question requires us to refine a bit what was said above about the new world of publicity after the turn of the century. The public spectacle of the commercial world, whose essence was in place by the twenties, became far more elaborate and pervasive than it had ever been before. This change was especially evident in the United States, which until the turn of the century had been an agrarian and small-town society where people (this is almost unimaginable to us today) actually made most of the goods they owned. By the twenties this was decidedly not the case, and the mail-order catalogue or "wish book" was something most families had and thought to use. The marketplace was national, advertising was inescapable, and resistance was futile. But why resist?[3]

To this aborning consumer paradise were soon added radio, a carnival barker's mouth continually soliciting the ears of a nation—and of course the movies. In the late teens and twenties, the growth of both of these entities meant that the tabloid journalism already in place was now supplemented by what has come to be called "electronic media." There have been many books detailing the differences between print and iconic media, and I do not propose to rehearse those many distinctions here. But the most important for the purposes of this study probably springs from the confluence of the national grid of marketing and the invention of these electronic forms of communication. The result is a curious loss, rather than gain, in the sense of reality.

On the surface, this seems paradoxical or just plain wrong. And in a way, it is wrong. After all, the radio and cinema carried into remote parts of the country images inaccessible hitherto: a newsreel could show the world, not just tell of it; a radio broadcast could provide a free ticket (minus advertising) to what earlier generations had to catch whenever it came to town. But at the same time, the dependence of these media on commercial sources lent an air of the meretricious to the most innocent proceedings—as for many of us it still does. As a result of this partnership between commerce and electronic imagery, there arises the fear that what is presented therein is somehow phony, either motivated by some hidden purpose unavailable to public view or itself a mere simulation. When commercial and government forces have the ability to put forward spectacles for our entertainment and edification, the suspicion that these processes can be, and then actually are, being manipulated by sinister powers seems less "paranoid" than just cautionary.

It may not require advanced psychological insight to see that the fear of lying in this instance is actually based on the suspicion of theft. By that I mean that what commercial processes have always done is to take the materials of already existing or prior culture (its songs, its myths, above all its prejudices) and in effect sell them back to the culture's members at a markup.[4] In the process commercialism also divorces the things of culture from the site of cultural transmission and denatures them, particularly minimizing their connection to the conscience (which does not sell well unless it is enjoined on people different from the audience). The fraud, in other words, resides not so much in any specific "lies they are telling us" or "things they refuse to tell us" (though assuredly both exist) as in the precondition for the commercial elaboration of culture itself, which is the borrowing or stealing of folk- and high-cultural elements and their recirculation in the marketplace, to be sold back to the people from whom they were taken. To be sure, for most people this does not seem like a fraud, or even an especially bad deal; as with tasteless produce shipped over great distances, cultural material that comes from afar can make up in abundance and convenience what it lacks in juice and fiber. Still, when cultural materials are disengaged from the social circumstances that *make* them cultural in the strongest sense—aspects of a way of life—there is always a feeling that what results is like advertising: a practice that quickly became paradigmatic for defining just what thing it was that this emerging commercial electronic apparatus of publicity actually *did*.[5]

Whether or not the suspicion of falsehood belies the reality of theft, it remains that the vast new amusement park of electronic media was born in tandem with the newly nationalized marketplace. The most immediate symptom of this conjunction is indeed advertising, for which radio from its inception was continually used: "And now a word . . ." completes itself for a reason. Yet in a way, advertising itself may be less weighty in its impact than this other, vaguer sense of simulation. The new commercial media have three properties that are found together: they increasingly come from far away, because the centers of commerce are few and centralized; they have the illusion of immediacy, chiefly owing to their iconic status, which gives the impression of actuality to what they are presenting (although radio does retain a role for the mind's eye); and above all, they are everywhere, assaulting the eye and ear, teeming with urgent messages that usually involve buying something. The net effect of the illusionistic materials, distant origins, and overwhelming pervasion of commercial electronic media is to blur for many people an all-important epistemological distinction, that between fiction and nonfiction.

It is worth recalling that fiction and nonfiction are not separated on the basis of truth and falsehood—fiction, of course, can be thought of as true spiritually, or as ringing true; and *The Protocols of the Elders of Zion* is no doubt found in the nonfiction part of the library. The basis for separating fiction and nonfiction, in conventional terms anyway, is that fiction is that discourse in which the question of truth or falsity is not radically implicated. In fiction, all of it can be true or false; but either way, all of it is assumed to be made up. This is one reason, though not the only one, of course, why novelists so often react badly to attempts to determine the real-life "model" for this or that character: theirs, you must understand, is a work of imagination. In nonfiction, the basis is assumed to be given from evidence, the assertions assumed to be truth claims about the world. The line between fiction and nonfiction has always been contested by the inevitable amalgam of the two, which I will call *facsimile*. (*Faction* has always seemed to me an ungainly term.) But the means of representation elaborated in twentieth-century America, together with what was suspected to be the motivations behind this elaboration, make both the possibilities of facsimile—and the paranoia about those possibilities—more fertile than ever. Interestingly, the flip side of this paranoia about what is real in that which presents itself as nonfiction (a paranoia summed up nicely in the bumper sticker "I never believe the liberal media [here clearly meaning news organizations]") is a queer disinterest quite frequently in the moral valence of fiction in its various forms: what is christened, and supposedly thus rendered nice and harmless, as "entertainment." Both the uncritical acceptance of entertainment and the paranoia about dark conspiracies behind the publicity facade arise from the defeat of reality testing. The reality behind the image is either indicated by appearances or belies them, and we are not given the means to confirm or deny. At the same time, electronic media intensify the illusion of reality afforded what we see and hear.

Our reaction to this state of affairs is threefold: we trust uncritically, we distrust completely, or we decide it does not matter. No reaction is favored, in the absence of any concrete means of testing what is presented. Thus do the rudiments of public life (and public spectacle is one of those rudiments) cease to belong to the realm of logical discourse or reflection and become instead phantasmagorical.[6]

Hence the view that the twentieth century in America can be summarized as the age of advertising is, in a sense, too benign. Advertising, after all, is relatively open about its object and is openly paid for. What I would argue, instead, is that the twentieth century has been in fact the age of public relations. If there is a presiding deity of the century, it could well be Edward Bernays. This nephew of Sigmund Freud has marketed himself as the father of American public relations, a claim whose success could itself be evidence of Bernays's skill in his field (some hold out for his contemporary Ivy Lee, who rubbed some serious tarnish off John D. Rockefeller's image in the teens after his paid troops massacred striking miners *en famille* in Ludlow, Colorado, in 1913).[7] Regardless of who started it, though, Bernays's philosophy certainly had the largest part in establishing the means and ends of public relations as it evolved. Briefly, Bernays saw public relations as a response to the threat of democracy. The role of public relations was to mitigate the rise of possibly critical mass opinion by catering to instinct rather than reason and reconciling people to rule by the few.

In an age when the word is applied far too promiscuously, Edward Bernays could with some precision be called an elitist.[8] What public relations consists of, in the end, is the conscious manipulation of "real life" (events assumed to be spontaneous or prima facie newsworthy) according to a hidden agenda. The twenties, which saw the marketplace grid firmly installed for the first time, also saw the rise of Bernays and his practices.[9]

This may seem far afield from the present study, but it is not. The issue here is not whether the entire field of publicity has in fact been "taken over" by hidden persuaders who manipulate the figments of reality placed before us, but whether the very structure of that field ministers to the sort of confusion between reality and appearance that Bernays and his heirs could exploit. My belief, as should be obvious by now, is that it does and has done from the beginning. We could even preliminarily divide recent decades into Early Public Relations (the era of James's literary tales), Middle Public Relations (the early- and mid-century U.S. background of West and Nabokov), and Late Public Relations, a term I prefer to *post-modernity* (the world inhabited by Pynchon, DeLillo and their readers). Roughly speaking, these eras parallel technologies: James's that of print journalism, West's and Nabokov's that of print plus cinema and radio, and Pynchon's and DeLillo's that of all the above plus television and computerization.

The more salient point for my purposes is that the vastness and mystery of the mass-culture landscape and its impact on the public sphere mean that the individual who questions it in any way adopts the attitude of a detective. James's heroes were caught in their marketplace worlds, but they knew fairly well what those worlds were and what their roles were to be. By contrast, Miss Lonelyhearts and Tod Hackett are each so disoriented, so alienated in their sudden immersion into mass culture that they must first assess the dimensions and intentions behind their worlds before even deciding what to do, whether to accept or reject their worlds. Their projects are a kind of reality testing, or attempt at it. I say attempt because this detective work "saves" none of the protagonists, and arguably only makes them more miserable. Why this is so I take up later. First, though, I reflect on the detective role taken up by these protagonists; what compels them to start decoding their situation, and by extension the larger publicity machinery of which their situations are small parts; and what larger ends they think their paranoid skepticism serves. For they confront the apparatus of illusion that is the American marketplace not as writers, but as readers. And what they read is the handwriting on the billboard of mass culture.

Reading and Redemption

It may not be exaggerating to say that the protagonists of these novels associate the quest for the meaning of publicity culture with salvation: salvation from it or salvation through it. But beyond this generalization, there are varying forms of predicament and equally varying hopes for manumission from the causes of that predicament. What is read, and how, depends on how one feels trapped in the first place. Each novel confronts its would-be detective with a different mystery, with its particular connection to the larger mystery of the public relations society.

Although the metaphor of detective work is convenient, is does not quite cover the case of Miss Lonelyhearts. For he starts the book under no illusions about the true nature of the tabloid newspaper whose cause he serves, nor about the role he plays toward the readers who ask him for help: that of base betrayer. So it is worth asking whether he has anything to discover at all. But in a way, the very fact that he has no illusions is his problem, because what he needs are illusions. His quest is for a transcendent meaning that can be realized through his flawed medium of the advice column. As mentioned, it is not strictly speaking an aesthetic redemption he seeks, although many have noticed a possible reply to those who insist on a salvific power for art in a book where the first phony reply Shrike dictates directs its reader to seek solace by its means. Miss Lonelyhearts's relation to art is not differentiated from that of his colleagues at the newspaper who, having believed in beauty as a personal ideal in college and shortly thereafter, have now "lost everything."[10] They are "not worldly men," and neither is he (14). What he does seek as an answer to the mystery of his predicament is the Christian faith of his youth, the only ideal that could possibly make his phony consolation sincere.

In one sense, then, *Miss Lonelyhearts* is the appropriate transition after the James stories, since of all of the reader figures in these twentieth-century novels, its title character most resembles one of James's artist figures. The essential difference is that he is not a highbrow purist trying to negotiate the waters of commercial compromise but a full-fledged citizen of the land of the tabloid trying belatedly to become good. He takes his part in the newspaper as a mercenary if risible necessity, until he starts examining it. This detective work has little to do with uncovering a hidden plot in an outfit whose cynicism is quite out in the open. Rather, Miss Lonelyhearts describes it as examining "the values by which he lives." It is only in the course of this examination that he realizes the extent to which "he is the victim of the joke and not its perpetrator" (32).

From that point on, his investigation chiefly involves trying to give a face to his readers' names, a breach of columnar fiction for which he pays dearly. He also experiments with incorporating his religious aspirations into his advice, with disastrous results. The interesting thing he does not explore is himself: why he seeks and avoids Betty, finally treating her essentially as a harmless child; why he refuses to read a letter addressed to him when it is the one thing that could have saved his life (with the clear symbolism that he has decided not to read himself); above all, why he never quits his exploitative job. While it is possible to see Miss Lonelyhearts's several dream sequences as tentative forms of self-evaluation, the meaning of them is less reflected upon by him than left for the reader to sort out independently.

Throughout this novel, the reader encounters an ironic tension between the attitude taken up by Miss Lonelyhearts toward his role in the media marketplace and that of his text, so much so that media critic George W. S. Trow identifies the tabloid substratum of twentieth-century America with the newsroom in West's novel.[11] Although its title character may believe that a change of attitude can rewrite the betrayal that is written into his column, the novel itself seems to know better. Miss Lonelyhearts's attempts to uncover his real relation to his readers as people, not merely as words and abstractions, have to fail because the fictional role, where for one thing he has a different gender, requires the distance of the apparatus itself to prosper. He can only unite with his readers in death, which in a way he does.

With Tod Hackett, the set designer of West's *Day of the Locust,* one can argue that he accepts the advice only put forward by jesting Shrike and never followed by Miss Lonelyhearts: "Art is a Way Out." Tod's relation to Hollywood seems, on the surface, more sophisticated than his counterpart's hysterical project of becoming a savior via his column for the lovelorn. What Tod does instead is to use his day job for money and pursue his artistic vision on his off-hours in his apartment. Further, whereas Miss Lonelyhearts seems to know only two modes—escaping the world of the newspaper altogether or fashioning his role in it into a messianic mold for which it is clearly not designed—Tod Hackett's painting, *The Burning of Los Angeles,* is in part a way of analyzing or dramatizing the repressed content of the Hollywood whose faithful servant he is during the day.

That having been said, though, the prophecy in Tod's painting saves neither others nor himself. Indeed, there is good reason to be dubious whether it really is prophecy at all, since at least his interpretation of his own painting is that it depicts an angry populace smashing its idols, and the actual riot that closes the book is far more amorphous than that. Beyond that, it can be argued that Tod is at least as much a split personality as Miss Lonelyhearts, if slightly less high-strung. The social circle he inhabits consists almost entirely of aspiring performers who are unable to get to the discovery stage, and his obsession with Faye Greener partakes of the same worshipful fandom his mural shows, turning ugly toward its objects of veneration. Still, in the end Tod Hackett is the only one of the reader figures who comes close to being an artist figure until the writer Bill Gray. In addition, though, Hackett definitely sees himself as some kind of prophet, although from a different testament from that of Miss Lonelyhearts, *The Burning of Los Angeles* suggesting Jeremiah rather more than Jesus.

It could be that the visual arts provided the distance needed for West to be able to inscribe the conflicts between artistic aspiration and commercial complicity so directly. After all, the passage from *Miss Lonelyhearts* to *Locust* describes a shift from print to electronic media that parallels West's own journey from New York to Hollywood to become a screenwriter. He started writing for Republic Studios for the money, as he cheerfully acknowledged, all the while continuing his serious work on his own with a view to critiquing the industry in which he was a small cog.[12] It may be film's status as a collaborative medium that allows a Tod Hackett to divorce his work as a set designer from his personal artistic quest. Miss Lonelyhearts's identity as the sole begetter of his column may be a clue to his delusion that he could somehow transform it into authentic expression.

Tod Hackett also has concerns about authenticity, a recurring issue wherever twentieth-century publicity culture is observed. It is fair to say also that the moving picture medium, with its greater effect of reality, seems to have heightened the specifically miragelike quality of mass-cultural product. Whereas in the former novel the most direct victims of the advice column are easy to define as the letter writers and eventually the columnist himself, by contrast the Hollywood depicted in *Locust* works to loosen the hold of reality itself, of collectively understood history. The running together of historical modes in housing styles parallels the eclectic approach to history itself as rendered by Hackett's studio. Where Miss Lonelyhearts's detective work sends him into direct contact with his readers, the closest Hackett gets to his audience, until the riot in which he is finally trapped, is the demimonde of actors and extras and an Iowan refugee, Homer Simpson. The audience he inscribes in his painting is truly a work of his imagination, into which he pours many of his own urges and fantasies.

This is what artists always do, but prophets are supposed to read more clearly. Tod thinks of art as a way out, and in a sense it is. One of the strangest moments of the ending occurs when Tod thinks himself back to his situation in the apartment painting his mural. It is possible that the crowd's incitement is causing him to think of new things to do to his canvas, but just as likely that he is using his imagination to return him to the scene of imagination itself rather than the reality. He is not able to escape the crowd or Los Angeles, as it happens. One would sooner say that it is Hollywood and its public that escape him. Tod does not make Miss Lonelyhearts's mistake of imputing the capacity for sincerity and greatness to the publicity mechanism within which he finds himself, but his faith is in the public as almost as mystical an entity—and as misplaced.

What has to be understood in looking at both of these West novels is that, while the intent of the author could be seen as satirical and even demystifying, neither of the protagonists is about the demystification business at all. In fact, arguably both of them start out disabused before the action gathers itself. Instead, what motivates their detective search is better thought of as a remystifying process, a desire to fashion the realities of the publicity machines within which they find themselves so as to accommodate the personal myths that Miss Lonelyhearts and Tod are pursuing.[13] The former hero imagines himself as playing out an essentially priestly role, with the ungainly instrument of the column for a pulpit; as a result, the novella does not address the question of the efficacy of art, at least not directly. Nor does it make room for the possibility of combining the whoredom of writing a phony advice column with the off-hours purity of another, more authentic writing situation.

Like Miss Lonelyhearts, Tod Hackett too yearns for authenticity. But unlike him, Hackett sees it as accruing to an artistic rather than a strictly religious vocation. For all that, he admits he cannot shake the mantle of "prophet," which makes his ambitions messianic in only a slightly less fanatical way than his counterpart's. But by crucial contrast, Tod also refuses to forsake his disabused stance toward the Hollywood enterprise in which he is enmeshed, and in fact pursues his critique of the industry he is involved in by means of his off-hours art. His solution, then, is to maintain the ironical stance of working for the studio by day and subjecting it to a withering irony by night. But, as it turns out, neither embracing the pregiven role nor doubling it with another, higher role is effective in surmounting the contradictions the publicity apparatus affords, at least for a West protagonist. The mantle of prophet is as hard for the artist to assume as it is for the would-be priest, which is why *Locust* may have to use a visual artist rather than the more obvious choice of screenwriter for its protagonist. To etch those contradictions as starkly for a writer would pose a more directly disabling challenge to the stance of the book's own author.[14] It seems in any case that whether one embraces one's fate like Miss Lonelyhearts and says, "I accept," or strikes the stance of the grand refusal and declares oneself an artist—in short, whether one cooperates with or undermines one's role in publicity, the ineffectual result is the same. This is so in part because both protagonists have another role they acknowledge less than their activist one: both are also consumers. Miss Lonelyhearts's advice to himself is, after all, not all that different from the sort of recommendations he makes to his victims: it is not for nothing that Shrike dubs Christ the Miss Lonelyhearts of Miss Lonelyhearts. As for Hackett, his obsession with Faye Greener, which is significantly twinned by that ultimate audience, Homer Simpson, proves that he is just as much caught up in the psychology of the movies as the people in his mural, that the mural looks within at the creator's mind while it looks out onto Los Angeles. And herein lies the essential difference between West's and James's cultural figures: the latter are finer sensibilities whose economic need forces them into the marketplace and indirectly into its corruptions as well, whereas the former are already formed by the media products they now put out and try to despise. The loop structure West describes is, if anything, even tighter than James's, because the mentality of the protagonist is already compromised. The engines of publicity have advanced too far, become too vital to everyone's formation, by the thirties. The prior innocence James seems largely to assume of his heroes is no longer as plausible, and its absence makes a stance of alienation from the marketplace, à la Hackett, as hard to sustain as an attempt to infuse the marketplace with sincere intention, à la Miss Lonelyhearts.

Sincere intentions do not burden Vladimir Nabokov's narrator, Humbert Humbert, whose fictional memoir forms the novel *Lolita* (1955). But a similar desire to read the deeper meaning of a shallow mass culture does persist here nonetheless, as does the aspiration to the status of artist. Since the relentlessly narrow aperture of the narrator's concerns almost entirely concerns his love object (when he mentions that he and Lo visit Mission Dolores in their travels, he adds that it would make a "good title for a book"), any larger social or cultural texture seems tangential somehow.[15] Still, since for his own purposes he has to fathom how Lolita's mind works, an issue that becomes more insistent when he writes his memoirs than he admits it was before, this in turn requires attention to the mass-cultural backdrop of her desires and interests: a mass culture that attains embodiment in the person of Clare Quilty.

Humbert, be it noted, is no creative artist, except for the memoir itself perhaps—which of course could be creative in a less honorific sense as well.

He is an academic and a translator. But he is, in his perverse way, an Arnoldian culture bearer, concerned that his Dolores Haze get a grounding in the classics and as horrified at Beardsley High's modernizings as it no doubt would be at him. As with the West heroes, though, Humbert not only wants to unravel Lolita's culture but also finds himself fascinated by it. At least part of what intrigues him in Lolita is what he calls the eerie mixture of vulgarity and grace, and the mass-cultural background of both is part of what attracts him to Lolita. (If one wished to be more psychoanalytic than Nabokov would wish, one could even argue that the complete imaginary identification Humbert posits between his Annabel and her later incarnation in Lolita is a screen perception and a handy way of obliterating the "American" part of her appeal to him. Though named after an American heroine out of Poe, Hum's early love seems in no other way a translatable entity into the American idiom.)

In one sense, then, Humbert's project of finding meaning in the illusions of his American Oz is really just one version of the immigrant parables making up this phase of Nabokov's literary career, the other two novels in this vein being *Pnin* (1957) and *Pale Fire* (1962). In all of these narratives, the alienation of the protagonist from American mass culture is not, first and foremost, aesthetic but rather a matter of deep identity. Timofey Pnin and Charles Kinbote confront things American with as much bafflement as Humbert, but they do not have a sexual object of comparable organizing power, unless one counts Kinbote's magnificent obsession with the poet John Shade, his neighbor across the road. Throughout what some have thought of as his American trilogy, however, Nabokov presents this country as above all a task of translation, a riddle to be unraveled by his heroes, albeit with varying degrees of success. (The degrees of effort also vary: by the time Kinbote commences his commentary on Shade's poem "Pale Fire," he has all but decided to read this *echt* American text as if it referred to his European childhood.) But what all three have in common is their immigrant predicament, the never-ending need to take what they experience in the United States and find some resonant equivalent from their own past. *Lolita* can be taken as the paradigmatic text for these émigré tales.

What I focus on, however, is the role played by the villain of the piece— that is, the other villain besides the narrator himself, Clare Quilty. Just as Charlotte Haze, the blocking figure for Humbert's seduction plans in book 1, embodies a certain American mid-century housewife with cultural aspirations and muddled, middlebrow results; the rival in book 2, more successful than poor Charlotte in thwarting Humbert's plans, is also burdened with a cultural association. Like Charlotte, he is middlebrow, but not through ignorance or impercipience so much as strategy. He is a deliberate hack, writing to the mass market; he is even a pornographer whose wish to debase Lolita darkly recalls Humbert's own desire to have filmed her, but solely for his own benefit rather than that of the anonymous masses. But to understand the full power of Quilty's role as Humbert's hated alter ego and scapegoat requires one to recall how Humbert construes his own *grande passion* for Lolita.

Humbert Humbert appears in this book the classic failed artist, who tries to borrow art's prestige for his own affliction and the crimes it occasions. Emblematic is the fantasy he confides of being commissioned by the Enchanted Hunters Hotel, where he has just seduced Lo, to paint a mural commemorating the event. His description of this notional mural, which is also of course Nabokov's, makes it sound far more idiosyncratic than even Hackett's mural. But he does not paint it, of course, nor does he compose any literary pieces that we know of. He does translate other masterpieces into English, a practice that as we have seen carries over (perhaps in reverse) to his love life and overall approach to his adoptive land. But he himself thinks of his attempt to relive the Annabel experience through Lolita not as translation but as the work of an artist: "I broke her [Annabel's] spell by incarnating her in another," he says (15). Even assuming this story to be valid, and there is no internal contradiction to it that I see, the objectification of Lolita here is near total, as is the violation. To use another person as the occasion for one's own "artistry," particularly for the less-than-artistry of a Humbert Humbert, adds to an already heinous act another aspect of baseness.

When he goes after the hated Quilty, the one who he says cheats Humbert of "my redemption," he does so in part for the obvious reason that he stole his girl. But Nabokov implies a deeper reason, which is Quilty's convenient embodiment of all of the lower artistic impulses. Humbert himself at first obliterates Lolita's individuality by thinking of her "as" Humbert's earlier lover, but later comes to see Lolita in herself as whom he loves; and Quilty is the reminder of all of the unworthy impulses that prompted Humbert's initial undertaking. Getting rid of Quilty for Humbert does not take on guilt so much as alleviate it. Edmund White even goes so far as to announce that "the murder of Quilty expiates Humbert of everything base," despite what opinion the authorities may have held in the matter.[16]

There are temptations to ally a Quilty figure with other Nabokov doubles such as Gradus in *Pale Fire*. But the difference is that his status as writer makes him a more intimately destabilizing element. After Lolita's abduction, Humbert literally becomes a reader of Quilty, searching the motel records for a familiar name, then trying to decode clues from the names he sees to the identity of the evildoer. Further, Quilty's form of writing is decidedly not literary but commercial: he does not write for television, but had *Lolita* come out a few years later he probably would have. His inability to see Lolita's individuality is made a symptom of his inability to see Humbert's identity either, a possibly Dantesque punishment for his protean agility at hiding his own identity. He is a slightly slicker article than Gradus, but the "mass man" label is just as easy to attach to him. It is also appropriate that Lo herself is more attracted to Quilty's vulgarity than Humbert's more high-end cultural capital: she is, after all, a child, and this preference is proof of it. Nabokov writes during a period when the things of mass culture can still just plausibly be ascribed chiefly to the world before the onset of full adulthood. (It is doubtful whether such an assumption could be made with verisimilitude today.)

In sum, it is true that Nabokov's antihero, like the other protagonists, is in a sense a cultural reader and a detective. But as is so often true, Nabokov's work is a special case. For one thing, Humbert is himself a criminal, which accounts for the strange relief the reader feels when attention turns to Quilty, a figure who actually seems more awful than Humbert does. For another, he is of course a terrible detective: after years of cogitating about presumably nothing else other than this worst event in his life, he has to be told by Lolita (we assume truthfully) who the culprit is. Finally, since the business of *Lolita* is only secondarily about the world of American publicity and its artifacts and primarily about a twisted postmodern turn on romantic love, it is fair to say that his riddle does not carry much direct epiphanic resonance for an understanding of the country as a whole. Humbert may change in his attitude toward Lolita but is touched by no palpable evolution in thinking about her country or culture. Ultimately, what Quilty's execution, real or imagined, accomplishes for Humbert has to do with his citizenship in another country from that of the United States: the realm of art. Everyone understands that Quilty represents some sort of double figure for Humbert, but his identity as a writer may be as important as his onetime interest in Humbert's love. For Humbert to purify and justify his feelings for Lo, it makes sense that he would have to say good-bye to the man who epitomizes the baser promptings that gave rise to those feelings in the first instance; but equally, for Humbert to justify his memoir, its fitness for "the refuge of art" must be fortified by severing all ties with his inner hack, all too well typified by

Quilty (309).[17] If his memoir is to be the artwork he has never achieved any other way, Humbert must purge it of unworthy or meretricious elements. (Arguably this takes a while.) Thus, ferreting out and symbolically cleansing Quilty from the narrative could also be to cleanse his kitschy practice from the narration as well. By deconstructing the text and then the person of Quilty, Humbert can finally go from reader to writer. Justifiable or not, this homicide is Humbert's twisted way of clearing the path to do right by his Lolita, and by his *Lolita* as well.

Thomas Pynchon's *Crying of Lot 49* (1966) contrasts to *Lolita* in many ways, the most notable for our purposes being its center of gravity, which rests squarely on the machinery of publicity and mass media. It is, fittingly, set in California. Nor should it surprise that the later novel of Pynchon's that is most obviously a commentary on *Lot 49*, his 1991 *Vineland*, also has a California setting. Oedipa Maas does have a relationship with the now-dead Pierce Inverarity, so that Pynchon's book is not without a romantic subplot. But that subplot is largely pretext for the detective work Oedipa begins as executrix of Inverarity's estate. In some ways, then, Oedipa's journey is the most complete realization of the reader-detective ideal. The structure of the narrative itself even recalls the West Coast mystery novels of a Ross MacDonald, though echoes of another California writer, Philip K. Dick, can also be discerned.

There is, to be sure, a tenuous relay drawn between her quest for American meaning on the one hand and the apparently unsatisfying, narcissistic liaison that has been Oedipa's career as Inverarity's mistress. But it remains essentially a metaphorical suggestion, not the sum and substance of the novel. Still, what prompts her to set out on her attempt to "read" or decode the expanse of the America she encounters is at root not unlike what has motivated the other readers described in this chapter. That is, her desire to read the artifacts of publicity culture are finally part of a deeper desire to transcend them—and something in herself as well. It is a desire for salvation that inspirits her quest.

Yet as with Nabokov's novel, Pynchon's to some degree lacks a heroic protagonist. Unlike Humbert, Oedipa does not seem willfully deviant or criminal, even though the man she was involved with appears to have been louche, to say the least. But it is not Oedipa's personality or even her fate that is the reader's primary concern. Rather, her quest is the excuse for Pynchon's bizarre take on postwar American mass culture, more than anything else. His is a kind of Menippean satire on a theme by Marshall McLuhan, and it does not require much more of its heroine than Voltaire required of his Candide.[18]

Perhaps because it is free of the burden of characterization, then, *Lot 49* may get as close as any of these books to the intricacies of the machinery of mass publicity and how its artifacts partake of the military-industrial complex of that era. In fact, just as Don DeLillo's *White Noise* (1985) draws much of the power of its evocation of nuclear tension from its refusal to directly indicate it, so Pynchon's reflection on Cold War ideology as a strangely religious underpinning for the otherwise relentlessly secular consumer society of the postwar period is powerful essentially because it is implied more than stated. Nevertheless, it is, I think, essential to the book's satirical strategy; chiefly through Oedipa's reaction to the Tristero system, Pynchon is able to depict the effects of Cold War thinking on the observer herself as well as what she observes. The mystery story, the unraveling of the hermeneutic code about Pierce Inverarity's estate, comes to reverse at least one aspect of the standard detective story: the dead man turns out to be the culprit, or at least one possible culprit among many.[19]

Oedipa herself is defined, more than the other readers, by her status as receptor, by her essential passivity. Despite some latter-day attempts to render feminist consciousness in the works of Pynchon, it would be hard to see Oedipa as any more of a feminist than, say, Nancy Drew. And indeed, her very fitness to serve as a detective looking into consumer society—that is, her own identity as the ultimate consumer (attracting as opposites must the ultimate "producer" or broker in Inverarity)—suggests a profound sort of passivity. Of course, she is our first "television age" heroine, and that is significant: the first thing she does when she finds out that Pierce Inverarity is dead is to stare at the TV tube and speak the name of God. Whereas the other characters I have discussed have been concerned with the publicity apparatus primarily for its impact on their own projects, their own fictions, Oedipa Maas by contrast has no discernible project or fiction of her own—unless the whole thing is her imagining, which has occurred to more than one critic over the years.

What Pynchon seems to construct in *Lot 49*, then, is twofold: a countermyth of mass publicity itself and also an implied consumer psychology in the person of Oedipa, who becomes more baffled as her journey questions the stability of her identity, a stability that consumer society has been set up to ensure, in exchange for her coin. However, Oedipa also has another identity, which ironically proves the more activist: it turns out that though a passive consumer, Oedipa is a very assertive reader because of her background as an English major. Beyond that, one of the quaint features of *Lot 49* is the way literature of long-dead eras seems to figure saliently in her search for clues to Tristero, as in the instance of *The Courier's Tragedy*.

Hence, one could say that the literary does give Oedipa a glimpse of the world beyond the confines of the media marketplace. At the same time, the tragedy presents a master myth that becomes a foil for Pynchon as much as anything, in part precisely because it was written so long before the present age. The world of the play, after all, is one of mutual enmity and ultimate destruction, of fight to the death; but the reality of Inverarity's world is more about co-optation of whatever seems in conflict with it, turning opposing cultural currents into just more vendible items in circulation. Although Pynchon does grant Oedipa a certain literary acumen, he may do this to enmesh her more thoroughly in her delusion somehow.

The seemingly heroic backdrop of World War II, which Pynchon will follow up more thoroughly in *Gravity's Rainbow* (1973), along with the Manichaean narrative of the Cold War that follows it, provides the theme music of mutual enmity and stark battles between good and evil; but the reality of commercial society is not moral so much as transactional. Oedipa's faintly transcendent yearnings, nicely indicated by the Pentecostal structure of the story itself, find it hard to come to terms with such banality; but it does not really matter what items are being auctioned off in Lot 49. What matters is the auction itself, the deals for which everything—from myths of warrior heroism down to the remains of the warriors themselves—exists only to be put into circulation, to be bought and sold.

Even her conspiratorial narrative, the sort of thing Pynchon does much more thoroughly in *Gravity's Rainbow* with its evocations of "They" and their machinations, may have the effect of romanticizing the real way America's masters work their will, which is through the manipulation of everyday perception; the way they run people's lives is through advertising and the public relations of engineering consent. Although Oedipa Maas has gotten as far as sensing this, and does in any case end up better than *Gravity's* Slothrop, she has, like her fellow consumers, too faint a memory of a culture that did not exist to be sold to escape the auction house of language in which we leave her. As the vastness of the conspiracy labyrinths is driven home to Oedipa Maas, the narrative finds her more and more isolated, incapable of reaching out: her previous contacts such as Randolph Driblette dead, her husband incommunicado. Her quest yields a great deal of insight, at least for the reader—but not definitive enlightenment. Oedipa's attempt to transcend the limitations imposed by the publicity apparatus only imprisons her more paranoically than ever within her own apprehensions and theories.[20]

This pattern of ill-starred questing seems to recur in just about every novel examined here, in fact. Perhaps the publicity apparatus is too much of an incubus and thus impossible to escape or transcend, or even understand.

(Here as so often Nabokov's novel appears to be the exception, and even here such transcendence as Humbert may have achieved is only possible by virtue of his accession to "the refuge of art," a consummation that is predicated on his and Lolita's physical death.) No doubt owing in part to realism, since all of these novels were written during the century when the electronic media and commercial markets joined forces to make mass culture inescapable, the way beyond this pale is never found. Even the standard form in which novelistic progress is rendered, that of imputing some characterological shift or change of heart in the book's center of consciousness, proves elusive. This pattern may also result from the likelihood that these texts, being satires, are primarily outward looking, leaving the central characters to a status reminiscent of Alice's in Carroll's tales, for instance. (Humbert again is the exception, his persona, however complicated or simple, the obvious center of gravity for *Lolita,* and the satire at the expense of mass culture secondary.) Does this pattern break itself in Don DeLillo's *White Noise?*

The short answer is that it does not. But what DeLillo takes as his province differs from the earlier texts because his narrator is himself an academic, and so in a position to register the depredations of postmodernity as they have compromised his realm of activity. In a strange way, J. A. K. Gladney's odyssey recapitulates those of Miss Lonelyhearts, Tod Hackett, or Oedipa Maas: like them he is driven by prophetic voices, harried by world-historical guilts and misgivings. He is, however, himself at least as tarnished as any Hollywood set designer; his new area of scholarship, Hitler Studies, is a transparent play for undergraduate enrollments, a fact he indirectly acknowledges when he insists that he is not seen as brilliant by his colleagues, only as shrewd. This status has not the effect of rendering his observation any less keen, though it does make his judgment less than reliable. Even when he finally does undertake his quest, which eerily echoes Humbert's Quilty hunt, his choice of quarry, a man named Willie Mink who supplies Gladney's wife with a death-denial pill and compulsively watches TV, has all the earmarks of a scapegoat—and unlike the Quilty project, the attempt on Mink miscarries and lands Gladney once more in his accustomed postmodern rut, little wiser if much sadder than when he set out.

Just as Miss Lonelyhearts's belief that he could turn his profane column into a religious experience comes to grief, and just as Tod Hackett's slightly more clever idea of being a prophet in his spare time is shown wanting, so Jack Gladney's attempt to kill his way into a more authentic being results only in a muddle. This desire for authenticity, very much a motive for Gladney's Mailerlike derring-do, wars with the obvious embarrassment that this adventure is itself a form of denial. It is odd that Gladney assumes a postmodern omniscience in Mink such that his pill actually works on Babette (it clearly does not work on Mink himself, nor does the magic of television), but Gladney's attack on him is in the service of denying death as well. His blow against postmodern publicity culture must glance off because he himself is too fatally implicated in it, and because he does not realize how factitious his desperate lunge at authenticity really is. DeLillo's seeming devotion to the existential *acte gratuit,* a gesture that animates not only this text and *Mao II* but also *The Names* (1982) and obliquely even *Libra* (1988), accounts for the allure of this pseudo-Armageddon.[21] But the overwhelming reality that arranges itself against these gestures—and the artificiality that permeates the gestures themselves—means that authenticity eludes them.

If there is a common theme to all of the books I treat, in truth, it may be that of the search for authenticity against the backdrop of the great machinery of fakery that is American mass publicity. Invariably the psychological urges and confusions of the protagonists are a part of the motivation, but the pervasive unreality of the newly electrified commercial culture in which all of us are now allowed to move, and which grew in size and power as the century progressed, is a predicament they all share.[22] The failed gesture of Gladney seems in the tradition of ineffectuality begun by Miss Lonelyhearts: a rearguard action partaking of its own brand of phoniness. Mass publicity's forms had, after all, gotten there first: one's own "authentic" responses had, in a measure, already been co-opted by the apparatus against which one interposed oneself. The very mythology of such gestures of rebellion, the individual vs. society Expressionism they imply, comes from mass culture, which is always "on the side" of the individual. Yet those who would write the great American novel are themselves often the most credulous believers in this particular myth, with its baggage of romantic originality. To set up as a serious writer, though, is always to affirm the possibility that individual judgment is capable of rendering true insight into one's time and place. It is an implied rebuke to the figments of mass publicity and our desire to accept them as real. But of course the embrace of "reality" can also be a flight from the reality of which mass publicity is itself an important symptom.[23]

The Writer's Portion

To sketch the quests of these novels' main characters is not necessarily to describe the quests that may animate their authors, and any such ascription must be tentative. What can be noted is that while none of the twentieth-century texts we treat have creative writers for heroes until *Mao II*'s

Bill Gray, nevertheless almost all of the central figures are resonant with analogy for the writing situation. Miss Lonelyhearts actually is a writer, just a thoroughly self-abased one; Tod Hackett is a set designer whose artistic training recalls a writer's apprenticeship in past classics of his craft; Humbert Humbert is a translator and critic; Oedipa Maas is a lapsed English major; Jack Gladney is an academic historian. All of the characters are observers who also bear their share of Arnoldian high culture, whose plights (again with the exception of Nabokov's hero) are essentially viewed sympathetically. How to distinguish among them?

In actuality, the distinctions among the main characters *as characters* matter less than the differences between texts that emphasize the characters and those that stress what they observe. All of the books strive to present some picture of mass publicity and the way its machinery impinges upon high-cultural observers. But the recipe of parts, how many of observer for how much observed, changes too. West's novels keep a rough parity between the needs of satirical anatomy and the sketching of psychology, though Hollywood is perhaps more fully explored than the *Post-Dispatch*.[24] Not surprisingly, the most solipsistic-seeming narrative of all is *Lolita*, whose events are often hard to disentangle from the narrator's fancy; by violent contrast, Oedipa Maas, though possessed of a sociological identity, the traces of a past, and even some quirks, is scarcely a character at all (she has to approach going crazy before the reader is mindful that the quest we get is all *hers*), and the focus is primarily on anatomizing mass media. DeLillo's heroes, Gladney and Bill Gray, are once again in more balance with their surroundings, or rather out of balance along with their surroundings. Indeed, as noted above, the observations of all of the central reflectors are compromised by their own enmeshing with the system they critique, a fact that the disturbingly high incidence of near insanity among these characters would only underscore.

Perhaps it approaches insanity to attempt a mapping of our mass-mediated world in the first place, it is so completely a part of what we ourselves have come to be. But the authors attempt such a thing, and seem to need characters from whom they can distance themselves in order to do it. After all, Gladney is already a bit of a hustler, and Oedipa the mistress of a dead billionaire and not much given (other than as a result of her humanist training, it is implied) to questioning the culture in which she finds herself. Miss Lonelyhearts has already forsworn the path of art, a fact Willie Shrike rubs his nose in by making it the subject of an inspirational Miss Lonelyhearts advice column. Of all of the novels under discussion, perhaps only *Day of the Locust* comes close to presenting directly the dynamic of the commercial hack who also insists on claiming the mantle of art for himself. But even here, West introduces the needed superficies of making the protagonist a visual artist.

By making their protagonists just close enough to their authors without tempting the reader (or writer) to identify them, these writers may gain the requisite distance and discretion to pursue a critique of the machine without explicitly having to engage their own implication in the system. This does not mean that we cannot suggest some aspects of that engagement as symptomatized in their products.

West is the most direct about such symptoms and the inability to overcome them.[25] This is why his novels provide models with which to look at subsequent treatments of mass culture. But Nabokov's novel is also implicated in the confrontation between Humbert and Quilty; indeed, I argue that Quilty becomes a convenient scapegoat for the text itself, which fortifies its own status as a proper literary story and not mere pornography precisely by visiting deeper guilt on the bad object that is Humbert's rival. In the same way, Pynchon's novel has its own agenda beyond that of its protagonist: to provide an anatomy of the mass-publicity apparatus of its day, possibly the most ambitious such mapping done to that point. Just as *The Courier's Tragedy* proves incongruously relevant to the perturbations of the postwar consumer society, so Pynchon's text clearly hopes to prove a kind of guide to the postmodern perplexed in its own right. And so it has done.

With Don DeLillo the ambitions are at least as pronounced, the anatomizing urge as all-encompassing. (Indeed, the novel most possessed of this ambition, his *Underworld* [1998], is so capacious that dealing with it would almost require a separate study of its own!) But as with West, DeLillo is as interested in tracing the psychological legacy of consumer society on his protagonists and their judgment as he is in describing the thing itself. Gladney is himself a symptom as well as giver of diagnosis, and part of the game of *White Noise* is deciding when his insights do and do not carry the authority of the text itself. Also, DeLillo may be better able to leave his hero to his minor-key fate if he is a mere academic historian rather than an author.

It is important, naturally, to keep in mind the fact that all of these authors are very disparate people: their decision to depict American mass culture at all is enough to vouch for their idiosyncrasy. But the gradual disappearance of the direct stake for the writer, for *any* writer, in the social dynamics within these novels may be owing in part to the ever more overwhelming force and pervasion of mass publicity in the United States throughout the century. A quick comparison of backdrops may help to indicate this. In both West novels, where creative types are most avowedly at the center of consciousness, the focus is actually limited to the newspaper office or Hollywood. So innocent is the public in *Miss Lonelyhearts* of the phoniness of tabloid journalism that its narrative representatives, the gullible letter writers, clearly believe sincerely that the advice they get is intended for their welfare and not as a circulation stunt.[26] Even the more media-savvy extras who occupy fame's anteroom in *Day of the Locust* are geographically restricted, being people who have come to California either to die or attain filmed immortality. As late as Nabokov's *Lolita,* Humbert's immersion in American mass culture is his compromise with Lolita's tender age, and the running joke is that the comic books and films they both take in are so many desperate ploys to keep her from the boredom and resentment always about to present.

By the time we get to Pynchon and DeLillo, however, the children's hour of mass culture has well and truly become a daylong affair, and all of us have become children at heart. Collaterally, the places where public relations are manipulated come to take up ever more of the space between sea and shining sea, no longer confined to either coast and a few radio stations. Between the early fifties and the mid-sixties, a kind of critical mass was reached as electronic media altered the terms in which literature could view these matters. The exitless Frankfurt School nightmare seems in retrospect a hyperbolic model for the mass-publicity apparatus of midcentury, but by the writing of *Lot 49* it has become less so. The paranoiac mapping that Oedipa is encouraged to do looks less bizarre in the "administered world" she confronts than a thirties version may have done—and after the conspiracies woven by *Gravity's Rainbow* is in any case hard to distinguish from her creator's.[27] Who knows? It may be that the crushing weight of consumer society and its simulations on the one hand, and the waning influence of the literary on the other, conspire between them to make a direct depiction of the literary life in those books too depressing for even their authors to contemplate.[28]

Since creative imagination as such is only obliquely represented in these novels, then, and since those culture bearers who are represented are compromised, sometimes fatally, by their marination in the mass market, one can legitimately ask whether we are in fact right to look into this aspect of their novels at all. Perhaps the true quest of the authors is not merely tangential but actually indifferent to the typical quest of their protagonists. I would deny this and point to one essential similarity: the active deployment of the fictive itself. To the public relations illusionism of American society they counterpose other, more salvific fictions and hope through those fictions to create a kind of alternate history to that of official consumer society. This aspiration may be less strong in Nabokov than in others.[29] But for West, Pynchon, and DeLillo, one could define one common project, which is to construct a counternarrative, or a supplementary narrative, to the implied world projected by the public relations apparatus. Authenticity may not be possible, either in the high art form or the cognitive form. But if a life's base lie cannot be rewritten into truth, as *The Courier's Tragedy* would have it, then at least another fiction can be erected to compete with the official version.

If this answering of figment by fiction is indeed a pattern for these writers, this assumes a hierarchy of fiction itself: an unavoidable preference for literary depth over mass publicity's superficial glance. Part of the postmodern quality of all of these authors, naturally, consists in their uneasiness about just such hierarchies; but rightly or wrongly, they are not as cavalier as some of their latter-day critics have been in assuming no such distinctions exist. In fact, I think it is part of the writer's portion that they must exist. Otherwise, there is little point in mounting these glum critiques of the given public relations realities. To depict the effects of this simulated world on a possible person is already to introduce an element that the celebrants of mass publicity's artifacts tend not to notice: Gladney's *timor mortis*, Oedipa's fear of isolation, Miss Lonelyhearts's messianic ambitions all shake up the prescribed structure of our culture industry. If their embroilment, and that of their authors, means that their observations can never pierce the absolute truth behind the illusions of mass publicity, still, the fact of their embroilment makes of that apparatus a human problem, not merely a social fact. This in itself is a gain, even if the price is forswearing a conspicuously literary hero paring his or her fingernails.

Miss Lonelyhearts is no literary hero in the first place, but his feeling of entrapment and sullying by a machine of language resonates well with the later novels. Add to that the fact that part of the legacy of the new publicity apparatus is to problematize the status of a literary hero anyway. By the time Don DeLillo allows himself a James-style literary center of consciousness in *Mao II*'s Bill Gray, it will be apparent that the machinery of publicity has succeeded in providing even the most reclusive and subversive of authors with his appropriate marketing niche. DeLillo himself has already shown the extent to which the society of public relations has taken all of our realms of authentic experience and made them material, and he records the impact of this on ordinary educated people.[30]

For what it is worth, when we return to the narrower concerns of the literary in *Mao II*, we have encountered a larger, more elaborated publicity apparatus than James could have dreamed of, and both Pynchon and DeLillo present a world where the dispossession and romantic alienation of the artist arise from the same situation of commercialized banality that afflicts everyone else. The vain nostalgia, the desire for authenticity, and the fear of being caught in the machinery of public relations that have traditionally characterized practitioners of high art come to haunt more and more people—who, at least as things are divvied up in postmodernity, are consumers rather than producers of culture.[31] This is why the sorts of concerns that motivated James can continue to inform Pynchon and DeLillo, without specifically literary concerns assuming center stage.

The historical period within which *Lot 49* and *White Noise* were written, though, is paradoxically one where the literary seems to have had less relevance than ever. As DeLillo eventually examines in his post–Cold War *Underworld*, the secular religion of Cold War national-patriotic culture had by the fifties joined forces with the public relations apparatus erected by corporate America. The principles of merchandising had been extended to a public sphere that had once been thought beyond the spell of advertising and manipulated spectacle.[32] Even at the time there were voices raised in alarm over this development, though nobody could then have predicted its overwhelming issue in the present age.[33] Suffice it to say that the dominance of electronic communications, which convey sight and sound more than words, and the sheer marginality of letters combine to allow writers to take distance from the works of public relations society, to turn a private eye to the public spectacle. But this splendid isolation is still isolation.

There is of course no privileged place apart from the realm of public relations available to literary critique, for two reasons. The trivial one is that in order to mount one's critique in the public sphere one must publish it in the first place, thus participating in marketplace machinations of one's own. It is trivial because there is no obligation to applaud a process one is forced to engage in, any more than a soldier conscripted to fight an unjust war must decide it is not unjust after all.

More disabling is the other major reason, that the very sources of symbolization have been already so debased by the culture industry that they cannot be turned effectively against those entities.[34] The only reply to this is that it must still be possible to arrange the received materials of mass publicity in fictions that counteract their typical forms, and that if those forms carry a critical power or insight these can work to resist the debasement of the materials. Simply put, if mass publicity works, as *Lot 49* tells us, by taking up already existing cultural materials from both high and folk culture and turning them into commodity items, then equally it should be possible for an artist to take up commercial forms and bend them to the uses of art. This is not to say it will be easy, though. Indeed, the sophisticated stance, of which for that very reason one should be suspicious, is that any position to one side of "mass culture" is hopelessly false, elitist, or nobly doomed—but never effective.

That said, it may be that the only real hope novelists of publicity have is the paradoxical one that so many other people share their vulnerability and sense of doom. As the dreamworld of mass publicity becomes the place all of us are being told to prefer to reality, the entrapment felt by James's artists becomes, willy-nilly, part of an all-encompassing dilemma for the public as well. Common victimhood at the hands of mass publicity confers a strange kind of solidarity, supplanting the sort of hostility toward the public we see in a "Next Time," for instance. Hence, before DeLillo ever introduces "the writer" as such as a center of consciousness, the previous novels have already described much of his predicament, only in the guise of describing everybody *else's* predicament. Reversing Flaubert's formula, we can truly say: "Bill Gray, *c'est nous.*"

chapter four

Letters and Spirit in *Miss Lonelyhearts*

The Scene of Typing

A n advice to the lovelorn columnist whose advice is often worse than no advice—and who knows it—has many reasons to want to escape into daydream. This pastor's son has as his most significant dream that of salvation through, and ultimately as, Jesus Christ. But before that consumes his life, there are smaller dreams, and although their goal is to take him out of an imprisonment, they often return him there more forcibly. In Nathanael West's novel *Miss Lonelyhearts,* all the title character's dreams, all his forms of escape, have a way of doing that.

One of the strongest dreams occurs as Miss Lonelyhearts, in typical paralysis before the newsroom typewriter where he produces his columns, sits and thinks instead of a desert: "A desert . . . not of sand, but of rust and body dirt, surrounded by a back-yard fence on which are posters describing the events of the day. . . . Inside the fence Desperate, Broken-hearted, Disillusioned-with-tubercular-husband and the rest were gravely forming the letters MISS LONELYHEARTS out of white-washed clam shells, as if decorating the lawn of a rural depot (25–26). "Desperate," "Broken-hearted" and the rest are of course the letter writers who send queries to his columns; but their names are created by and for the newspaper, and the fence that rings them in with the day's events is the newspaper itself: that which imprisons both the columnist and the readers and binds them to one another. They exist for him only through their letters, he for them only in his replies. Yet not content with the stories these characters invent for themselves, he invents his own for them. In his story, they spell out his name as an object of worship which shows, ironically, that they are as much Miss Lonelyhearts's creators as his dupes. In dreaming his readers' dreams of him, Miss Lonelyhearts realizes that their dreams allow "Miss Lonelyhearts" to exist as a name and its bearer to pursue his trade.

Paradoxically, this scene recalls him to his task; after all, the readers' faith in his name requires Miss Lonelyhearts to help them form its letters by forming his own letters. His typing, however, is again interrupted: "He could not go on with it and turned again to the imagined desert where Desperate, Broken-hearted and the others were still building his name. They had run out of sea shells and were using faded photographs, soiled fans, timetables, playing cards, broken toys, imitation jewelry—junk that memory had made precious, far more precious than anything the sea might yield" (26).

The column, it appears, consists of the mutual effort of writer and reader to construct a saving name, not from nature but from the runic fragments of discourse and human fabrication: timetables, photographs, playing cards. The name they build must somehow yield the meaning of the junk of its decay. The prospects for genuine redemption, as opposed to temporary balm, are not good, though, because Miss Lonelyhearts soon has another dream of detritus, and here it is he who does the forming, not his readers. His daydream features the cultural remnants similar to those of the earlier dreams. He finds himself "in the window of a pawnshop full of fur coats, diamond rings, watches . . . the paraphernalia of suffering" (30). They are not such in themselves, certainly, but only by virtue of their situation in the pawnshop. Still, Miss Lonelyhearts, sensing a "tropism for disorder" among these objects, joins battle with chaos: "First he formed a phallus of old watches and rubber boots, then a heart of umbrellas and trout flies. . . . But nothing proved definitive and he began to make a gigantic cross. When the cross became too large for the pawnshop, he moved it to the shore of the ocean" (31).

This dream, parallel with the first, makes it clear that Miss Lonelyhearts is a Miss Lonelyhearts reader. Like the others, he uses the "paraphernalia of suffering" of a pawnshop to erect a variety of symbols by which the suffering can be redeemed: a project for forming legible meaning from the spoor of failure. He carries his readers' projects of redemption back to the life-giving sea in an attempt to transcend the desert of the newspaper office, and his way of getting there begins with a sexual symbol and ends with a religious one—a development that will be seen to mime that of the book as a whole. Whether in practice he ever actually gets to the life-giving sea of renewal is explored below.

In addition to the fact that Miss Lonelyhearts's way of retrieving meaning from cultural debris is the same as his readers,' the setting is also very similar, the pawnshop suggesting the newspaper office as did the fenced-in desert. This columnist's fantasy visions, whether of his readers' attempts to give meaning to their suffering or his own, can only exist within the prison of the newspaper office. He can be a savior, they a faithful flock, only insofar as the paper allows both to exist linguistically, as words. Indeed, whenever Miss Lonelyhearts confronts his readers in the flesh, the results are disastrous.

The pawnshop image itself is a clue as to why this dream may well end in disaster. A pawnshop is a place where its customers' misfortunes are exploited for money, just as the Miss Lonelyhearts column has its origin as a cynical circulation gimmick, where his replies to his readers' problems are cruel jokes that function as further posters on the fence of the desert. Thus does every attempt to escape this doomed condition return Miss Lonelyhearts all the more forcibly to it.

The World According to Shrike: Origin as Parody

The dreams may be Miss Lonelyhearts's invention, but his column is not. It is the brainchild of the newspaper's city editor, Willie Shrike, to whom Miss Lonelyhearts owes his name (and so his identity); and like his name, the words he writes are not his, though he writes them, owes his existence to them. His first reply in the novel, in fact, is dictated by Shrike:

> Art is a Way Out.
> Do not let life overwhelm you. When the old paths are choked with
> the debris of failure, look for newer and fresher paths. Art is just such
> a path. Art is distilled from suffering. . . .
> For those who have not the talent to create, there is appreciation. . . .
> (4)

It is ironic that Shrike emphasizes Miss Lonelyhearts's bondage by dictating a letter that speaks of a spurious "way out" through suffering, doubly ironic that he dictates a recommendation of the saving, creative power of art. It is a complete perversion of the "personal expression" in language that not only Miss Lonelyhearts but also his colleagues and his boss once believed in: "At college, and perhaps for a year afterwards, they had believed in literature, had believed in Beauty and in personal expression as an absolute end. When they lost this belief, they lost everything. Money and fame meant nothing to them. They were not worldly men" (14).

At the newspaper they are as far removed from personal expression as possible; the relentless mechanism of the paper and its cynical relation to its audience are personified by Shrike, and the other newspapermen are the objects of his sinister ventriloquism: "Like Shrike, the man they imitated, they were machines for making jokes. A button machine makes buttons, no matter what the power used, foot, steam or electricity. They, no matter what the motivating force, death, love or God, made jokes" (15). They all imitate Shrike as machines would, but Shrike himself is a kind of mechanism: All are caught in the infernal machine of the paper.

Miss Lonelyhearts's project is to forge from this empty language the possibility of genuine redemption: if the cynical fictions he is required to write are actively taken over by the writer, then perhaps they will be rendered true. The relentless machine of the typewriter must be sublated, and the Promethean pen must replace subservience before the typewriter (where an earlier draft of this novel has a bemused Miss Lonelyhearts mention he composed his first love letters!).[1] If the joke can, by a change of intention, cease to be joke, then the writer's pledges can be redeemed along with the suffering of his readers in the same way that the paraphernalia of suffering in a pawnshop can be redeemed. It is important to understand that at no point does Miss Lonelyhearts conceive a determinate alternative to doing this: quitting the newspaper job, say. The Dickensian change of heart is the most he considers.

That this change of heart might not succeed in reversing the columnist's role from victim to savior is clear from another dream, related to those above, in which Miss Lonelyhearts is a magician who makes doorknobs flower and speak at his command. But when it comes time to "lead his audience in prayer," ventriloquism once again intervenes: "But no matter how hard he struggled, his prayer was one Shrike had taught him and his voice was that of a conductor calling stations" (9). Not only Miss Lonelyhearts's language but also the circumstances in which he enunciates it are determined by Shrike (or rather, by the same cynical exigencies that determine Shrike's behavior). However sincere, his prayers come out as Shrike has dictated them.

Shrike constantly refers to the need for the circulation to multiply; Goldsmith, one of Shrike's imitators, tells Miss Lonelyhearts to respond to a sexually frustrated letter writer by determining to "get the lady with child and increase the potential circulation of the paper" (26). The reproduction of life is to serve the newspaper rather than vice versa. And indeed the general pattern in this text is that the manic productivity of civilization has produced no spiritual regeneration. The protagonist sees the explosion of productivity that produced the city as destructive frenzy: "an orgy of stone-breaking," he calls it. And the existing civilization is the stone that "would someday break them [i.e., the Americans]" (27). Many of Miss

Lonelyhearts's readers have also been financially and psychologically broken by the repetitive activity of the economic system; one thinks of Doyle the cripple and also, inevitably, of the text's 1932 publication date.

Miss Lonelyhearts, then, is broken like the readers of his columns, but over his typewriter, not the wheel. The same mechanism that can reproduce language to infinity without sympathy or even comprehension adheres to Shrike's own discourse, machinelike letter without spirit. Shrike's name is already, of course, a parodic anagram for "Christ," but he is not sufficiently demonic to be an Antichrist: he is at best, as one of the chapters calls him, a dead Pan.[2] The nickname works on two levels, since in Shrike one finds the incarnation of the boundless capacity for parody and joke telling founded on the failure of Eros. If his practical jokes seem to have an air of the sadistic, this should not be surprising; they are used as compensation for the lack of true sexual power, in a pattern that Miss Lonelyhearts also imitates (at least at first). Shrike's relation to his wife bears out this sadistic hint: unable to please her himself, he still maintains dominion over her in a parody of the male role. As Mary Shrike tells Miss Lonelyhearts: "Do you know why he lets me go out with other men? To save money. He knows that I let them neck me and when I get home all hot and bothered, why he climbs into my bed and begs for it. The cheap bastard!" (22). Shrike's lovemaking at best pleases himself at the expense of frustrating both his wife and her other men; and it is a question whether it even pleases Shrike. ("Sleeping with her is like sleeping with a knife in one's groin," he tells Miss Lonelyhearts [21].) Shrike's victimization and his glib rhetoric are of a piece, and his sadistic ironies shield his own impotence.

In taking out Shrike's wife, Miss Lonelyhearts indulges in a bit of sadism himself; one suspects the real quarry here is Shrike rather than Mary. But the columnist becomes a part of the scheme whereby Shrike, in his own inadequacy, victimizes others in turn. As Miss Lonelyhearts attempts to "drag Mrs. Shrike to the floor," she demands to be released: "Then he heard footsteps . . . the door opened and Shrike looked into the corridor. He had on only the top of his pajamas" (24). It seems that even in his off-hours, Miss Lonelyhearts still works for Shrike, is still his victim.

This sadism has as its condition the unredemptive, unregenerative sexuality that is imaged in the text by various distortions of nature: "there were signs of spring. The decay that covered the surface of the mottled ground is not the kind in which life generates" (5). The Eliotic wasteland imagery has been remarked by other critics, and the title character in this text bears some resemblance to Eliot's Fisher King.[3] One could even say that Shrike is a walking wasteland of cultural detritus, though that fact indicates some of the difference between West's world and Eliot's. Whereas in Eliot the reclamation of the Indo-European cultural heritage would revivify the wasteland with the "peace which passeth understanding," West by contrast presents a universe where that attempt has already fallen under the ban of Shrike's sterile parody. Though the iconography remains, it cannot inspire the belief of other times. The fragments Miss Lonelyhearts has shored against his ruin are themselves already ruins.[4]

The fact that the culture is decaying would explain the decay Miss Lonelyhearts finds in his urban park near the office: the little park that he says needs a drink. For all his girlfriend Betty's conviction that his problems are city problems, their weekend in Connecticut confronts images that partake of the city park: "Although spring was well advanced, in the deep shade there was nothing but death—rotten leaves, gray and white fungi, and over everything a funereal hush" (38).

To bring renewal to this decay, Miss Lonelyhearts wishes his readers would "water the soil with their tears. Flowers would then spring up, flowers that smelled of feet" (5). This comic image is an ironical use of what, like the sea, are potent symbols of regeneration. The agent of this flowering is his readers' tears, suffering its own means of redemption. Indeed, the park vision in its essence is feminine: not only because of the Mary Magdalene images of tears and feet but also because it is initiated by the "shadow of a lamppost" that pierces him "like a spear" (4). But this confusion is a part of his dilemma: how to make passive suffering the agent of overcoming. The appeal of Christ as a model for this *via negativa* is obvious, and upon returning from Connecticut Miss Lonelyhearts endeavors to propose the Christ vision explicitly but cannot: "He snatched the paper out of the machine. With him, even the word Christ was a vanity" (39).

Christ's name is early on identified with the redemptive power of language: "something stirred in him when he shouted the name of Christ, something secret and enormously powerful" (8). He also figures the triumph of the soul through suffering, of course, and Miss Lonelyhearts hopes that his linguistic bondage to the repetitive dead language of the paper will yield redemptive discourse not only because his own suffering makes him similar to his readers but also because remorse over his own complicity in their exploitation will bring the necessary humility to accept the mystical solution. If those two reasons sound contradictory, they are; but both spring equally from a situation of writing that breeds suffering equal to that of his correspondents. Still, it is his complicity in the initial exploitation that keeps Miss Lonelyhearts from really fusing with his readers; true, he suffers as his readers do, but for him suffering is indissociable from guilt. The readers are unknowing victims, but the columnist is know-ing: a party to his own exploitation and, to the same extent, that of his readers. His female name expresses the predicament: he is the perpetrator of a hoax, but also a passive sufferer under it.

The price, then, of bondage to Shrike is an emasculated language that increasingly takes over Miss Lonelyhearts's life. The fraudulent discourse becomes its own curse after a while. (As mentioned earlier, his colleagues are also riddled with self-contempt. The revealing exchange in which var-ious newspapermen at the speakeasy fantasize "gang bangs" of famous women novelists is fitting, since for a woman to attain something of their own forsaken ideal of personal expression must be further unwanted proof of their linguistic emasculation.) The glib rhetoric and endless punning of Shrike signify the same impotence as that displayed by the readers with their "inarticulate and impotent" (18)—and ungrammatical—letters. His abdication of any true self-expression is the precondition for Shrike's ster-ile patter. In a way, the empty articulateness of Shrike or Miss Lonelyhearts is more severe a condition than the words of the letter writers or the bal-letic hands of Doyle as they shadow forth his suffering. At the least, they give some voice to grief. Shrike, by contrast, manages this only once, in evoking the true hell of life with Mary. But both glibness and inarticulate-ness contain formidable latent aggressions, as becomes clear below.

Miss Lonelyhearts is different from Shrike in that he wishes to break through glibness and cliché to some ideal of authentic speech. When he attempts such speech, though, his tongue becomes a "fat thumb" (11). Like his readers, he loses the ability to articulate his thoughts at precisely the moment when they are most important to him: as he is explaining to Betty his position on the newspaper and his attitude toward it. He begins to "shout at her, accompanying his shouts with gestures [that resemble] those of an old-fashioned actor" (12). This scene is repeated later when he is at home with Betty, and Betty advises him to stop "making a fool of yourself" by avoiding his job. He replies with his own Miss Lonelyhearts story, told in the third person, recapitulating his absurd vocation to the point where he "discovers that his correspondents take him seriously. For the first time in his life, he is forced to examine the values by which he lives. This exam-ination shows him that he is the victim of the joke and not its perpetrator" (32). Though more articulate than his first attempt, it is still blunted on Betty ("he saw that Betty still thought him a fool" [32]).

Like his dreams, the story he tells Betty is an approach to his predicament. He is not usually in the position of asking for advice or expressing suffering, as he here does; more typically he gives advice or alleviates suffering (in theory). The column begins as exploitation disguised as service; but encounter with his victims as individuals gives his own culpability some clarity. This is why his formulation that he is victim and not perpetrator could be amended; he is both victim and perpetrator: indeed, victim *insofar as* perpetrator.

Ironically, this figure is seen by Shrike as a priest of twentieth-century America (44); his characteristic posture is that of hearing confession. In a society where failure is sin, advice for its banishment is absolution. But if Miss Lonelyhearts could genuinely absolve his readers with healing speech, his own pain would be removed along with theirs. The trouble is that the remedy has been poisoned before the fact by its origin as parody. Much as he mocks Betty's belief that all evil is sickness to be cured ("No morality, only medicine" [13]), her medicinal approach is not far from his own naïveté in assuming that words used with the proper spirit can heal.

When Miss Lonelyhearts tries to transmit his own belief in the efficacy of suffering for redemption, he becomes inarticulate like his readers, but in his case it takes the form of the slick rhetoric of the column. His readers' tongue-tied sincerity wars against the cynical patter of Shrike, producing a strange combination. He sees it at one point as owing to his avoidance of Christ: "he had failed to tap the force in his heart and had merely written a column for his paper" (49). Yet when he tries to bring up Christ at the Doyles,' the results are even worse: "This time he had failed still more miserably. He had substituted the rhetoric of Shrike for that of Miss Lonelyhearts" (50). The figure of Shrike and the column provide the measure of his failure to give genuine healing through speech. It is not that his hysterical speeches to the Doyles are not sincere, just that their form has already been inscribed by the pen (or typewriter) of Shrike's paper. When the columnist attempts to play his savior role straight, the conventions within which he must do it—determined by the newspaper's management and ratified, despite the falsity of those conventions, by the readers—betray the pathos of that role. When he tries to legitimate his false role toward his audience, it only becomes more false. This is the paradox concealed in the fact that it is only when he understands that he is being *taken seriously* by his letter writers that he realizes he is also the victim of the joke he has helped to perpetrate.

Stages on Miss Lonelyhearts's Way

Given this understanding of his own position as a writer addressing an audience under false pretenses, is there a pattern to Miss Lonelyhearts's attempts to work through the predicament that haunts his dreams, daydreams, and language?

The fitful alternation between frantic activity and catatonic passivity in the character of Miss Lonelyhearts has been noted by others.[5] Some have traced this trait to that psychology associated with hysteria, that "snake whose scales are tiny mirrors in which the dead world takes on a semblance of life" (9). The violent imagery of West seems to support this view.[6] One of the commentators on *Miss Lonelyhearts,* Randall Reid, has pointed out that the febrile imagery is not only indicative of the protagonist's hysterical state but also of a genuine state of affairs; so what Reid calls hysteria, and what we might call passive-aggressive behavior, reflects Miss Lonelyhearts's imprisonment in a situation that requires him to parody a redeemer's role.[7] It is his status as a *writer* that compels his behavior: behavior that oscillates between passive withdrawal and active delusion in an attempt to transcend an enforced false relationship with his readership. Roughly speaking, there are five stages that lead up to the protagonist's final ironic apotheosis:

1. Anger at his impotence in the face of Shrike and his paper, with two results: the attempt to use his position to sexual advantage and sadism directed against various targets. (The two are related, since sex, as we have seen, is generally used here in an aggressive way.) He tries unsuccessfully to seduce Shrike's wife in an indirect foray against the editor, but this sally only confirms his bondage to and victimization by Shrike. The second, more fateful, attempt involves a letter writer, Fay Doyle.

With Fay's letter, a complaint about being married to a cripple, the prospect of spiritual nourishment looms again in adulterous sex. This time he is successful, though Fay is as much the seducer as seduced: "He had always been the pursuer, but now found a strange pleasure in having the roles reversed" (28). Mrs. Doyle is a sea image, of course (Miss Lonelyhearts crawls out of bed "like an exhausted swimmer leaving the surf" [28]). Thus when he cannot advance his own aggressive interests on those who have rhetorical and institutional power over him, he practices his designs on a reader over whom he has some power. But even this sadistic move is only partly successful, ending with a lengthy tale of woe related by Fay, to which, as usual, Miss Lonelyhearts must listen sympathetically. The climactic incident in the speakeasy with the Clean Old Man brings these sadistic impulses to a head, as Miss Lonelyhearts viciously twists the old man's arm to torture him into telling the "story of your life" (17). The frustration and sadism of the columnist's role are clearest at this point, and the scene will be echoed later in the text.

2. Attempt to escape the columns and the attendant sense of futility: what could be called the "suburban solution." He retreats first to his room

(in the chapter "Miss Lonelyhearts in the Dismal Swamp"), then to Connecticut with Betty. Of course, Shrike, who bursts into Miss Lonelyhearts's sickroom before he leaves, has already satirized this possibility of escape (along with the escapes of hedonism, the South Seas, suicide, art, and drugs) in a series of bombastic set pieces (35).

Despite Shrike's malediction, Miss Lonelyhearts and Betty go to Connecticut for a pseudo-pastoral interval. It is not only nature but nature's story that is competing with his gloom, as Betty's stories of her childhood on a farm are proffered as an antidote to his own story. This itself gives a clue to the failure of nature as an escape: Betty has already made a cliché of nature, one that has been parodied by Shrike. Nature as an imagined scene of plenitude is a figure of cultural fantasy, and so his union with nature and its story, figured in his sexual union with Betty— now "wholesome" rather than "sick" sex—is still not proof against the Bronx slums through which they return from Connecticut's impossible suburban space.

3. Decision to use the new fully conscious sense of his own degradation to effect his readers' salvation. He feels at this stage that he has not allowed the Christ dream to emerge "not so much because of Shrike's jokes or his own self-doubt, but because of his lack of humility" (39). He begins cultivating his humility and avoiding Betty as well. His visit to the Doyles is the culmination of his attempt to bring the message of suffering as redemption through Christ. It is initiated by accident and ends in disaster. Miss Lonelyhearts is trying to read the cripple Doyle's letter, which he has been handed, when their hands inadvertently touch: "He jerked away, but then drove his hand back and forced it to clasp the cripple's. After finishing the letter, he did not let go, but pressed it firmly with all the love he could manage. At first the cripple covered his embarrassment by disguising the meaning of the clasp with a handshake, but he soon gave in to it and they sat silently hand in hand" (47).

This kind of grotesquely painful social awkwardness is something that starts the elaborate series of false steps and misinterpretations between Miss Lonelyhearts and Doyle that melodramatically recurs in the last chapter. Nor do the cross-purposes augur well for the session at the Doyles' in which, amid the couple's ill-concealed mutual hatred, Miss Lonelyhearts tries to "find a message" to give them (48). It is at this point that he realizes he has only written a column for the newspaper and imitated, against his intention, the rhetoric of Shrike.

4. A second retreat from the column, this one more severe. This sequence is presided over by the image of the rock: a metaphor for passive

withdrawal. When Shrike bursts into Miss Lonelyhearts's room during his work stoppage, as is Shrike's wont, Miss Lonelyhearts does not yield: "Shrike dashed against him, but fell back, as a wave that dashes against an ancient rock, smooth with experience, falls back" (51).

The nature of Miss Lonelyhearts's withdrawal, his passivity, is worthy of note: a withdrawal from speech and specifically from the narratives of his column. The false reciprocity of his column has been a story of redemption in exchange for a story of woe, but by this point Miss Lonelyhearts has clearly abdicated his part of the exchange. In the chapter entitled "Miss Lonelyhearts Attends a Party," he utters not a recorded word. But then the party is just another ploy to humiliate him, in the form of a game called "Everyman his own Miss Lonelyhearts," which involves a batch of his (presumably as yet unanswered) letters from the city room. Says Shrike: "'First, each of you will do his best to answer one of these letters, then, from your answers, Miss Lonelyhearts will diagnose your moral ills'" (52). It so happens that the letter he distributes to Miss Lonelyhearts is Doyle's death threat, prompted by his wife's contention—which, ironically, is untrue—that Miss Lonelyhearts tried to rape her. The letter is read by Shrike, because the letter's intended recipient has silently left the party without removing the letter from its envelope.

In rejecting the letters, in refusing to read the message and abdicating his Miss Lonelyhearts role, he does not "get the message" of his own peril. The letter is a prediction, the more because its addressee has not read it. Everyone in the book has a Miss Lonelyhearts story, including columnist and editor. Both the columnist's professional and his sexual lives have relied on an exchange of stories: Mary Shrike has a tale of woe, Betty a tale of innocence, and so on. In the wake of failure as a healer, he is now weary of the surfeit of narratives that endlessly repeat the stories of the tellers' lives without ultimate cure. So he withdraws from the letters, from his professional position, and from his own past exploitation. This break with his past writing situation he sees as a way of detaching himself from Shrike's joke.

But his refusal to be the butt of Shrike's joke only ensures that he will be the victim of a more earnest joke with a fatal punch line. Miss Lonelyhearts has refused to read the story of his own life: of his past complicity in the deceptions that made his linguistic life possible and of his future peril from an admirer who has discovered his fraudulence and illegitimacy. (Fay's rape story is a lie, but its profounder truth is that Doyle has been cuckolded in a sexual betrayal that is also a linguistic one: Doyle could, after all, be any reader whose trust Miss Lonelyhearts has transgressed.) His renunciation of letter in favor of the spirit of a Christ that he will not have to "handle . . . with a thick glove of words" seals his doom (33). His own past is inscribed in Doyle's letter and, because the message is not received, his atonement as well.

In the next chapter, Miss Lonelyhearts's conversation with Betty only confirms his divorce from language. Although he does speak with her, he blandly fobs her off with things he feels she wants to hear: he tells her he is working for an ad agency, begging her to marry him for this reason (55). He feels guiltless about this because his withdrawal from language (that is, from any connection between language and truth) is complete: "He did not feel guilty. He did not feel. The rock was a solidification of his feeling" (56). Ironically, this dialogue with Betty is a further negation of his own past ties to his earlier aggressive sexuality. In this sense, his position parallels that of Betty, who offers to abort their illegitimate child and so remove a reminder of the common burden of their past.

5. A "religious experience" (as West acidly calls it), the culmination of Miss Lonelyhearts's momentary dyslexia. In another failed dialectical reversal, he rises, after lying abed for three days, on the third day and foresees a new career as Miss Lonelyhearts, only now twice-born. His call to grace takes the form of a repetition of his previous writing situation, with God taking Shrike's position:

> God said: "Will you accept it, now?"
> And he replied, "I accept, I accept."
> He immediately began to plan a new life and his future conduct as
> Miss Lonelyhearts. He submitted drafts of his column to God and
> God approved them. God approved his every thought. (57)

Miss Lonelyhearts's letter to Christ—dictated by Shrike earlier in the text—has now been answered.[8] The passive-aggressive oscillation has now swung back to frenzied acceptance of the columnist-savior role, but on a mystical plane that will somehow transform shoddy advice into revelation: in the extreme of his delusion, Miss Lonelyhearts is indistinguishable from God ("His heart was the one heart, the heart of God. And his brain was likewise God's" [57]). The aggressiveness of his mission is signaled by the "mentally unmotivated violence" that changes the rock into a furnace (56).

The promise is fulfilled by the arrival of the cripple Doyle, but lacking the message of Doyle's note, Miss Lonelyhearts radically misconstrues the meaning: "God had sent him so that Miss Lonelyhearts could perform a miracle and be certain of his conversion. It was a sign" (57). A sign it surely is, but of rather a different sort. How different becomes clear when one sees that this ironic climax is the repetition of the climaxes of two previous chapters: chapters that suggest the dissonance between the true import of Doyle's actions and the victim's interpretation of it.

Doyle's act itself and its intent have been prefigured in the sordid close of the "Clean Old Man" incident. That scene directly depicts the frustrated sadism practiced by Miss Lonelyhearts at first against his editor, his fiancée and, of course, his readers. His seduction of Fay belongs to this early phase, though it occurs before he meets her husband. Doyle's revenge is thus the mirror of Miss Lonelyhearts's earlier impotent rage and is also the fulfillment of a chain of events begun by Fay's seduction.

Miss Lonelyhearts sees his role as the opportunity, in the fullness of his divinity, to enact fully what he only awkwardly enacts in the scene wherein he and the cripple meet. He thinks: "He would embrace the cripple and the cripple would be made whole again, even as he, a spiritual cripple, had been made whole" (57). As he was at the beginning, so now the born-again columnist is confronting his specular image in that of his readers; but he assumes that he has been healed, and so misreads the nature of his resemblance to Doyle. To be specific, this misconception allows him to ignore the "something wrapped in a newspaper" that Doyle is carrying, which is a pistol (57). Ignoring this is symptomatic of his refusal to acknowledge the aggression lying within his *own* writing position, along with the equally aggressive consequences. (It is not surprising that, deluded as he is, Miss Lonelyhearts is incapable of "reading" what is really in the newspaper.).

Trapped in the narrative of the Christ story, he does not recognize the story he is really in: the oldest story in the book, the adulterous triangle. He misunderstands Doyle's warning as a cry for help. His attempt to escape his past involvement with stories takes the form of another story, the Christ legend, which he persists in enacting and which only causes him to misread his own peril. His fate is a parody of the Christ story, wherein resurrection on the third day is followed by crucifixion: the Christ story as Shrike no doubt would have written it. Miss Lonelyhearts is most completely the victim when he believes himself the savior, and he is, of course, never more distant from his readers (whom Doyle represents) than when approaching his mystical union.

In Miss Lonelyhearts, the central narrative of Western culture produces no revivification, only the bloom of fever. It only makes possible the endless parodic repetitions of Shrike (who is conscious of the parody) and the manic delusions of Miss Lonelyhearts (who at the last is not). Miss Lonelyhearts's Christ dream betrays him as much as Shrike's Christ joke has betrayed his readers; he is in this respect as well Doyle's semblable.

Rather than allowing Miss Lonelyhearts to exchange his soulless typewriter for a Promethean pen producing life-giving language, it leads him only to repeat Christ's role in his own subservient columnist's role, and the two roles fail to cohere. Like many narratives Miss Lonelyhearts tries to escape, the Christ legend is doomed to the same fraudulence; as long as Miss Lonelyhearts is who he is, even the Christ dream is compromised fatally, like a compulsively recurring dream that ends only with the end of the dreamer.

The stories we tell ourselves, like the stories we tell others, are as necessary as they are fraudulent; and the more irrelevant they become, the more necessary they may well seem. The narrative of *Miss Lonelyhearts* is the story of this cruel calculus. At no point in the story can Miss Lonelyhearts conceive of an alternative to his scene of typing, and so his solutions must all bear the mark of his imprisonment. In this tale, all of Miss Lonelyhearts's "escapes" assume the conditions that must be escaped, and so become ever more desperate as they fail. It is a tale in which Shrike has the last laugh, because he has already written the first line.

chapter five

Promise and Prophecy: The Artist's Vision in *The Day of the Locust*

Sea Dreams

A mong its many concerns, Nathanael West's novel of Hollywood, *The Day of the Locust,* treats of the false relationship between an artist and his audience. In this respect, there is a little-noted affinity between this problematic and that of *Miss Lonelyhearts,* although what in the latter text was a writing situation is here transposed (some might say disguised, if they were biographically inclined) into a problematic of the visual field.[1] Regardless of the shift's motives, the fact that the novel's protagonist Tod Hackett is a set designer seems appropriate for what is, after all, a novel "about" the movies, that most visual of media. Beyond that, the process of exchange in *Miss Lonelyhearts,* of a story of redemption for a story of woe, is not quite what occurs in the movies. There, a sum of money is exchanged for a *promesse de bonheur:* a radiant, shimmering mirage, an image of ecstasy and fulfillment. (The often violent content of the films' narratives, for reasons discussed below, is paradoxically all the more a part of this process of exchange.) Still, both Tod and Miss Lonelyhearts are figures of the active artistic imagination, one visual and the other literary, imprisoned with its own complicity in a situation that betrays the belief in "Beauty and in personal expression as an absolute end" (14).

Each protagonist has his project for coping with this complicity, this imprisonment. Miss Lonelyhearts's goal was to infuse the forms of his advice to the lovelorn column with sincerity and, ultimately, even with salvation: to use the circumstances of his own indenture to produce true redemption. Tod is less sanguine about the ability to make Hollywood spectacle into a salvific vision: one of many ways in which he is less deluded, more worldly perhaps, than his counterpart. Instead, he cynically accepts his job in its own crass terms, preserving his prophetic impulse for off-hours, where by night he mentally destroys the dream sets he constructs by day. Thus, one tries fitfully to embrace his role's limitations to turn them to other ends, while the other tries to distance himself from that role.

It is, psychology aside, the divergence between the situations of the respective men that suggests such diverse strategies. This divergence is dramatized in the two kinds of sea meditations indulged in by the heroes. In Miss Lonelyhearts's newspaper office, for example, he daydreams of a sea without the usual oceanic properties. Rather, it is a "dismal swamp," a slough of despond (30). Still in all, in his reverie he is able to "make a gigantic cross" from all the "marine refuse" he gets from the sea waves: "bottles, shells, chunks of cork," and so on (31). These waste products, mixed in his dreams with pawnshop items, are the spoor of suffering and decay, but he envisions his labor as redeeming them, making them mean something. It is a kind of second-order retrieval system, taking junk and recuperating it for greater glory. By contrast, Tod's sea image for the back lot of the studio where he works is that of the Sargasso Sea. Whereas Miss Lonelyhearts sees himself as on the shore of his ocean, able to use its effluvia, Tod's famous "dream dump" is self-contained and impervious to much intervention by him or anyone else: "A Sargasso of the imagination! And the dump grew continually, for there wasn't a dream afloat somewhere which wouldn't sooner or later turn up on it, having first been made photographic. . . . no dream ever entirely disappears. Somewhere it troubles some unfortunate person and some day, when that person has been sufficiently troubled, it will be reproduced on the lot" (132). The characterization of the back lot is also a "history of civilization" (132), which suggests the larger canvas of Western culture and history: here, though, all the available cultural material has been retrieved not by religion or by art, but by show business. The recuperative movement is unceasing, its manic, pointless productivity resembling an industrial process wherein nothing goes to waste. Hollywood needs no Miss Lonelyhearts to operate a retrieval system, for it has one ruthless in its efficiency, able to assimilate even its own refuse to advantage. The Western world's dreams, once reproduced by Hollywood, make perfect sense, and they can be recycled. These dreams, however, are in no ways regenerative; they only add to the capital accumulation of the dream dump. Tod makes nothing out of these dreams and cannot. Anything he would do with them would only augment the "dream dump" the more. Residing on the shore to form a second order of meaning is impossible, since the materials never reach the shore.

Miss Lonelyhearts's reflections are occasioned by letters from "real" suf-
ferers: the exchange is genuine on one side, cynical on the other, and it is
this initial disparity that leads Miss Lonelyhearts (mistakenly as it turns out)
to believe that sincerity on both sides would even up the situation, despite
the way the whole enterprise is framed by the paper. That is why, for
instance, he pictures his letter writers as forming his own pen name out of
detritus (false redemption) but himself as forming a cross (true redemption). But in the movies, of course, no such collaboration obtains; the film,
already a fictive construct, is designed *for* the audience, not *by* it. Distraction
and entertainment ("only a movie," as people say), such material does not
even pretend to speak to the spectator's own problems but instead presents
merely another scene, often one inspired by some historical event or exotic
locale. Though it may seem more innocent than the outright gulling of the
lovelorn column, film may be more insidious finally. The "naturalistic"
paraphernalia of movies—the authentic costumes, the period decor—are
largely guises for the real business, which is to allow the spectators to project their own inmost wishes onto the exotic "other scene" enacted before
them in the dark. The real anxieties that are fled at the movies are precisely the constant elements that ensure that the dream dump will only accumulate and recycle its stock of novelties but never draw it down.

Against this system, the heir to high culture cannot work inside the
dream factory to produce higher-quality dreams but must destroy the idols
of the marketplace. Tod's zeal is nowhere near messianic in Miss
Lonelyhearts's vein, but he does have the occasional religious vision of himself. Appropriately, while Miss Lonelyhearts's active extension of his healing task leads him to assume Christ's mantle, Tod's belief that the "dream
dump" of mass culture must be extirpated root and branch leads him
instead to an Old Testament role model, Jeremiah. Unlike so many
prophets, though, Tod is a legend only in his own mind. He is not dis-
honored in his own country so much as simply unknown. Before gauging
Tod's curious prophetic stance close up, I will first pan back for a better
view of his milieu and fix him within the constellation of characters peo-
pling West's show-business novel, if "constellation" applies to a group
notably lacking in stars other than the self-styled variety.

Seeing and Being Seen: Public Space and Private Lives

West refers at some point to "the peculiar half-world which I attempted to
create" in *Day of the Locust.*[2] Since he uses it to defend the selectivity of his
social canvas—his refusal to include "the sincere, honest people who work

here and are making such a great progressive fight," among other things—
one can safely assume "half-world" to mean that realm of would-be society on the fringe of notoriety. Of course, this is Los Angeles, not Paris; and
the half-world here has little one could characterize as bohemian. But as
the book progresses through what are more like a series of blackouts or
spectacles than plot turns, it becomes clear that these figures inhabit a half-
world in another very strict sense; they are forever at the threshold of performance and spectatorship, of seeing and of being seen.

The group West portrays, the lower depths of the industry, partake of the
two major groups into which West's protagonist has divided Los Angeles in
the very first chapter, starers and masqueraders. Tod notes the distinctions
between the gaily dressed "evening crowd" in Norfolk jackets and Tyrolean
hats (worn by the sadistic dwarf Abe Kusich as well) on the one hand, and
on the other "people of a different type" whose clothing is "somber and
badly cut" and who stare at the others, "their eyes filled with hatred" (60).
These are of course the people who have "come to California to die," whom
Tod desires to make the subject of his prospective painting, *The Burning of
Los Angeles.* The social space created by these two classes of people, with its
imaginary proscenium arch, seems similar to the *theatrum mundi* where all
have a mask and a part to play, and some all-encompassing social ritual is
enacted. But it is actually very different, since the relation between the two
groups is so distant and so unequal, at once symbiotic and hostile. The masqueraders and the starers do not participate in some ritual affirmation of
commonality, but rather the uneasy coalition between narcissistic exhibitionism and vicarious voyeurism.[3] Spectatorship is the mode the public
adopts, insofar as the public emerges in any way; those who present themselves as performers do so only insofar as they separate themselves from the
public. They come to the coast to realize some purely private dream to live
as the characters in the movies or as the stars are alleged to live in their often
equally manufactured "offscreen" lives. (The fact that these dreams result
from a mass-production industry does not make them any the less private,
even solipsistic.) When they find they cannot, they are reduced to staring at
those who seem to be; they both admire and resent the others.[4] This
ambivalence springs from the nature of the mass-media image as propagat-
ed in the cinema, as will be clear later.

Among those foregrounded characters in the novel, perhaps Harry
Greener, Faye's vaudevillian father who now sells "Miracle Polish," is closest to the pure performer, a category that can functionally be equated with
that of masquerader.[5] He performs compulsively: "like a mechanical toy
that had been overwound, something snapped inside of him and he began

to spin through his entire repertoire" (92). Even when he is genuinely sick, he convinces himself that was an act, too: "He pushed all thought of sickness out of his mind and even went so far as to congratulate himself on having given the finest performance of his career" (92). His very head is "all face, like a mask," which "could never express anything either subtly or exactly" (119)—a face, in short, designed to be seen from beyond a stage. He cherishes what he wishfully takes to have been a favorable review from his vaudeville days and, like so many failed actors who become proportionately more actorish in their daily lives, Harry stages even the arguments he has with his daughter, one of which is witnessed by Homer Simpson: "Homer was amazed. He felt that the scene he was witnessing had been rehearsed. He was right" (96).

As for Homer himself, he is the closest of the major characters to the audience in its purest form: his trajectory is one way of indicating that the audience role can be as taxing as that of performer. He seems the perfect audience, though, being a refugee from the Midwest, like that "barber in Purdue" that screenwriter Claude Estee posits as the recipient of Hollywood product (72). He is easily entertained (he finds it "very amusing to watch" a lizard on his property for hours [89]) and obliging even when he isn't (when Harry as salesman goes through some unfunny physical business, Homer understands "that this was to amuse," and so laughs [90]). He indeed eventually tires of his role, especially after having been Faye Greener's hapless audience; but he does not cross the footlights except in his attack on Adore Loomis at the conclusion, for which transgression he pays a heavy price.

Most of the people depicted, however, cross the threshold between performer and audience with some frequency. It is not that they synthesize these two roles; far from it. Instead, they gyrate back and forth between them in a kind of wilderness of mirrors. Unlike Harry, who despite failure never relents his role as performer, most of the other figures in the text take turns, informally of course, as performers and as audience, acting out their fantasies. Faye Greener herself enacts this sort of duplicity, and her singing of the song "Viper" and her sex life—not to mention her comportment and manner—suggest somebody who imbibes dreams at least as furiously as she produces them. This trait, though, is shared by most of the characters who inhabit West's half-world, and for two main reasons.

First of all, the obvious reason for the desire to be seen is to fulfill a dream of oneself as another, and for this an audience is needed to complete the self-fulfillment. But bit players like Faye or Earle Shoop realize they must play the audience in order to perform in their own turn. Thus Faye, for example, allows the Mexican Miguel to believe that she is his audience—that is, that he has taken her by seductive storm—in order to experience not so much the seduction itself as its refracted image within the audience. As usual, that audience is the cuckold Homer, who in his *style indirect libre* monologue to Tod remarks: "The door wasn't locked. You'd have thought she would have locked the door because the Mexican was in bed with her, both of them naked and she had her arms around him" (170). Quite the contrary, for it is not sex that Faye is after but its appearance for others. That she works as a prostitute, in a job requiring the appearance of desire in order to be the object of desire, tallies with this need to see oneself as an object in another's field of vision.

The second reason why these figures can be seen at the threshold of performing and spectatorship is that they are still molding their self-images, and their other fantasies as well, from the models of mass-culture cliché before they embark on careers in Hollywood in the first place. One might even say that their dreams of success *in* pictures are only a small part of the dreams vouchsafed to them *by* pictures. They are as much consumers of fantasy as producers of them, maybe more. Again, the unattainable love image Faye has her own unattainable love image: that of a Tarzan photo from a movie theater. When Faye is bored, her daydreams take the form of possible film scripts: "She would get some music on the radio, then lie down on her bed and shut her eyes. She had a large assortment of stories to choose from. After getting herself in the right mood, she would go over them in her mind, as though they were a pack of cards" (104).

Because the very terms of these fantasies are drawn from mass culture such as movies and radio, the people who perform for each other in this text are not viewed through a folkish lens, as participants in some sort of carnival. Instead, the primitive technique, the face-to-face relation between performer and audience, the rapid shifts between producer and consumer of fantasy, the fact that performers select all their own material—all of these things, not necessarily bad in themselves, flow from the fact that these people are not successful in pictures. Folkloric forms such as the singing of the blues or the cockfight are out of place and a little passé in the city movies built; submitting to the machinery of the dream factory (from which their own dreams largely emanate anyway) would suit the denizens of West's half-world far better than this parody of artisanal culture, since in the end most of them would rather be talking to the camera than to one another.

A seeming contrast to this ragged edge of filmdom, this twilit Valhalla of extras and starlets, is the Hollywood establishment, the successful hierarchy of scriptwriters and producers whose embodiment is the sardonic Claude Estee. Sophisticated, even cynical about pictures, his rhetoric and overall stance of detachment recall Willie Shrike, prepossessing city editor in *Miss Lonelyhearts*.[6] His habitual comment, "It's not for pictures," at least implies the ability—not noteworthy in several of the other characters—to separate "pictures" from life. However, the distance between successful Hollywood and its lower depths should be modified in a couple of respects.

For one thing, all the Hollywood sophisticates go to Mrs. Jenning's house not for sex (none of her women "lived on the premises" [73]), but rather for another film, this one with more risqué matter and a foreign title, unlike Hollywood's standard fare.[7] Additionally, of course, they are audience for one another's stunts, such as the illusionistic dead horse in the pool at Claude Estee's. In that sense, then, the sophisticates are closer to the half-world than we at first may think.

Furthermore, their houses are themselves simulacra, means by which the owner tries to "be" someone else, just as do the actor for fame's sake and the spectator for escape's. To look at the landscape of Los Angeles's residences, including its mansions, is to confront "Mexican ranch houses, Samoan huts, Mediterranean villas, Egyptian and Japanese temples, swiss chalets, Tudor cottages" (61), monuments to the warped urge for exoticism. The same desire to flee one's own existence by acquiring an exotic home motivates Estee as it does the actor to adopt a character or an audience member to imagine him- or herself on the screen. The desire to live somewhere else without the requisite courage to quit where one already is produces this urge:

> Claude was a successful screenwriter who lived in a big house that was an exact reproduction of the old Dupuy mansion near Biloxi, Mississippi. When Tod came up the walk between the boxwood hedges, he greeted him from the enormous, two-story porch by doing the impersonation that went with the southern colonial architecture. He teetered back and forth on his heels like a Civil War colonel and made believe he had a large belly.
>
> He had no belly at all. He was a dried-up little man with the rubbed features and stooped shoulders of a postal clerk. The shiny mohair coat and nondescript trousers of that official would have become him, but he was dressed, as always, elaborately. (68–69)

Estee has certainly not stepped serenely outside of the wilderness of mirrors inhabited by the others, though he may be more conscious of its ironies; and to the extent that he may somehow figure West himself (rather than, as seems at least as probable, West's hunting buddy William Faulkner), it still cannot be said that "Claude is clearly West's ideal vision of himself."[8]

If the Hollywood hopefuls and the Hollywood establishment are both equally prey to this dual role-playing of exhibitionism and voyeurism, it may still appear that Tod himself—West's painterly eye—is scarcely either performer *or* audience. Coming from the eastern seaboard, imbued more with high art than with folk or mass culture, he has not consumed (or been consumed by) the cinema's dreams, at first at least. He is not a performer, either, nor has he any desire to be a producer or scriptwriter like Claude Estee. He stands on the periphery of show business and observes: the logical perspectival focus in the text. His status as an artist also makes this observer's role central, both for the obvious fact that painting involves depicting observed reality in whatever form, and because his prophetic powers depend on accurately seeing the situation before him and not fleeing from it into some exotic daydream. Tod's eccentric position at first bids fair to make him ideal to see more clearly than others what is really happening, and his judgments in the orienting first chapter are Olympian in their certitude.

In fact, Tod is compromised more than he prefers to think both as producer and as consumer of dreams. His job, obviously, compromises him as a producer, as a part of the dream factory (the reader is first introduced to Tod "around quitting time" [59]). *The Burning of Los Angeles* project is in part a reaction against this complicity, but also a rationalization for it—after all, he has to be in California in order to portray those people coming there to die, who are "the people he felt he must paint" (60). It may be as well that in addition, this complicity explains part of why that project remains, throughout the novel, only a project.[9]

Similarly, Tod is a consumer of dreams despite his armor of high culture. His infatuation with Faye, above all, shows this to be true; and the relationship to Faye, whether through Tod's optic or through Homer's, is the central form of interaction thematized in the novel. The point-of-view switches between Tod and Homer have been much maligned in criticism, but apart from whether they "work" dramatically, their thematic function, at least, should be clear. It is Faye who is the star (that is, object) for both the least sophisticated observer, Homer, and the most sophisticated, Tod Hackett.[10] With this in mind, and by examining the nature of Faye's appeal to both Tod and Homer, we may reach some conclusions about the source of appeal of that mass culture of which she aspires to be a bearer.

Screen Play: Projection and Frustration of Desire

When the film breaks at the showing of *Le prédicament de Marie,* the evening crowd in attendance stages a near riot: "The old teaser routine!" says one of them (75). The only way in which this particular "teaser routine" differs from the one carried out in other parts of West's Hollywood is that here the breakdown or interruption of the film is the tease, whereas elsewhere the ongoing performance is itself the source of frustration.

Faye Greener's central role makes this feature somewhat plainer and also suggests why there is such a strong admixture of violence in so many of the Hollywood fantasies—and indeed in the fantasy life in general as portrayed in this novel. For Faye is the person in the book who has worked the most to mold herself into an object of desire along motion-picture lines. The relationship of the various men in the narrative, chiefly Tod and Homer, to Faye follows a trajectory of desire and frustration that can be divided into four stages.

First of all, there is the fantasy of total union with the desired object: a fairly brief stage, no doubt. Tod's image for this union is violent, indeed, but interestingly it is masochistic at this point rather than sadistic: "Her invitation wasn't to pleasure, but to struggle, hard and sharp, closer to murder than to love. . . . If you threw yourself on her, it would be like throwing yourself from the parapet of a skyscraper. . . . Your teeth would be driven into your skull like nails into a pine board and your back would be broken" (68). This violent image is really one of radical rebirth, a change of identity figured in the plunge from a window: by uniting with the desired object, the subject imagines sudden and swift transformation of his own life.

The second stage is deeper self-abasement before the fantasy or desired object as its unattainability becomes increasingly acute and painful. Although Tod himself exhibits many symptoms of this stage, it is Homer Simpson who portrays it best. His desires are presented as wholly displaced from his conscious waking life, to the point where they become localized eerily in his hands, which take on a life of their own.[11] Sexual dissatisfaction and repression are not the whole story behind Homer and the masses he is supposed to stand in for, though they are surely a major part. But the chastity that is said to be his armor may be his best qualification as an audience for the coquettish Faye. Even Homer's tears have no climax, since "to those without hope, like Homer . . . no good comes from crying" (103). Lacking the ability or the will to attain his fantasy, Homer's relation to his idol becomes ever more subservient as she grows more distant: "Homer realized that the end [of their friendship] was in sight even before she did. All he could do to prevent its coming was to increase his servility and his generosity" (143).

The mounting frustration with the desired object causes a shift to the third stage. Satiation of desire may reduce the desired object and postponement elevate it for awhile, but eventually this deferral spawns fantasies more bitter and forcible, combining possession with degradation. In Tod's case, this stage manifests itself in those rape fantasies that increasingly recur as he contemplates Faye. He pictures himself throwing himself on her later in the novel, for example, but here the target of violence is not himself but Faye: "If he only had the courage to throw himself on her. Nothing less than rape would do. . . . It was her completeness, her egglike self-sufficiency, that made him want to crush her" (107). A later elaboration on this theme is even more detailed and graphic, and there is a nice detail accompanying the last rape fantasy, which Tod spins out while seated in a restaurant: "The waiter came back. Todd [*sic*] looked at the steak. It was a very good one, but he wasn't hungry any more" (175). As the fantasies aggrandize themselves, reality is more and more impoverished, just as the inadequacy of reality at first encouraged the fantasy as compensation.

This vicious circle—blending anger at the object of fantasy and self-loathing at being weak and gullible—yields the final stage along this arc of frustration, which the rape imagery prefigures: the desire simply for destruction, not even possession and degradation but annihilation, the attempt to cancel what had attracted. Homer's attack on the androgynous child star Adore Loomis after Faye leaves him is a stark instance: it is hard to deny that Adore recalls Faye and that that is why Homer is maddened by her.

The apocalyptic rending of the desired object on this level of private frustration is generalized to the itch for apocalypse that possesses the vaster hordes in West's Hollywood. This itch is put there by the mass media, of course, but not only by virtue of their content (those "lynchings, murder, sex crimes, explosions, wrecks, love nests, fires, miracles, revolutions, wars" [178] that both papers and films feed their publics); the itch is also an inevitable by-product, or rather an enabling condition, of the mode of mass-culture fantasy, quite apart from its content. If Faye's vapidity and self-sufficiency make her ideally suited to personify this mode, then the movie screen provides the ideal medium for a mode of fantasy combining superficial flatness with the hieratic aura of distance.[12] The daydream projections of mass culture all rely on the separation between the observer and the object: a kind of screen that at once projects the fantasy of the viewer onto another scene and puts up a barrier protecting viewer and fantasy from colliding.[13] When that screen is penetrated, the result may violently alter the fantasy as well as the observer, just as the extras who collapse Mount St. Jean during the shooting of a battle scene are as damaged as the scenery itself, as both "carpenters and ambulances" are required (135). The double function of the screen surface as both the place where fantasy is projected and the barrier to its fulfillment makes it the chosen instrument for the Hollywood dreams—that *promesse de bonheur* whose blatancy gives it the illusion of accessibility, but whose true mission lies in perpetual titillation. Thus the fragility of specific dreams does not endanger the operation of the dream factory or the recycling of old dreams in the future. Like Marcel Duchamps's *machine célibataire,* the film image prompts one to imagine oneself in it and also forecloses the consummation of that process, which produces a compulsion to repeat. The promise within the medium itself ultimately matters more than its specific embodiment.[14]

Prophecy and Iconoclasm:
Tod Hackett's Destructive Element

Tod himself, then, has a dual status inside and outside the Hollywood nexus. As one smitten by Faye Greener, he knows the psychological dynamic that the screen siren, and by implication the screen itself, set in motion; and as heir to a tradition of art less sullied by commerce, he is equipped to use his own frustrations as clues to the mass psychology of entertainment as well. He embodies this in a vision (although "embodies" may be strong, given that he never paints his picture). This vision, in any event, stands in polemical relation to the dreams manufactured by Hollywood (and of course himself), and such a vision at once accounts for and counters the movies. Where mass culture offers a perpetual, teasing promise, Tod will erect instead a prophecy of the destruction of that promise: *The Burning of Los Angeles.* He has art-for-art's-sake reservations about this stance, but they are not overwhelming: "He told himself . . . he was an artist, not a prophet. His work would not be judged by the accuracy with which it foretold a future event but by its merit as painting. Nevertheless, he refused to give up the role of Jeremiah" (118). His justification as an artist partakes of the accuracy of his prophetic powers, inevitably.

Like the other masqueraders and performers, Tod has also his models, but he draws them from the tradition of high art, another painterly discourse: Goya, Daumier, Magnasco, Guardi and Monsu Desiderio (142;

131–32). There has been considerable research into these allusions in past West criticism.[15] These portrayers of "Decay and Mystery," war and the grotesque, are the art that, in Tod's eye, the life of Los Angeles tends to imitate.

While these models are surely not realistic in the conventional sense of the term, still it is Tod's belief that his predilection for them is dictated, oddly enough, by their appropriateness to the situation around him. It is when he first glimpses the people who had "come to California to die" that he realizes that "despite his race, training and heritage, neither Winslow Homer nor Thomas Ryder could be his masters and he turned to Goya and Daumier" (60). Later, he decides that Magnasco would be better than Daumier, because that way he could "paint their fury with respect, appreciating its awful, anarchic power and aware that they had it in them to destroy civilization" (142). It is not the fact that Tod's vision is violent that distinguishes it from the Hollywood product; after all, we have seen that Hollywood's fantasies often use a generous dollop of violence themselves, as witness the Waterloo scene that is a famous set piece in the novel. Rather, it differs from the commercial vision in two related respects. First of all, whereas the historical styles and allusions of mass culture are used largely as forms of exotic escape, Tod by contrast is trying to find the nightmare most apt to apply to the place where he lives; where the logic of daydream has taken over, phantasmagoria is realism. Second, unlike the movies, Tod's project is precisely to include the audience in the picture, indeed to grant it the starring role onstage, even if it means that what it is doing is striking the stage. Those who have come to California believing that by metonymy the city that has produced their fraudulent dreams is the place to realize them sense they "have been cheated and betrayed" and have "slaved and saved for nothing," and their eruption onto the canvas will be a return of the repressed, the piercing of the screen—a final iconoclastic sundering (178). Hence the resultant vision is motivated by a clear-eyed enunciation of the logic in what Tod sees, not by some sort of yearning, as is the case with movie fantasy.

Even this nightmare vision is undercut by West's narrative, however. Tod's self-understanding as prophet is based in large part on ignoring the psychological wellsprings of his vision, and it fails the test of predictive power as well. As to the initial motives, it becomes evident that Tod's own desire to have done with the contradictions involved in having to work for Hollywood is displaced onto the audience, whose members become the collective agents of his own desire to destroy the idols he himself creates. It is true that Tod's attitude toward the crowd he envisions is highly ambivalent—but then, it goes without saying, so is his attitude toward the burning of Los Angeles, the dismantling of the dream factory itself. Tod's vision, finally, is less satirical prophecy than it is another kind of exotic space wherein to resolve and forget the contradictions of his own situation. The fact, mentioned at the outset, that Tod never even paints his picture, much less broadcasts his prophecy, shows two things: first, that his own impotence as an artist is no doubt part of the impulse leading to this iconoclastic vision, perhaps on the grounds that if he can no longer make images nobody should; and second, that Tod is not someone who could activate public space in prophecy but rather remains in his own daydream of that role, just as the extras dream of being stars.[16]

As to the predictive power of his vision, the actual riot at the movie premiere, which concludes the book and which at first may seem to be Tod's nightmare vision coming true, does not really obey the implicit laws of his prophecy. Most significantly, the rage of the rioters is not directed against the movie theater or the stars who are ushered inside; in fact, the riot is directed (at least at first, when it is directed at all) against Homer for harming a rather obvious symbol of show business, the child actor Adore Loomis: "'A pervert attacked a child,'" explains one woman (183). Ultimately, though, the crowd in this Walpurgisnacht directs its rage not against Homer or against the movies that have cheated it, but everywhere and nowhere—and there is an undercurrent of sinister jocularity to the riot as well. The Dionysiac revelers have not sundered the proscenium separating them from the stage, as Tod thought he foresaw, but turn on one another implosively. Tod himself is victimized as he foresaw, but not because he works in films. It is simply because he happens to be in the way. Even the apocalyptic note of prophecy seems overdrawn, since this melee seems unlikely to lead to civil war.[17] It is during this riot, in fact, that the escapist nature of Tod's own supposed prophecy becomes most clear, as Tod thinks of his picture precisely in order to block out what is happening: "He had almost forgotten both his leg and his predicament, and to make his escape still more complete he stood on a chair and worked at the flames in an upper corner of the canvas, modeling the tongues of fire so that they licked even more avidly at a corinthian column that held up the palmleaf roof of a nutburger stand" (185). At the last, this artist figure is capable neither of promise nor prophecy. The destruction of Hollywood's daydreams has been his daydream, but for all his acuity as to the psychological turmoil exploited and worsened in mass culture, Tod has erred in one crucial respect. He has assumed that people would be able to step out of the charmed circle of illusion. The crowd that ends West's novel is not acting in concert to uproot the source of its misery: even if the rioters' frustration is stoked by the teasing of mass-culture dreams, they are not apparently aware of it.[18] Tod overestimates the audience's powers of perception and so its ability to wrest public space back from those who use it only to project private fantasy. The mob with which the book ends, in short, is not really even a mob, at least not in the way Tod hoped and feared it would be.

To the sirens of teasing promise put forward by the film industry, Tod replies by taking as his model that of a warning siren instead. But once he has misperceived the nature of the passion unleashed in movieland, Tod is reduced, his prophecy unheeded and unfulfilled, to repeating in madness the sound of a warning siren after the fact, having already forfeited its prophetic function: "The siren began to scream and at first he thought he was making the noise himself. He felt his lips with his hands. They were clamped tight. He knew then it was the siren. For some reason this made him laugh and he began to imitate the siren as loud as he could" (185). To judge by the fate of the artist who is the novel's chief viewpoint, the prospects put forward in West's novel of exposing the mass-culture "lie" by means of the higher truth of art (such as satirical fiction) are about as realistic as those for the aspirations that spring from cinema itself, whose Sargasso Sea, in video libraries and DVD collections, continues to grow as surely as it did in Tod's day.

chapter six

Quilty the Guilty:
Scapegoating Mass Culture in *Lolita*

As Humbert Humbert and his Lolita are journeying westward for the last time, she maneuvers them into stopping in the "kurortish" town of Wace, where a "summer theater in full swing" greets them. The play they attend there is largely forgotten, at least by Humbert, but the authors who are called up onto the stage afterward provide a central clue to the identity of Humbert's pursuer and Lo's ultimate seducer: "authors Clare Quilty and Vivian Darkbloom" are presented to the audience, which causes Lolita to lag behind her companion on the way to the exit, "in a rosy daze, her pleased eyes narrowed" as she looks stageward.[1] Humbert later remarks that "Vivian is quite a woman," to which Lolita replies, falsely, that "Vivian is the male author, the gal author is Clare" (223). This statement, obviously at variance with the entry in *Who's Who in the Limelight* earlier mentioned in the book, is combined with a mention of Ramsdale and dentist Ivor Quilty, which should remind the reader that Lolita's interest in Clare Quilty is of long standing, despite her denials. It is one of the strongest hermeneutic signals that Humbert's bête noire is indeed Clare Quilty.

It also sends a signal, though considerably more mixed, about the identity of the author of *Lolita*. What does it mean that Vivian Darkbloom is an anagram of Vladimir Nabokov, other than that Lolita, though misleading about the fictional writer, is accurate about her own creator? Could it be that Vivian's appearance on the public stage with Clare Quilty dramatizes some feared misperception on the part of Nabokov's readers that his delicate book participates somehow in the coarser, more commercial world of Quilty's endeavor? If so, the process by which Vivian the woman becomes Vladimir the man, to those in the know, should parallel the understanding that, surface resemblance to one side, Nabokov's text has meanings not only different from but opposite to those available to its popular reception. *Vive la différence,* indeed![2]

Without insisting on this passage as the key to Nabokovian anxiety, I would assert that the author was unquestionably concerned, throughout his life, to justify his novel as both a work of art and a highly moral endeavor. Since he had lent a copy of his novel to Edmund Wilson, only to find the author of *Memoirs of Hecate County* disgusted by its coarseness, Nabokov had been anxious lest his peers in the literary world mistake his narrative for pornography (few did that, considering its paucity of arousing passages) or for a merely smirky, shock-comic treatment of sexual transgression (many suspected this and still do). He was not unaware that *Lolita,* which would make him financially independent, would always be perceived as, or suspected of, pandering to low public instincts. Such is his awareness, in fact, that the ex cathedra pronouncements of his afterword on "aesthetic bliss" being the artist's only proper goal can be attributed at least in part to plain defensiveness.[3] At other times, his view of his efforts appears more rounded. Contemporary critics of Nabokov, no doubt in contrast to earlier figures more taken with the project of modernism, have outdone one another in stressing the highly moral content of his corpus in general and *Lolita* in particular.[4] Nevertheless, as of old, critics continue to treat the novel as an exercise in examination of the vexed relation between aesthetics and ethics.

They are not inaccurate to do so: like all good critics, they go nowhere to which the author has not led them. It is, after all, neither Pope nor Stevens but Nabokov himself who is the "old poet" Humbert cites in his famous couplet: "The moral sense in mortals is the duty / We have to pay on mortal sense of beauty" (285). Still, this relation between aesthetics—and, more to the point, the aesthetic attitude—and ethical action is not quite so simple as it seems. The reader's moral questions about the narrator are many and self-evidently the stuff of the fiction; but those about the novel itself, disguised like Vivian Darkbloom though they be, also present themselves, detaining our attention for reasons other than Lolita's. Yet so many critics neglect just that inevitable entanglement of the novel itself in the moral ambiguities to which a doctrine of aesthetic formalism was hoped to be the answer. That entanglement, and the means by which *Lolita* symbolically disentangles itself, form the subject here. It will emerge that Vladimir Nabokov, so close and yet so far from Vivian Darkbloom, gains legitimacy by making her partner a writer figure who contrasts not only *Lolita's* protagonist but its author as well. Before exploring how this turn of the symbolic economy is arranged, though, I examine "this tangle of thorns": the interlacing of aesthetic and ethical discourse that the figure of Quilty is called upon to unweave (11).

Drunk on the Impossible Proust: Scripting and Encrypting

Julian Moynahan has pointed out that Humbert Humbert comes to America in much the same spirit as others before him: to replay the past, only with better results.[5] This is not Humbert's project in coming to North America—avoiding World War II is—but it is a project he begins to implement after he arrives. When he tells the reader that "Lolita began with Annabel [Lee]" (16), Humbert acknowledges that his infatuation with her has nothing to do with qualities specific to Lolita, or at least not ideally. The qualities that certify her for nymphet status are those that recall Humbert's long-lost pubertal love, which means that the living girl serves almost solely as a kind of projection screen for the earlier, now dead girl from Humbert's past. The past is recaptured in a way Marcel Proust would not have attempted, despite the novel's many homages to him. For all *Lolita's* famous verbal complexities, its narrative drive is remarkably simple to summarize in popular culture form. It is the old story: In book 1 boy meets girl, boy loses girl, boy recaptures girl "by incarnating her in another" (17). Then, in book 2 boy loses girl again, recapturing her for the final time solely in his memory. There has been argument that the primary structure of the narrative is quadripartite: first, the pursuit of Lolita, followed by attempts to secure her allegiance and fend off competitors, then efforts to elude capture, concluding with manhunts for both Lo and Quilty.[6] This is one way to define the plot, as in effect a series of romantic quests. Still, what is relevant here is how Humbert the failed living (and then successful posthumous) artist works out his writerly difficulties by means of the events of his life. The experiments that succeed, particularly in contrast to those that fail, indicate the text's aesthetic as well as anything can.

The mere fact that Humbert translates the present of Lolita's life directly into the past of Humbert's muse tells us that his first form of recuperation is not artistic. Further evidence is that the means are not literary at all but visual: "I recognized," "With awe and delight I saw," and so on. Indeed, his shock of recognition is explicitly twinned by the visual image Humbert believes himself to be forming in Lolita's view: "my adult disguise (a great big handsome hunk of movieland manhood)" (41). Although Humbert may wish to contrast the superficiality of her attraction to the depth of his, the commonality between them is a seduction by surface. The role of the visual, and of its mechanical reproduction, as a substitute (or competitor) for the imagination is one to which we return in discussing Quilty. But as Humbert pursues Lolita, his clear purpose involves making her over in the psychic as well as physical image of the earlier, pubescent love: a process not unlike translation itself and a perversion of artistic fash-ioning. Although Humbert is liberal with his allusions to the tropes of courtly love and to the ladylove as inspiration for the poet's endeavor, in reality his project almost completely reverses the model from which it claims to derive.

Petrarch's passion renders legitimacy to Humbert's, and his Laura (or "Laureen") forms one famous precursor of the similarly dubbed Lolita (21). But Petrarch used his unreachable love as a muse to inspire his artis-tic endeavor, while Humbert defines his artistic endeavor as grafting his lost love's essence onto Dolores Haze's body. It is in this larger sense that he "solipsizes" her, in his famous neologism (62). In fact, the davenport sequence from which that word comes demonstrates exactly why Humbert is the reverse of the troubadour poet, although he compares his "physio-logical equipoise" at the point of orgasm to "certain techniques in the arts." His guile and craft are employed to attain her rather than to write about her, and even the sort of calculation required to avoid violating her in this sequence is not really the same as artistic technique. He even imagines Lo to have "noticed nothing," when his own account suggests that it is the narrator to whom this applies (63). His confusion of seduction with art is, of course, symptomatic: he is creative only insofar as he is delusional, and his reproduction of the past is a kitsch knockoff of the original.

Briefly, then, whereas the poet in the courtly love tradition may use his unattainable love as inspiration for his art, Humbert's imagination is employed in trying to construe his conquest of Lolita as an artistic project, and secondarily to mitigate his own guilt. If the poet's sexual frustration is projected into his work, Humbert's frustration as an artist is projected onto his seduction, or rather rape, of Lolita. Comically, this dual agenda comes to fantasied fruition after he satisfies himself with her at the Enchanted Hunters and imagines a mural he would be commissioned to paint, a "list" of disjointed and vulgar "fragments," naturally (136).

Certainly Humbert follows the Proustian mode in reacting to the inau-gural sight of Lolita with the sudden recognition that transports him to the lost past: "The twenty-five years I had lived since then [his loss of Annabel], tapered to a palpitating point, and vanished" (41). But his pur-suit of Lolita changes the scenario of memory and desire from one of thwarting and sublimation through art to one of conquest as a substitute for artistic retrieval. Even his decision to pose as Lolita's father marks artis-tic ambition as well as practical design. It is not so much Petrarch as Pygmalion whom Humbert resembles as he constructs his lost love out of his existing love.

Admittedly, Annabel is, strictly speaking, no more resurrected and attained than Petrarch's Laura is conquered. It is this melancholy fact, as much as the famous statute of limitations on nymphancy that condemns even college girls to the nunnery, that gives Humbert's project the appearance of an artistic quest, at least for him. But the essence of his quest, focusing on an experience that is to complete in fantasy the coitus interruptus of years ago with Annabel Lee, is not so much artistic as merely fictive; and its desire to reverse the passing of time to reattain adolescence is as self-destructive as it is deeply felt.[7]

Even though both the artistic and the merely fictive are in some sort parasitic upon reality, the difference here is, for one thing, that the artistic process augments the surrounding material, and the memory of it, with imaginative depth; the fictive merely attempts to reduce one aspect of the already existing surrounding world to the function of reproducing another experience. Humbert's discourse on the otherworldly charm of "nymphets" is justly famous, but it is probably this seeming afterthought that accounts for much of the true appeal: "since the idea of time plays such a magic part in the matter [of nymphet allure], the student should not be surprised to learn that there must be a gap of several years, never less than ten I should say, . . . between maiden and man to enable the latter to come under the nymphet's spell" (19). It is here that he recurs to his time earlier with Annabel, leading us to the other crucial difference between the artistic and the fictive: the role of nostalgia.

The quest for Lolita by Humbert is close kin to Gatsby's pursuit of Daisy Buchanan in the Fitzgerald novel—only the gallantry is missing. The goal of Humbert's "solipsizing" project is to repeat the past, with the difference that a crucial missing piece will now be supplied. The point of "Lolita" (as opposed to the "Dolores" she is "on the dotted line" [11]) becomes allowing Annabel finally to fulfill Humbert's desire, thus adding necrophilia to the already long list of his accomplishments: "Lo. Lee. Ta." His incapacity or disinclination to distinguish between artistic creation and the employment of one human being as the screen for another marks Humbert's pursuit of Lolita as the enactment of the fictive attitude.

The quixotic attempt to realize fantasy in reality makes for most of the narrative thrust of book 1, whose point of suspense is whether Humbert will actually bed his love. The piquancy that informs the narrative drive of this section derives from the overlay of two competing traditional plots: the melodrama of seduction and captivity on the one hand, and the comic plot of courtship and union on the other. The tension this dual narrative attitude introduces into the (male) reader accounts for much of the discomfort this section arouses. Adding to the irony is the employment of standard melodramatic devices, such as coincidental last-minute reprieves, to further precisely the seduction and captivity that are the worst outcome of melodrama. Charlotte Haze's grotesque death, as she runs heedlessly to mail letters incriminating the protagonist, is only the most striking of these reversals.

To put this generic tension into the human terms it implies, the reader's tension springs from the dual status of the title figure as Dolores Haze and as Lolita: as actual human being and as fantasy object. Parsing the two is far easier than relating them for Humbert, who has decided that what he does to Lolita has little or no effect upon the real-life Dolores Haze. But it does, certainly. Let us consider Humbert's morning-after description of Lolita: "It was something quite special, that feeling: an oppressive, hideous constraint as if I were sitting with the small ghost of somebody I had just killed" (142). Since he is about to inform her of her mother's death, Charlotte is a possible nominee for the "somebody" here. But the likelier victim is Dolores herself, whose spiritual death repeats eerily the physical death that deprived Humbert of the one whom the present girl is to impersonate. This glossing predicts the next phase of Humbert's project, which is to make good his spiritual loss of Lolita just as he has initially tried to recuperate the physical loss of her predecessor. For once, Humbert gets it right: "Whether or not the realization of a lifelong dream had surpassed all expectation [clearly it had not], it had, in a sense, overshot its mark—and plunged into a nightmare." Humbert is already on the way to losing his love a second time, even at the point of possessing her.

There remains, then, a barrier, as one would expect from the courtly love tradition. But the barrier is not public morality, which is easily subverted; it is the love object's spiritual distance. The endless replication of motel rooms in which Humbert consummates his relationship with Lolita can be read as perpetually renewed attempts to stage a seduction scene rather than a rape, a fact that makes it harder than ever for Humbert to bear returning to their room in Chestnut Court, only to find her brimming "with a diabolical glow that had no relation to me whatever" (216). Finally his Lolita has been seduced in a motel room, but clearly not by him. Mission Annabel has at some point been supplemented, perhaps usurped, by "Mission Dolores: good title for book" (160).

Curiously, the vagaries of the fictive attitude are explored in the fateful play of Clare Quilty's in which Lolita performs, called *The Enchanted Hunters* and one of the many unsubtle clues Humbert does not take to heart. One of the hunters is "a Young Poet, and he insisted, much to Diana's annoyance, that she and the entertainment provided . . . were his, the Poet's, invention." She proves rather that she is "not a poet's fancy, but a rustic, down-to-brown-earth lass," with a "last-minute kiss" to "enforce the play's profound message, namely, that mirage and reality merge in love" (203). Such a dual notion is close to the heart of Nabokov's work as well as Quilty's, and Humbert is very close to the Young Poet of the play in his insistence on the primacy of his fancy over Dolores's reality. At the same time, there is a sense in which, just as the whole of the play is indeed a poet's invention (or at least that of a writer, Quilty), similarly the novel we read is an invention as well—and not only the novelist's but also the memoirist's.

The play predicts the second career of Humbert, who goes from trying to resurrect Annabel Lee by means of Lolita to capturing Lolita's memory by means of pen and paper. The first fictionalizing, based on ignoring the difference between a living woman and a figment, has miscarried; but the second succeeds as a way of concocting memory into artistic form. Not only does Humbert reconstruct such documentation as his early diary, he endows himself, the principals, and most of the supernumeraries with made-up names. In that sense, John Ray Jr., in his pompous foreword, is right to describe Humbert's story both as a "case history" and as a "work of art [that] transcends its expiatory aspects" (7).

Humbert's Writing Lesson: The Use and Abuse of Memory

To return to the distinction at the outset of the previous section, then, the first major story, of Humbert in pursuit of Annabel through Lolita, is overlaid by the second, of Humbert in pursuit of Lolita's essence through the "local palliative of articulate art" (285). The story told, which is of Humbert's and Lolita's doomed union, is less edifying somehow than the story's telling, which is Humbert purging his own "rust and stardust," the degradation he both inflicts and suffers in realizing his fantasy (259). But in what does this edification consist? How to distinguish ethically between those two ways of fictionalizing reality—turning Lo into Annabel as against turning one's own past into a narrative—apart from the obvious distinction between intervening in someone else's life and refraining from doing so?

With the discretion that may or may not be the better part of genius, Nabokov does not allow his memoirist to disclose any road-to-Damascus moment of conversion, nor to limn a process of deepening reflection for that matter. Some have actually seen Humbert's remorse as itself so melodramatic as to be parodic, so little is it seemingly prepared for. The instability between the content of the reminiscences and their tone is central to reading

Lolita, and almost every critic remarks somewhere the off-balance quality of assessing the narrator's attitude.[8] Most do concede that self-justification makes way ultimately for contrition. But what accounts for the ultimate turn to remorse? The candidates for influence are various, but none seems decisive. Whether this gap arises from Nabokov's famous abhorrence of the didactic (about which more anon) or a lacuna in fleshing out Humbert's characterization, readers all feel compelled to fill it by accounting for the seeming tonal shift as Humbert's memoirs proceed. One possibility is the dialectical shift that seems to announce itself within Humbert's and Lolita's original relationship. What begins as a mere obsession with revisiting the physical scene of his first love (his "kingdom by the sea," in the book's working title) becomes a concern for Dolores Haze's intellectual and spiritual nourishment. He sounds almost like any harassed parent who wants the best for his child when he says, "no matter how hard I pleaded or stormed, I could never make her read any other book than the so-called comic books or stories in magazines for American females. Any literature a peg higher smacked to her of school, and though theoretically willing to enjoy *A Girl of the Limberlost* or the *Arabian Nights,* or *Little Women,* she was quite sure she would not fritter away her 'vacation' on such highbrow reading matter" (175).

Although he does seem genuinely concerned with Lolita's education, however, Humbert's concern can also be traced to the larger original, or rather secondary, project of making her over as his first love: "The spiritual and the physical had been blended in us [Humbert and Annabel] with a perfection that must remain incomprehensible to the matter-of-fact, crude, standard-brained youngsters of today. . . . Oh, Lolita, had *you* loved me thus!" (16). The "affinities" he claims with Annabel are based on conversations whose talking points include "the plurality of inhabited worlds, competitive tennis, infinity, solipsism and so on" (14). Hence his attempt to get Lo to read may be related to his equally problematical attempt to inflict "tennis coaching . . . on Lolita" (235) as a further means of reproducing the emotional as well as the physical sensation of the earlier affair. With this suspicion in mind, it is hard to credit his efforts to improve her mind as so many signs that he is outgrowing his initial self-absorption— any more than she is taking to his program of instruction.

There are other candidates for the scene of conversion, though. Many, including Nabokov himself, have made much of Humbert's final interview with Lolita in Coalmont. The author has said of the paragraph where Humbert renders his "*petit cadeau*" of four thousand dollars to a now overgrown and pregnant Dolly Schiller that it "stings the canthus, or should sting it," being "the most pathetic thing in the whole book" (430 n). One can only speculate why Nabokov singles this scene out for attention; but Humbert's hopeless love of a superannuated Dolly, "pale and polluted, and big with another's child" (280) though she be, is surely decisive in its importance. Lolita has exceeded the age limit for nymphet status by several years, and in seeing her Humbert knows, "as clearly as I know I am to die, that I loved her more than anything I had ever seen or imagined on earth, or hoped for anywhere else" (279). This presumably is what tells us that true love is here. But how does it come about?

Again, the evidence is provided only by Humbert, as is the case with all information but that in the foreword. But this generosity of Humbert's is immediately preceded by Lolita's revelation of her other lover, along with a description of the crowd with whom he spends his time and a hinted intention to return to him if necessary. This scene may be enough to demonstrate that Humbert, after years of deprivation, has displaced the image of Annabel with that of Lolita, as he insists at the novel's outset (13). This displacement is the essential index that the first Humbertian quest has been completed and overcome, considering that the initial inspiration for his pursuit of Lolita was the reenactment of the earlier scene with Annabel.

The mere fact of Lolita's image trumping Annabel's, however, is not enough to announce some profound shift in Humbert's ethical status. Even if the fading of Annabel's face is not solely owing to time passing, Lolita's ascendance does not necessarily imply Humbert's remorse for his past deeds. After all, the fascination with surface image remains in this formulation, even if the original basis for the fascination is lost. One could even suspect that his stakeout of Clare Quilty is a sure sign that he is not taking on the burden of his guilt but is instead making someone else into its carrier: the scapegoat, in effect.

The spectacular lack of psychological insight into the narrator in book 2 has led some readers, accustomed by now to seeing Humbert as unreliable, to posit that the seeming change of heart toward memoir's end is just as rhetorically shrewd and manipulative as the more overt protestations of goodness, addressed to the "ladies and gentlemen" of his interior jury, that mark the rest of the story. "*Qui s'accuse s'excuse*," some mutter when confronting Humbert's final agony. This is a possible interpretation, but an unsatisfying one. It smacks somehow of bad faith, like insisting the narrator is mad or lying when the story takes a strange or incongruous turn.[9]

The best explanation for Humbert's turn is twofold: dramaturgical and thematic. It makes a certain rhetorical sense to end the book on a note of magniloquence and even the hint of insight, and surely Nabokov understands the reader's desire, so long thwarted, that Humbert Humbert display not only chagrin at losing his love (he does that from the first) but the necessary contrition at his own effect on her short, unhappy life. The conventions of melodrama, inverted in book 1, are played relatively straight, then, by the conclusion of book 2.

More importantly, however, the Proustian theme, that of the recuperation of lost memory through art—and specifically "articulate [i.e., literary or discursive] art"—is served by Humbert's dawning awareness, as expressed in specific moments of past time retrieved, "smothered memories, now unfolding themselves into limbless monsters of pain" (286). Thereupon several instances from his relationship with Lolita are retailed, with the eventual realization: "Now, squirming and pleading with my own memory, I recall that . . . it was always my habit and method to ignore Lolita's states of mind while comforting my own base self," he acknowledges, further gaining the insight that "the parody of incest" was, "in the long run, . . . the best I could offer the waif" (289).

In classic Nabokov fashion, Humbert's very obsession with Lolita, the thing that causes her harm, becomes also his means of recognizing his impact on her. (Lolita herself, naturally, helps: Humbert's lengthy review of his life with her follows his final interview with her in Coalmont, where she essentially repudiates his offer of love eternal.) What he appears to have done in this latter-day reflection, though, is to see his love for the first time as a person with her own history, and not primarily as a screen for the projection of his own history. The fictive attitude that informs most of his memoir, or at least most of the story that memoir tells, is for the first time extensively critiqued and overcome. There are, of course, earlier hints, often very powerful. "I catch myself thinking today that our long journey had only defiled with a sinuous trail of slime the lovely, trustful, dreamy, enormous country that by then, in retrospect, was no more than a collection of dog-eared maps, ruined tour books, old tires, and her sobs in the night—every night, every night— the moment I feigned sleep," he remarks fairly soon in book 2 (177–78). Still, it is the later reflections that form the drama of conversion.

These culminate in the famous scene, the last of the novel, wherein Humbert, shortly after having lost Lolita, hears the voices of children in a valley and knows that what he regrets is "not Lolita's absence from my side, but the absence of her voice from that concord" (310). Admittedly, this regret can be read as the nymphet lover's disappointment that his love object will have aged if and when he ever again sees her. But it is more likely that, combined with Humbert's loyal response when he visits Coalmont, his reaction betokens a late awareness that "a North American girl-child named Dolores Haze had been deprived of her childhood by a maniac" (285).

Such awareness is, I suppose, worth something: and it is, in dramaturgical terms anyway, arguably necessary. If the only alternative to cynicism is mawkishness, as Humbert seems to imply, then mawkishness, or even pathos, should be given a chance by the conclusion. On the other hand, it is difficult to credit this turn with great psychological insight: after all, Humbert only arrives after great travail at an ethical understanding that one would hope most of his readers already possess intuitively. Further, the process by which he arrives there, as I have suggested, is sketchy at best. The passage of time and the final interview, assuming it has actually occurred, would help account for it indirectly, but amazingly little is given the reader as to the narrator's reasons for his change of heart and subsequent remorse.

The critics are right to defend Nabokov's contention that his novel is moral, in the strict sense that his narrator comes to realize that what he did was wrong.[10] Yet this ethical awareness, as if in illustration of the author's contention that the novel "has no moral in tow," is a mere by-product of the fact that he has fallen hopelessly (apt adverb) in love with her (316). One of the few succinct statements the author has made about the larger structure of his novel is that the novel's "tragedy . . . is that having started the affair from purely selfish motives, [Humbert] falls in love with [Lolita] when she is beyond loving."[11] Tragic it is. But it can hardly qualify as profound psychologically, or for that matter morally. What it does qualify as is necessary, in the implicitly Proustian structure of the narrative, to Humbert's artful rendering of Lolita in his memoir: "Oh, my Lolita, I have only words to play with!" (34).

This is, as I say, necessary. However, it is not sufficient. Humbert himself points to one further requirement for the memoir to proceed: "And do not pity C. Q. One had to choose between him and H. H., and one wanted H. H. to exist at least a couple of months longer, so as to have him make you live in the minds of later generations" (311). The death of Quilty may be needed for Humbert to go on living and writing; but equally the story of Quilty itself is needed to secure the moral allegiance of the reader for Nabokov's tale. For Humbert's rationale, his self-exculpation, is entangled in some measure in that of his text.

Needed for the Defense: Clare the (Obs)cure

It has been an apparent tenet of the Nabokovian worldview that in the categorical contest between the aesthetic and the moral, the former either trumps the latter or, failing that, moves inexorably toward the latter without friction. Depending on which critic is examining the book at any given time, either the one version or the other prevails. But most have obediently followed the author's ordering of realms, accepting that Humbert's obsession turns forthwith, and without need of much explaining, into true love. This exaltation of the particular makes plausible that an obsessional singularity could lead to a concern for the object of the obsession, and little is done to demonstrate how or why.

This blankness of causality at the center of the narrator's shift is further justified, no doubt, by the author's suspicion of general principles, as strong as his love of the empirical instance. Sigmund Freud is Nabokov's old enemy in part because he seeks to apply general laws to affairs of the heart and loins. Nabokov's own impeccably modernist abhorrence of the overtly didactic contributes to this prejudice. Note how frequently the teacherly as such is satirized, either as ineffectual (Lo, given literature, returns happily to comics) or as downright harmful (Miss Pratt, the comically sinister Beardsley headmistress, decries Lolita's lack of interest in "the process of mammalian reproduction" [197]). It is striking, given this sort of lordly dismissal of all pedagogical content in artworks, how frequently, and stridently, Nabokovians insist on the "morality" of this novel. Are they wrong to do so? And is their very occupation with the question a sign that they somehow "haven't gotten" the idea of *Lolita* to begin with?

I think not. For one thing, in obsessing on the "moral" point, they only follow, in this as in so much else, the lead of their author. Nabokov often recurs himself to the essentially moral thrust of his novel. He asserts in his very afterword what every reader seeking it soon glumly finds out: that *Lolita* has few erotic bits or pornographic passages (315). Further, we discover in Brian Boyd's biography that Nabokov was very disturbed by Robert Girodias's misreading of the novel as some sort of manifesto for pedophilia.[12]

At the same time, there is a reason why such mistakes get made—and of course the suspicion that the novel might not be moral is part of the justly praised "instability" that *Lolita* is said to cause in its hapless reader.[13] In short, the suspense not only attends the main character but the author as well. We now know that Nabokov's literary friends, including Morris Bishop and Edmund Wilson, were less than smitten with the book, in each case because of moral qualms.[14]

Such qualms, and worse, continue to bedevil *Lolita's* reception to this day. To some, such controversy bespeaks the novel's ever fresh power to unsettle readerly complacencies. Still, the queasiness of some—for instance, feminists—in approaching the work should not be written off as

the mere effects of simpleminded moralism. There is genuine reason to suspect this novel of falling prey to the fictive attitude whose excesses it seems
merely to describe. After all, while few serious readers see the work as
pornographic or even, with one or two exceptions, especially erotic, its hint
of low-minded cynicism, the fact that its witty narrator plays so much
tragedy for so many laughs, has caused more than feminists to note its
unsavory aspect—and to assign blame for it to more than the narrator.[15]
Nabokov, perhaps sensing the justice of this suspicion, was apparently ran-
kled all his life by comparisons to what he perceived as lowlier purveyors
of black humor such as Terry Southern and Joseph Heller.[16] Despite such
protestations, though, the handling of such figures as Charlotte Haze, in
whose life and death Humbert reposes such misogynist schadenfreude, has
raised questions as to just how much responsibility for the novel's black
humor can be conveniently sloughed off onto its reptilian teller.[17] Perhaps
another scapegoat is in order, as after two hundred pages Humbert
inevitably grows too old in the service.

In fine, the question as to whether this book is actually the "highly
moral affair" that the author insists it is has not been the province of
squares and bluenoses alone, not from the start.[18] The easy assimilation of
moral and aesthetic excellences wrought by a generation of formalist critics under the ratification of the modernist master is not a program to
which all literati have subscribed, by any means: the fact that Humbert, in
producing his memoir, becomes the artist he only pretends to be in his
affair with Lolita does not seem sufficient recompense for forcing the reader into complicity with him in the first place.[19]

Such art-for-art's-sake claims, compelling though they be to Nabokov
and to some formalist critics, are not in themselves enough to enlist the
reader's sympathy. For indeed, as demonstrated above, little moral benefit
can be seen deriving from the artistic process: even the realization on
Humbert's part of the harm he has done is at least as plausibly ascribed to
the fact that Lolita ultimately refuses his offer to renew their relationship
as it is to any epiphany conferred by the writing of the memoir. As for
Nabokov's own insistence on the essential morality of his work, without
doubting his sincerity one can note the obvious facts that he hoped to
make a great deal of money on the book, and that at least at first he wanted to publish it anonymously. Since even Nabokov's literary friends had
reason to doubt his motives, the confusion, if it is that, of Humbert's
attempt at rehabilitation with his author's is understandable.

Beyond that, even if the reader were to concur, however tacitly, with
such an aesthetic view of morality, this would still not resolve the question

of whether *Lolita* was moral. To accomplish this, the book would have to be adjudged good art. The moral question would entail aesthetic judgment more so than it typically does. It is, then, not so surprising that when Morris Bishop objects to the subject matter of *Lolita*, Nabokov's reaction is to defend the quality of treatment.[20] If the author thought his moral defense rested on his artistic success, then Humbert's status as memoirist, for all his character flaws, would have to vouch for that success. But such reliance on the repugnant narrator introduces a kind of instability so fundamental—and so compromising—that it alone could not carry the day. Rather than letting the proof of the moral pudding reside solely in the aesthetic consumption, then, the possibly wavering sympathies of the reader (and particularly of the learned reader) would have to be enlisted more crudely. That is one of the reasons why, whether his character exists or Humbert invents him, Nabokov at least would have had to invent someone like him.

In the end it appears (despite his letter to Girodias, which may endeavor to convince himself as much as his recipient) that Nabokov did not seem to desire a serious success as opposed to a succès de scandale: he wanted both. He seems very much to have wanted both the sort of wide readership that goes with a "taboo" subject and the plaudits of more cultivated, more literary readership. Such a high-wire act can indeed send "frac-tails flying," and the remarkable fact is that, by and large, the strategy has succeeded (319). Regardless of his original thought of anonymity, the publication of Lolita assured both his financial independence, which he clearly sought, and his literary reputation. Surely he is not the only writer to want it both ways; he is just one of the few to actually achieve it. Clare Quilty's presence in his text plays a considerable part in letting his (no doubt grateful) creator do just that. To garner the considered regard of the few while appealing to the prurient interest of the many is doubtless the dream of many writers. Nabokov arguably attains it in *Lolita,* though at the price of a certain rhetorical incoherence. It is this incoherence that Quilty is instrumental in helping the novel to address, or to avoid.

We recall the description Humbert renders of his slightly dim chess partner in Beardsley, Gaston Godin. He apologizes even for bringing up such a "glum repulsive fat old invert," but "I need him for my defense. There he was, devoid of any talent whatsoever, . . . highly contemptuous of the American way of life, triumphantly ignorant of the English language—there he was in priggish New England, crooned over by the old and caressed by the young—oh, having a grand time fooling everybody; and here was I" (185). What Humbert erects, rather transparently, is a

doppelgänger against whom to array himself, both in chess and in his project of rehabilitation (hence the double meaning of "defense," no doubt).
Humbert senses just enough about public relations to know that, by contrast to a homosexual pedophile such as Godin, there are some who will
see Humbert as less in the wrong anyhow. Arguably, Clare Quilty, figment
or otherwise, represents a similar sort of antagonist. Yet there are a couple
of major differences. For one thing, he is probably not homosexual, even if
not actively heterosexual. For another, though generally cynical, he cannot
be held contemptuous of the American way of life: he embodies one aspect
of it all too well.

For *Lolita* has always, in the reader's experience and so in its critical
reception, been in a sense two stories: one the highly personal, even solipsistic record of one's man obsessive erotic project; the other a faintly satirical treatment of the postwar world then being created, and now having
been perfected, by American mass culture. The longueurs that for readers
who prefer the first story slow everything down at the outset of book 2,
with the first chapter's magisterial catalogues of billboards, motel names,
and tourist traps, further the second story, of course. So does the retailing
of films seen by Humbert and Lolita during their excursion, evincing as it
does the same taxonomic mania: "Her favorite kinds were, in this order:
musicals, underworlders, westerners" (172). The illusionistic landscape of
America on the road does complement the private hell that Hum and Lo
share, but equally it has a hellish allure of its own, an evocation of larger
forces at work.

Early on Humbert sees them as his rival, at first for money and then for
Lolita herself, of whom he says: "She it was to whom ads were dedicated:
the ideal consumer, the subject and object of every foul poster" (150). One
recalls the blank melancholy of Dolly Schiller's fate and the apparent gap
between the poster's promise and that reality: a gap attributed by some critics to American society and by others to *poshlost*.[21] But one also recalls the
poster in Lo's Ramsdale bedroom, of Clare Quilty advertising Dromes cig-
arettes. The role of Quilty as the herald of the commercial culture that
Lolita is called on to consume may at first be obscured by his playwright
status. But the nature of his skill, and the uses to which it is put, suggest a
whorish talent. Appel notes, for example, that whereas Humbert is moved
to rhapsodic poetry by Lolita's tennis playing, which he wishes he had
filmed, Quilty by contrast sees only its use in debasing schemes.[22]

Much ink has been spilled over the question of whether Quilty actually exists at all. His miragelike appearances in the trademark red car (a
flashy consumer emblem anticipated by his *Who's Who in the Limelight*

entry divulging his love of "fast cars" as well as "photography" [33]), the trail of supposed clues Humbert divines in the "cryptogrammic paper chase" he is convinced Quilty is leading him on (252), the jumble of impersonations and voices that make up his interpersonal style—all of these have suggested a figment of Humbert's imagination, or a sort of double figure.[23] Critics have claimed that Humbert shoots Quilty because he exemplifies a rival, of course, but in a larger sense he is a threat to what Humbert holds dear—which then leaves one to contemplate the fact that Humbert does hold something dear.[24]

The confrontation between Humbert and his real or imagined antagonist (it does not matter which it is, by design) serves to bring the suspense of the second book to a head. Once the identity of the pursuer, who is fittingly "a specter from the movie world," is established, it only remains to hunt him down and do him in.[25] First he traces his prey to Pavor Manor, a kind of poor man's San Simeon where Quilty is temporarily between debauched parties. Humbert then proceeds to shoot, having first made him read a bad pastiche of Eliot's "Ash Wednesday," with its theme of deathbed conversion. Despite the high-culture touch awkwardly provided, the killing scene as such echoes, and seriocomically inflates, the hyperbole of "underworlders," one of which Humbert descries on an outdoor movie screen as he journeys to Quilty's house: "on a gigantic screen slanting away among dark drowsy fields, a thin phantom raised a gun" (295)—as if to emphasize the ritual character of Humbert's act and its indebtedness to mass culture. This is doubly ironic since Quilty is himself a carrier of that culture and is being killed, it is implied, in part for that reason.

It has not escaped critical notice that the pulp-fictional staging of the death scene, so blackly comic and reminiscent of the "underworlders" wryly described by the narrator, ironizes the act of killing Quilty, as if to stress the comic-strip artifice of the entire sequence. This ironization should not detract, however, from the way in which the confrontation with Quilty subtly alters the reader's sympathies with respect to the protagonist (who finally has a worse antagonist than the helpless Lo or hapless Charlotte)—and, more crucially, resolves the threatening instability within the peaceable Nabokovian kingdom where the ethical and the aesthetic lie down together.[26]

Consider what the figure, and fate, of Quilty do for Humbert Humbert himself, both within the event structure of the novel and in terms of readerly sympathy. It is incontestable that the killing of Quilty, assuming as always that Humbert actually does the deed as he claims, is the precondition for the writing of the memoir. Humbert's declaration that "C. Q." had to die for Lolita to live in art is to that extent true, for without being arrested, Humbert would have neither the time nor the audience to craft a memorable tale in which to make her live. On the psychological level, Michael Bell, for one, is right to note that dispatching Quilty is presented as a heroic ordeal or agon, in this case a purgative that allows Humbert to come into his own as an artist.[27] Nevertheless, the killing remains cold-blooded murder. Why does its completion cause so many critics to shift their sympathies Humbert's way?

For one thing, Quilty, in the romantic idiom favored by the novel (especially as it concludes), stands accused of the ultimate sin, which is to be incapable of enchantment.[28] (His play's moral, it appears, applies above all to its author.) His use of Lolita for smutty films at Duk Duk Ranch is not only the climax to the imagery of photographic reproduction, as already suggested, it also treats Lolita herself as reproducible, as substitutable for any other pretty girl. Quilty's reason for breaking Lolita's heart is, in the economy of the novel at least, infinitely inferior to Humbert's compulsion for breaking, however squalidly, Lolita's life. Thus in one figure Nabokov combines the cheap facility in writing, the interest in mechanical reproduction of imagery, role-playing, and the lack of any deep emotional sentiment to make a far more complete expression of the fictional attitude than Humbert's. By contrast, the obsession that drives Humbert at least exalts the singularity of Lolita, first as a physical or erotic presence and then, belatedly, as a person. Humbert has been invested with the trappings of courtly love and *grande passion*. Quilty, from the start, views Lolita as a commodity and as a commodity to be viewed: "Where the devil did you get her?" (129). He is, additionally, hated by Humbert as an emissary of Humbert's own earlier attitude toward Lolita, only exaggerated. No more selfish is he in his designs on her than Humbert was before true love dawned, even if lacking the excuse of overmastering compulsion. This doubleness, this vestige of similitude to Humbert, is precisely why some have seen it as symbolically crucial that Humbert murder him.

These defects of Quilty become unbearable to Humbert, furthermore, at just the time that they become apparent in the first place to the reader. It takes one most of the book to be convinced that Quilty is Humbert's pursuer; once it becomes plain, Lolita's complicity with Quilty in escaping Humbert's grasp has in turn been established. The fact that Quilty was all along feigning true concern for Dolores Haze so that he could trick her into performing in pornographic films is revealed by her just before Humbert makes his journey to Pavor Manor. (Easily lost is the awareness that Humbert has already purposed to kill Lolita's collaborator in any event.) This reversal changes the fairy-tale function of Quilty from help-meet to villain in one stroke and makes the equally fairy-tale solution of extinguishing him seem only his just desserts. What intrigues is the readiness of so many serious Nabokov readers to accept that this is the case, even within the strange world of *Lolita.*

I think that this readiness has reasons beyond these narrative reversals, although they prepare the way for it. In a way, Nabokov's more loyal critics have a stake in their author's way of construing the artistic role—a role that, as we have seen, assumes that the aesthetic either conjoins seamlessly to the ethical realm or else, failing that, somehow transcends it. This is difficult to sustain as a stance throughout most of *Lolita,* though, since after all it is an aesthete's role that Humbert Humbert quite consciously adopts as he makes over Dolores Haze into his Lolita. Yet that fascination with appearance, carried to sufficient length, is supposed to yield loving concern for the person behind the appearance. The rhetoric of particularism, of individual experience, which at first verges on solipsism (and in Humbert's case teeters into it) is vindicated by the dialectical reversal whereby love of "*this* Lolita" emerges.

We have seen that the alchemy by which Humbert's fictional attitude ceases to be harmfully selfish and transmutes into something more tender is left largely to the imagination. Moreover, the text itself relies for much of its effect on the reader's complicity, admittedly queasy, with the narrator as he puts down and profits from the suffering of the other characters. Though not pornographic, certainly, the novel betrays an undeniable prurience and ghoulishness of humor. The transformation of Humbert is bound up not only with his own rehabilitation but also with his author's justification. The murder of Quilty defines an enemy against which Humbert can prove himself and in his own mind redeem himself. In the same moment, the figure of Quilty provides the text with a nice embodiment of both evil and lowly artistic ambition. Specific embodiment of this lowly ambition is offered by his commitment to spectacle: to photography, film, and the stage. His is the very model of the "public" version of writing, as opposed to Humbert's private, even secret, mode of writing, whose publication is predicated on his own death.[29] Not without reason does Humbert acidly call Quilty a "scenario writer" (301). Indeed, as Humbert closes in on Quilty, Chum in hand, the sops Quilty offers to fend off fate are almost all forms of spectacle: "I have an absolutely unique collection of erotica upstairs . . . [such as] photographs of eight hundred and something male organs . . . and moreover I can arrange for you to attend executions," and so on (304). The author of "fifty-two successful scenarios" (300) understandably thinks to offer up imagery as his most precious commodity. Like Scheherazade or any TV executive, Quilty believes that if he can only help his pursuer to beguile the time he may be allowed to survive. It may be for that reason that he never sheds the patchwork quilt of roles that he donned long ago. Even as he flees Humbert's fusillade, he maintains his "phoney British accent" (305).

If the combination of role-playing and pornographic spectacle indicates why Humbert might see Quilty as a representative of his own past life— recall Humbert's analogy, with respect to the davenport scene, of Lo to "a photographic image rippling upon a screen" and himself to "a humble hunchback abusing myself in the dark"—then his debasement of artistic ambition to the needs of "public" commercial distribution qualifies him as a foil to Humbert's creator as well (64). This is the second function played by the goatish scapegoat that is Quilty: that of stabilizing the reader's sympathy not only for the narrator but for the very text of *Lolita*.

It may be that it is in Quilty's contrast to Humbert as a writer specifically that his greatest service is rendered to Nabokov. After all, if Humbert's rehabilitation can only truly occur insofar as he becomes a true artist in the Proustian mode, as opposed to his earlier confusion of art with life as retailed in book 1, then that salvation, however partial, comes about only to the extent that *Lolita is* in fact a genuine work of art, not a counterfeit. By figuring a writer who produces counterfeit art—and who is himself a counterfeit—Nabokov is well aware of the risks that someone might unkindly analogize himself to that writer (just as, more realistically, some have wondered how different, in the end, he really is from his memoirist). This danger returns us to the joke with which this analysis began, where a collaborator with Clare Quilty is given a name that anagrammatizes the author's. Such mockery of identification indicates how confident the author is that everybody in the know will dissociate a true artist, such as Nabokov, from a kitsch maker with a phony British accent, such as Quilty.

It is an audacious strategy in its way, but it works, at least for those critics who bother much about Quilty at all. This understanding, that Quilty is ultimately the enemy of high culture and so of both Nabokov and his discerning reader, is based on a set of common assumptions shared by both: we realize that this man is irredeemably vulgar. His closest counterpart from these years is probably Jakob Gradus in the later novel *Pale Fire*, who shares Quilty's numbed sensibility and his disinclination to distinguish individual beings one from another. Once we join forces, united in hatred of the cultural Other represented by the crass Quilty, the earlier ethical qualms we may have about the affiliations of Nabokov's own louche

text are put aside. For, as I have suggested, the justification of his art on
aesthetic grounds alone that Nabokov puts forward in his afterword is hard
to sustain logically or intuitively.

Few critics manage to confront the question of *Lolita*'s moral effect, or
for that matter intention, in terms of the wider public. Aside from the constant insistence on the essential morality of the narrative, few care to confront the issue. Martin Green is one of the few, and he acknowledges that
its effects on the average (as opposed to discerning) reader may well be
deleterious. He goes on to insist, though, that such an effect must be
accepted as the price of having a wondrous work of art which, for those
who penetrate its inner sanctum, is in its essence moral.[30] Few are as explicit as Green in giving the back of their hand to any consideration of public
effects in examining fiction. But readers, as we have said, are made queasy
by *Lolita* not only because it questions their assumptions but also because
it relies on titillation for much of its appeal: its humor, for instance, is often
cruel and degrading.

Under these circumstances, Quilty becomes an easy place to assign these
potentially disabling worries about Nabokov's project. It is not surprising,
then, that his most loyal critics, such as Alfred Appel Jr., make so much of
the crestfallen mass reader who expects a Quiltylike rendering of
Nabokov's theme and discovers that the book is that hated thing known as
literature.[31]

The implicit question that threatens to disrupt Nabokov's conflation of
taste with virtue—whether singularity of sensibility confers in itself any
special ethical status—cannot be answered directly from the example of
Humbert. If anything, he just aggravates the anxieties that would give rise
to the question, and his late conversion raises other questions. But Clare
Quilty is made to embody both aesthetic shoddiness and commercial facility—and also moral insentience. It should not surprise that Bell, whose
thesis is that Humbert indeed becomes a genuine artist by the end of the
events he narrates, sees Quilty's killing as a precondition for that status.[32]
After all, if he is the rejected earlier part of Humbert's own personality, and
if he is a cheap artificer to boot, then he has to go. But the confrontation
is also needed, I think, by the novel. Almost by a kind of syllogism, if
Quilty stands simultaneously for a degraded American mass culture satirized throughout the novel and also for a lack of the love whose impulse is
the basis for morality, then eliminating him must provide his vanquisher
with both moral and artistic legitimacy.

For the critic, whose sympathies for high culture embattled by crass
American kitsch are subtly enlisted by the fact that Lolita actually thinks

Quilty a more sophisticated figure than Humbert, it is easy to overlook the obvious possibility that, in carrying out this execution, he is of course projecting his own inner needs on another human being just as he did earlier on Lolita herself, and with even deadlier consequences. But even here, Nabokov seems to have stacked his deck somewhat, since for a variety of reasons (including how the composition of the memoir is dated) the existence of the Quilty death scene is always disputable.[33]

For once, Nabokov's ironic ambiguity seems here in its way too easy. The reader is permitted the symbolic victory of high culture over mass culture, and collaterally of courtly love over sleazy sex, without confronting the reality of murder. Even the rendering of the scene itself is brutally comic, a scene of which one could say after Wilde, only without irony, that only a man of stone could read it without laughing. But the laughter is tinged with self-righteousness—and perhaps a measure of relief. Quilty has cured the novel of its identity crisis by playing his last, best role: that of the hack writer who is also an amoral lout. Being against Quilty, cheering his ignominious death, gives Nabokov's novel and its reader a way of affirming assumptions that, left only to themselves, have a way of disintegrating from their own contradictions. To that extent, Clare Quilty may be dying not only for his own sins but also for those of Humbert, and—who knows?—maybe for more than his.

chapter seven

The American Way and
Its Double in *Lot 49*

Thomas Pynchon's *The Crying of Lot 49* presents itself in many ways as kind of detective story, a fact not lost on its critics. Tony Tanner, for example, opts for the Southern California variety, especially those by Ross Macdonald.[1] In a standard Macdonald plot, a crime in the very recent past is shown to have been engendered by conflicts a generation old: the past has been, in many if not most of Macdonald's books, a prologue. Similarly, Oedipa Maas, Pynchon's protagonist, searches for the answer to a crime and discovers that it leads not only to herself (one register of her filiation with Sophocles' Oedipus) but also backward to the past generations that have spawned both her and the culprits (another register of that filiation). At the same time, this novel also presents itself as a kind of anatomy of postwar American consumer society and the legacy it inherits.[2] It has been frequently noted by more than one critic (and by more than one cheated and sullen undergraduate reader) that the novel fails to deliver on the promise implied by the detective format.[3] However, it is partly through its very failure in this respect that it delivers on the second aspect of its agenda: that of describing the land inherited by Oedipa and her kind. To show how such failure aids such success will be my purpose. To do this, a detour from the narrative—brief but important—is needed, the better to return the reader to the world from which Oedipa sets forth on her quest. This world, never far from the foreground of Oedipa's journey, is of course itself a bellwether of postwar American middle-class culture as a whole: that of the media-soaked Mecca of consumerism that is California.

Cultural Meaning: Closure, Control, and Maxwell's Demon

Oedipa's world as she starts out, succinctly stated, is the "administered world," in a Frankfurt School phrase.[4] This is a realm of administered goods and services guided and circulated for the many by those few with the resources to arrange it. It is a commercial system—a "cash nexus," as Oedipa remarks—but because free choice is a part of the necessary ideology, the goods must be coded in such a way as to make them desirable. As a result, one buys as much the signs of the goods as the goods themselves. French sociologist Jean Baudrillard makes this point when he remarks that even in primitive cultures "objects never exhaust themselves in the function they serve," but rather in their "excess of presence . . . take on their signification of prestige," hence not only serving the needs of the possessor but also designating his "being and social rank." This assigning of prestige to objects has always been a social process of encoding, which Baudrillard calls the symbolic process. What has happened with the advent and perfection of consumer society is that what was once a manifestation of "the transparency of social relations" (as for instance the gift in a primitive gift exchange) has become, as a commodity in the administered world, a "sign [that] no longer gathers its meaning in the concrete relationship between two people." In lieu of this direct acknowledgment of the way objects are caught up in the social relationship, this fact is instead rendered indirectly, through the commodity-sign's "differential relation to other signs."[5]

The goods on offer and the media that promote these goods—and that is their chief function—become instruments for the normalization of consumer patterns by providing a fantasy for the consumer to fulfill through purchase. It is, of course, fashion and its vagaries that provide the most obvious case of the way in which the administered commodity system can take up styles—and, by implication, the self-images those styles project—and present them as if for the consumer's taking.[6] The various media of radio, film, and TV, not to mention such things as automobiles and tract homes (treated in Pynchon, as in Marshall McLuhan, as forms of sign making, communication), are presented in all their profusion in this novel, both commodities and vendors of fixed meanings.[7] For this process to be properly controlled, a closed system must be approximated (though, as we shall see, "approximated" is definitely the operative word). The closed system will always tend toward stasis, which is one of the points about the Second Law of Thermodynamics so dear to early Pynchon; and this danger is always present when the circulation of meanings and goods is controlled too tightly. Consequently, the masters of the closed system must themselves constantly be on guard to keep the exchange process going.

The starkest model for this activity is that of Maxwell's Demon, whose sorting and circulating functions slow and reverse entropy within a closed system. The demon is the figure who "keeps it bouncing," as Oedipa's ex-lover Pierce Inverarity says is crucial.[8] To normalize the responses of the buying public in Pynchon's world, three things have had to be accomplished: the atomization of consumers into individual units of consumption, the elaboration of means of making all the goods circulating within that closed system roughly commensurable by a common measure, and the normalization of tastes and habits. The problem for managers of the consumer culture is that all these tendencies tend toward stasis and away from active exchange in the long run. Like the closed system treated in the Second Law, that of administered goods and their meanings can get suffocating for all concerned if the closure is total.

Consequently, constant effort must be made to inject the system with novel forms of social prestige and interest. One of the points about Maxwell's Demon is that there seems to be an inverse relation between energy and information. The canny manipulation of meaning by the demon is to compensate for the loss of differential energy: "there were two distinct kinds of entropy. One having to do with heat-engines, the other to do with communication. The equation for one, back in the '30's, had looked very like the equation for the other. It was a coincidence. The two fields were entirely unconnected, except at one point: Maxwell's Demon. As the Demon sat and sorted his molecules into hot and cold, the system was said to lose entropy. But somehow the loss was offset by the information the Demon gained about what molecules were there" (105).

As applied to the commercial world commanded by people like the dead man whose estate Oedipa is in turn to administer, Maxwell's Demon is needed to use his intelligence and information (both passively, in soaking up data about the consuming public, and actively, in communicating with that public) in order to keep the exchange of money and goods bouncing: "that's all the secret," as Pierce Inverarity says. "Therefore, they are constantly dependent on what lies outside the immediate realm of the culture industry, on which they parasitically draw for their stock of codes, values, and meanings. The values/codes manipulated and circulated with the goods and services of the American consumer culture are not just made up, in Pynchon's novel.[9] Rather, they are taken from an already existing first-order process of symbolization—a process where "meaning" is chiefly a gerund rather than a noun—a process that occurs in society at large with or without the interventions of consumer culture. This process of symbolization is open to hazard and the miraculous confrontations of one meaning with another: in any case, an open process of communally shared labor. The close of this essay treats one such confrontation. Such an open process provides the administered world's closed system with its stock of meanings (in this case more usefully thought of as a noun rather than as a gerund), and from these stabilized meanings the chief point of "creativity" lies in recombining those codes and attaching them to commodities.[10]

This process of recombination is itself a constant labor: a hidden but all-pervasive labor of advertisement, commerce, and shaping of mass taste. The most deleterious effect of this labor is not its uprooting of the commodity from its function; as Baudrillard has suggested, the ancient gift and the equally ancient object of barter were always more and other than their narrowly defined use. It is in its vampiristic seizing upon the socially transparent labor of symbolic value for the purposes of appropriating that process to its work in circulating its own meanings. This appropriation becomes so complete that at times—as *Lot 49*'s Mr. Thoth remarks of the Porky Pig cartoon on TV—it "comes into your dreams, you know" (91).

Unlike the initial process of symbolization on which it piggybacks, though, this second-order process of sign making works to hide the labor that is put into its production. A luster of value is retained from the social symbolization it draws on for its resonances from, but the administered world of commodity-signs uses those meanings as if they were products themselves, the better to attach them to products and the better to preclude the consumer from altering those meanings. The second-order process of meaning making engaged in by the Maxwell's Demon of consumer society in Oedipa's California is a social labor, just as is the first-order process the demons must draw on. The difference is that whereas the first-order process is explicitly social, open to chance and change and productive of mutually created meanings that are in turn subject to alteration, in the second-order commodity-sign process, the meanings are presented as if completed before the fact: simply there, like the objects to which they attach, for the taking (or, if one is displeased, the leaving). The social process of meaning making on the second-order level is occulted: the consumer sees only as much of it as the producers judge will incline the consumer to buy. The consumer's role is not to respond to these symbolizings with his or her own, but rather to subject him- or herself to the fantasy world prescribed in and by the goods for sale.

In extremis, the consumer may attempt to live what is presented as a life by the various media. Pierce Inverarity's lawyer Metzger and his friend Manny Di Presso are aware of this lure of prepackaged values and shamelessly thrive on it. After Oedipa chides him for his part in the "cash nexus," Metzger argues their partnership is part of a media nexus as well:

> But our beauty lies . . . in this extended capacity for convolution. A lawyer in a courtroom, in front of any jury, becomes an actor, right? Raymond Burr is an actor, impersonating a lawyer, who in front of a jury becomes an actor. Me, I'm a former actor who became a lawyer. They've done a pilot film of a TV series, in fact, based loosely on my career, starring my friend Manny Di Presso, a one-time lawyer who quit his firm to become an actor. Who in this pilot plays me, an actor become a lawyer reverting periodically to being an actor. The film is in an air-conditioned vault at one of the Hollywood studios, light can't fatigue, it can be repeated endlessly. (33)

This hall of mirrors replicates itself without cease, and the real lives of these figures seem excuses for the thrill of becoming what they can then see on television or in the movies . . . But this is not a socially symbolic labor of cultural meaning for either man: it is finally each man's relation to his own ideal image that founds his interest in the other (Manny must play Metzger, Metzger must be played, each wants to be famous). Even those who produce the administered meanings of the media are prey to their parasitic fascination. These meanings rely for their power not on interaction between people so much as on each person's desire to buy for him- or herself an ideal self-image.

This ideal self-image is in its essence the functional equivalent of someone else's ideal image, which the consumer then appropriates for his or her own. Pynchon illustrates this process very early in the text through the reflections of Oedipa's husband on his previous job at a used-car dealership, selling that most Californian component of the American dream. For Wendell ("Mucho") Maas, as for McLuhan, the automobile is best understood not only as a vehicle for one's own projection through space and time but also as the vehicle for the projections of administered identity onto the buyer: in short, part of the apparatus of controlled communication, a kind of medium. As he sees his trade-in customers, he sees how "each owner, each shadow filed in only to exchange a dented, malfunctioning version of himself for another, just as futureless, automotive projection of somebody else's life" (14). Curiously, what "depresses" Mucho Maas about this is not the sameness of the cars themselves so much as the human detritus collected and inhering in them. But at least part of the reason that the "new" cars cannot renew identity is that they would be projections of somebody else's life, even if they were new.

The narcissistic hope of self-renewal held out by these trade-ins is always withdrawn: after all, if someone else's dream had not failed, it would not be available in exchange for one's own. The Easter cycle is the period during which this book's actions occur, but the seasonal promise of renewal—when tied to the products of the administered market, at least—delivers only endless repetition. That this repetition, this mechanical reproduction, is mistaken for renewal is one of the crucial features of the narcissistic self of consumer society.

Narcissus and Echo: Identity and Iterability

One of the oft-heard complaints about the character of Oedipa Maas is that the reader gets so few indices of her psychological or social background: no mention of parents and little of education (although we are led to believe that, like the author, she attended Cornell)—very few points of identity at all except for the fact that she is an upscale Californian, plugged into mainstream culture, and the former mistress of a wealthy speculator.

What we get, to the extent we get anything, is her profile as a consumer: "a buyer of Tupperware, tearer of romaine and garlicker of lasagna, reader of *Scientific American*," as Molly Hite characterizes her first appearance.[11] But if the concerns I have noted are central to the text, that profile is more than enough to know about her. She is a happy participant in consumer society and knows little else, but for the occasional feeling of isolation and sadness. On the whole, her process of plugging in to the media has yielded back a reassuring self-image. Even the fact that "a fat deckful of days . . . seemed (wouldn't she be the first to admit it?) more or less identical" guarantees a certain solid selfhood for her (11). The narcissistic subject is reassured of his or her identity by two forms of repetition: that in space—either through mirror or through duplication by another—and that in time, through the infinite reproducibility of image or sound. Yet this promise of an approved "lifestyle" is, while constantly renewed, constantly betrayed by the same token.

The isolated status of the subject, as the point of consumption for the commodity, is what ensures that the narcissistic appeal will be effective. On the one hand, the consumer desires the illusion of self-sufficient power; on the other hand, the consumer needs approval of others (which the media, as much as possible, would presume to give or withhold). Most of the major figures in the novel—Metzger and Di Presso as mentioned, but also Mucho Maas and of course the Californian attempt at a Liverpudlian rock group, the Paranoids—have tried to complete the promise offered by the media by becoming themselves active replicators of media sound and image, and in various ways they manifest the dangers of doing this. Oedipa does not succumb as they do; she is at least smarter than that. Further, she is not wholly content with the position that has been assigned to her by the administered world. But to what she attributes this discontent, and what she does about it, are in their turn also circumscribed by some of the assumptions from which she starts out.

Oedipa knows that she is the victim of a certain sort of narcissism: this is the sense of her famous encounter with the Varo triptych. But symptomatic of her media-induced narcissism is the fact that even as she cries Oedipa wants to "carry the sadness of the moment with her that way forever, see the world refracted through those tears, those specific tears" (21). To freeze such a moment in life is harder than to freeze it in an air-conditioned vault like a movie, but the same desire to repeat the past and to stop time inheres either way. Interestingly, although the triptych portrays girls in a tower weaving "a kind of tapestry which spilled out the slit windows and into a void, seeking hopelessly to fill the void," and Oedipa applies this to her own isolation, the reverse image—of a consumer in a tower confronted with an already woven tapestry to fill the void—is closer to her predicament at the story's start (21). After all, the first place Oedipa searches for meaning after learning of Pierce's death and her executorship is the "greenish dead eye of the TV tube" (91).

Oedipa's isolation is thus at one with her desire for wholeness and self-sufficiency: this in turn is the province of the body, which "will become for each individual an ideological sanctuary, the sanctuary of his own alienation."[12] Oedipa is most foolish to believe that Pierce Inverarity could ever have been "the knight of deliverance" from the tower she is trapped in, since it is people like him that have built and sustained such a tower in the first place (22). Similarly, although discontented and not without reason for being so, Oedipa cannot so easily remove herself from that tower either, because that tower is also one of pride fortified by and for the consumption of goods and the appropriation of values and meanings attaching to those goods. As Adorno says, the problem for the subject when he or she would undo these media-induced bonds of isolation is that "the bonds it [the subject] would have to tear, the bonds of dominion, are as one with the principle of absolute subjectivity."[13] It may be true that part of her malign fascination with the Tristero itself springs from its profile as an organization founded on alienation of a sort: the difference being that it is alleged to have alienated itself from the administered world but not necessarily from other human beings as such (for Oedipa, to do the former is to do the latter).

Just as Oedipa herself is prey to narcissistic yearnings, she is also the victim of others' narcissistic tendencies as they pursue ideal self-images that are at once complete and accessible. All of the men in her life chase a fantasy of wholeness through the administered images of the media: her husband, who crosses "the bridge inward" with the help of LSD and who manages to identify himself wholly with the sound of a radio commercial saying "rich, chocolaty goodness"—the medium here quite literally becomes the only possible message ("Everybody who says the same words is the same person if the spectra are the same" [142]); Pierce Inverarity, whose ventures in self-projection begin in San Narcisco; and, as mentioned, the lawyer Metzger.

When Metzger seduces Oedipa, Narcissus has found for a moment his Echo (the seduction scene is Echo Courts). He reclaims his lost youth, then, not only by running his old movie on the local channel (by a possible arrangement with the station) but also by possessing Oedipa: it is naturally ambiguous to what extent he uses the movie to beguile Oedipa and to what extent it is for his own amusement.

Insofar as there is a clue to what she will find when she intuits the "Tristero system," it is in the way "that night's infidelity with Metzger would logically be the starting point for it; logically" (44). The "logic" here would in direct plot terms derive from Metzger's status as Pierce's lawyer and from the fact that the TV screen that prompts the seduction doubles the World War II mythical fiction of the film *Cashiered* with the map of Pierce's artificial lake "with real human skeletons from Italy" that contain their "promise of hierophany: printed circuit, gently curving streets, private access to the water, Book of the Dead" (31). The fact that the TV tube blows during their climax seems portentous of escape from this administered meaning; and indeed, the fact that the film itself is a surprise—her bet that it will end badly for the heroes is, shockingly, correct—would appear to suggest that the quest she initiates after this seduction will break out of the official version of history implied by this Hollywood war picture.

But what is significant about the coupling of Metzger and Oedipa—and by extension, as I propose to show, about the quest whose genesis, in part at least, lies with that coupling—is more what it portends to be but is not.

It is, to start with, not much of a relationship: her "sharp breath" at seeing the map of Fangoso Lagoons is mistaken by Metzger as being for him, one private hierophany getting in the way of another (31). If she desires "to bring to an end her encapsulation in her tower" by being seduced by Metzger, then an affair with a fellow mirror gazer will hardly do it (44). If she traces her interest in Tristero back to this affair with Metzger ("it's all part of a plot, an elaborate, seduction, *plot.* O Metzger" [31]), then just as the affair they conceive offers the promise of deliverance from self and the reality of the self's doubling, so also the Tristero obsession for which that affair is "logically the starting point" offers the promise of deliverance from the consumer society's fixed meanings—but the reality of an imaginary other system mirroring in reverse the dominant system and its values. What fascinates her in Tristero may be the possibility of a "real alternative to the exitlessness, to the absence of surprise to life that harrows the head of every- body American you know" (170); but as with Metzger, what she really finds in her version of Tristero is the double of the world from which she began.

The Demon of Analogy: History as Theater

Upon Pierce's death with its miraculous violence, Oedipa has been shocked into being an active reader of the past and of cultural meanings: in addition to a will to administer, Oedipa develops a will to read.[14] What she desires to read in sorting out Pierce Inverarity's estate, though, is the "book of the Dead" (31), whose "hierophany" is bound up with the San Narciso devel- opment: its "hieroglyphic sense of concealed meaning, of an attempt to communicate" gives Oedipa the feeling that "on some other frequency . . . words were being spoken" (24–25). Oedipa senses that the secular pattern of "lifestyle" and its cash nexus contains the revelation of something, in much the same sense that her husband the DJ is "trying to believe in his job" but still feels excluded from "the faithful . . . knowing that even if he could hear it he couldn't believe it" (25).

The death of her lover does pierce Oedipa's sense of insulation, where- in her own life feels "as if watching a movie, just perceptively out of focus" (20). The shock of death, along with the attempt at posthumous meaning by which presumably Pierce and definitely Oedipa hope to recuperate that loss, provide what motivation there is for her to "execute a will" rather than remain will-less.[15] Still, it is at first in loyalty to Pierce's memory that she does it, searching for her revelation through his testament as his disciple.[16]

The very form of executing a will implies a retracing of the past, assess- ing a legacy: a final act echoing to a dead Narcissus. But rather quickly, this more reverential mode is augmented by the role of detective, retracing the past in a different key. The strange ending of *Cashiered,* an altogether too raw conclusion for a part of America'a mythic past, presages the more skeptical attitude toward the postwar past that Oedipa soon adopts; such an unhappy ending suggests the possibility of a less glorious beginning for postwar America as well. More narrowly, this movie, together with its commercial, prepare for the mystery of the dead GIs made into charcoal: a process that seems rather outside the one portrayed in the official World War II imagery. Such treatment serves also as a warning that some ways of recuperating the loss of death do anything but justice to the memory of those who died.

It is the desire to find out what the fates of those dead GIs may mean—not so much a conventional detective's question of who killed them (the assumption is it was starvation and the Germans) but rather the question of the meaning of their deaths and subsequent fates—that makes Oedipa pay attention when one of the Paranoids' girlfriends remarks the similarity between the story of their fates and "that ill, ill Jacobean revenge play we went to last week" (63). When she attends a production of that play, it is part of her will to read the book of the Dead.

In the *Courier's Tragedy,* the analogue for the dead GIs is the Lost Guard of Faggio. In an apotheosis of the dead as speakers of the truth of the past, the Lost Guard themselves are used to reveal how they died: Niccolo, a rival of Duke Angelo, is killed carrying a letter from the duke that had assured him (falsely) of his good intentions; when his body is recovered, the letter accompanying it has undergone more of a sea change than Niccolo himself:

> It is no longer the lying document Niccolo read us excerpts from [earlier in the play] at all, but now miraculously a long confession by Angelo of all his crimes, closing with the revelation of what really happened to the Lost Guard of Faggio. They were—surprise—every one massacred by Angelo and thrown in the lake. Later on their bones were fished up again and made into charcoal, and the charcoal into ink, which Angelo, having a dark sense of humor, used in all his subsequent communications with Faggio, the present document included. (74)

There is also evidence that the dead guard have themselves written the document: "A life's base lie rewritten into truth [as they describe the document] / That truth it is, we all bear testament, / This Guard of Faggio, Faggio's noble dead" (74). At first Duke Angelo has turned the dead guards into the raw material for a self-promoting lie, but when the actual historical scene is returned to, the truth of the past is revealed, Angelo's lie is reversed, and the dead revise and edit the living. That it occurs in the sea fits Oedipa's notion that the sea is "redemption for Southern California. . . . no matter what you did to its edges the true Pacific stayed inviolate and integrated or assumed the ugliness at any edge into some more general truth" (55). If others, in preserving their dead, have turned them to ill uses, then Oedipa can use their remains as clues to the truth about their fate and what their fates portend.

The power of the Tristero model arises because it contains a metaphor for the dead men at the bottom of Fangoso Lagoon. This metaphorical transfer, a form of the circulation of meanings, convinces Oedipa that this is not coincidence but equivalence.[17] One clue to her breathtaking ability to make historical hypotheses on the basis of fictional evidence may be found in her attitude toward metaphor itself, which is not characterized for her by its ability to force together two disparate semantic force fields but rather by whether it is true or false: an odd requirement to place on a figure of speech, one would have thought. To her it is "a thrust at truth and a lie, depending where you were: inside, safe, or outside, lost. Oedipa did not know where she was" (129). Oedipa makes what discoveries she does and the novel gains the reader's interest precisely because she does not know where she is: a not unadmirable state given the results. The problem is that Oedipa overlooks the miraculous possibilities within the "act of metaphor"—the miracle that Jesus Arrabal defines as "another world's intrusion into this one" (120)—in favor of trying to decide what truth claims that act can make. By turning the act of metaphor from a process open to hazard into a puzzle with a predetermined solution, Oedipa turns a matter for wonder into a mere question of belief.

Oedipa pursues the historical possibilities and paths not taken, not for their own sweet sake but for how they can further the revelation of meaning by returning to the origin of meaning. In like fashion she explores the various subcultures of the West Coast not because she wants to join— indeed, her isolation during her tour of San Francisco is striking—but because they may reveal the truth behind what cannot be assimilated to the official version of history for postwar America: truth that if absent would leave these groups as mere "storm-systems of group suffering and need" amid the always "prevailing winds of affluence" in the culture (178). Oedipa's interest in these groups is prompted by the notion that they may continue a history posited by the play she attends. That play, by proffering a word ("Tristero"), gives Oedipa a means to sort all of the unassimilable remnants of subcultural defiance and indifference, despite their diversity, into one box, and so provides the needed double or Other (Randolph Driblette the director would say "Adversary") for the administered world.

The connection between the play and the truth of history is strengthened by the further transfer of meaning *within* the play itself, which works in two fashions: first, the use of the product of the crime as the vehicle for denying one's criminality (by Duke Angelo), and then the miraculous use of the lying document itself as the vehicle to reveal the criminality. In the same way, Pierce Inverarity uses the dead GIs—and by extension the sacrifices of others in the war that laid the groundwork for postwar prosperity—to advance his own designs, turning the past to his own use along with its dead; but the completed legacy, written in the ink of that neglected past, could itself be used as the vehicle for revivifying that past, "as if the dead really do persist" (99).

The readiness with which Oedipa transfers meaning from the play to history ignores the crucial disjunct between the dead in Fangoso Lagoon and the Lost Guard of Faggio. The latter had their bones turned to the ink that was used to deny the history that produced what was being used to write it, and so the literal truth that was part of the material of the duke's document took its revenge on the lie they were used to construct. But the easy opposition of truth and lie that works in the play does not work in the case of the dead GIs. The meaning of their sacrifice has been somehow occulted or distorted, perhaps, but it is not a matter of a revelation to be affirmed or denied, a crime to be proven. It is rather a much more pervasive matter of cultural conditioning, a kind of collective amnesia, rather than the aftermath of a specific crime and cover-up.

Symbolic of this difference is the fact that there is no document comparable to that found in the play accompanying Niccolo that is ever produced from the Pacific. The dead men are not repositories or the victims of a lie, either one; nor are they truth or lie themselves. They are rather counters in a cultural play of metaphorical substitution in which they take their ever changing positions as commodities. Their bones have become part of the circulating system of goods and have taken no revenge comparable to that of the dead in the play. The dead of the *Courier's Tragedy,* having been turned to the purpose of lie, reverse the purpose by revealing the historical truth; the dead GIs, having been turned to the purpose of commerce, reveal no similar truth themselves.

At this point, though, Oedipa still believes that in sorting her lover's estate she can, while executing his will, reverse whatever "base lies" distort historical truth; this way, the parchment of Pierce's own testament can also become the document in which the dead rewrite deceit into truth. (The fact that the criminality of Tristero may have implicated the will's testator rather than posing a mere external threat occurs to Oedipa quite late. But even when it does she must persist in seeing that words and meanings be governed by their relation to a transcendental signified: a revelation that authorizes a closed system of meaning, or at least patterns a stark struggle of order and reverse order, truth and deception, good and evil.)

The only alternative Oedipa would credit to this pattern of revealed meaning is that of solipsism. This is precisely the threat posed to her by the director she meets after the play, Randolph Driblette: "'If I were to dissolve in here,' speculated the voice out of the drifting stream, 'be washed down the drain into the Pacific, what you saw tonight would vanish too. You, that part of you so concerned, God knows how, with that little world, would also vanish. The only residue, in fact, would be things Wharfinger [the playwright] didn't lie about. . . . But they would be traces, fossils. Dead, mineral, without value or potential'" (79–80). He eventually is washed into the Pacific, but although his actions repeat those of Niccolo in going out to sea, he assigns the opposite significance to the possible result. Whereas revelation emerges from the sea in the play, Driblette expects that the world revealed by the play would vanish. The textual meaning exists only if it inhabits someone's spirit, confers identity: the other side of the bargain that he give the "words and a yarn" some "life" is that they grant form to his life in turn. But it is a form that, as with the mass-culture consumers elsewhere throughout *Lot 49,* requires isolation of the bearer to achieve. Hence Driblette walks into the Pacific wearing the costume from the *Courier's Tragedy.* For him, the historical reality is "residue," only "traces, fossils"; they produce a significance only when he activates them as the projector in the planetarium, and when he goes, their significance disappears.

The solipsism of this view is the furthest extension of the media-induced narcissism of the rest of the book. At first it would seem as if Driblette is the reverse of the narcissist, creating a world rather than accepting one by finding himself in it. But in fact this appearance of mastery is the reality of submission; and as with Mucho Maas's fantasy of world harmony, it is enacted only in the interior of the self, which is why it will vanish when Driblette becomes a driblet in the vast Pacific.[18] The analogy to Niccolo seems appositely drawn, since Niccolo is "the rightful heir and good guy of the play" (65) who "hears the tale of the Lost Guard" (68) and is pursued for his knowledge by a band of evil figures finally named Trystero. Just as Niccolo's murder by Trystero reveals the origin of the plot against the Lost Guard by the illegitimate duke, so Driblette's walk into the Pacific—murdered, in a sense, by his own absorption into a play about Trystero—should yield similarly spectacular results, similar revelation. Oedipa tries for them when attending his funeral, trying to "reach out, to whatever coded tenacity of protein might improbably have held on six feet below. . . . She waited for the winged brightness to announce its safe arrival. But there was silence" (161–62). In a binary formula of the type that becomes manically typical of Oedipa, she concludes: "Either she could not communicate, or he did not exist" (162). It is true that Driblette is the director, but he enters the Pacific wearing the costume of the character he plays: the "colorless administrator, Gennaro" (75), who is left alive and alone at play's end. It is not revelation she receives, then, but as he predicted only "traces, fossils," and "words."

That this analogy breaks down so completely is itself clue enough to the inappropriateness of the play as the crucial means of suturing a historical narrative together; "Trystero" does not necessarily carry across to "Tristero." But beyond that, the metaphysical armature within which the original Trystero is presented is equally misleading. Part of Driblette's spoor, seemingly the essential, is the evidence that the version of the play Oedipa attended, which utters the word "Trystero," has its origin with the so-called Scurvhamite Puritan sect, whose essential tenets are as follows: "Their central hang-up had to do with predestination. There were two kinds. Nothing for a Scurvhamite ever happened by accident, Creation was a vast, intricate machine. But one part of it, the Scurvhamite part, ran off the will of God, its prime mover. The rest ran off some opposite Principle, something blind, soulless; a brute automatism that led to eternal death" (155). This metaphysic is just about what Oedipa adopts herself as she explores the question of the supposed "Tristero" conspiracy: the stark opposition of a destiny for the saved and a dire death of the soul for the damned. Indeed, the fate of the Scurvhamites parallels in many respects Oedipa's own: "The idea was to woo converts into the Godly and purposeful sodality of the Scurvhamite. But somehow those few saved Scurvhamites found themselves looking out into the gaudy clockwork of the doomed with a certain sick and fascinated horror, and this was to prove fatal. One by one the glamorous prospect of annihilation coaxed them over, until there was no one left in the sect, not even Robert Scurvham, who, like a ship's master, had been last to go."

This passage puts the reader in mind of the final pages of the novel, where Oedipa is described as considering joining the Tristero. But the entire metaphysical baggage of Manichaean-style division into good and evil principles, with their opposite machineries, bears strong resemblance to what Oedipa is left with, perhaps because she finds its assumptions congenial. It turns out that it is only the Scurvhamite version of the play that includes the ultimate reference to Trystero, and further that there is no rational reason to assume that the Trystero of the play has proceeded down to the present day: "the libraries told her nothing more of the Tristero. For all they knew, it had never survived the struggle for Dutch independence" (162). Yet somehow the analogical power of the play as a medium of revelation makes Oedipa believe, in the teeth of evidence to the contrary, that it provides the interpretive clue to all of the subcultures she encounters in San Francisco: to the muted post horn signal, the Peter Pinguid Society, Inamorati Anonymous, and the like.[19] Mendelson has pointed out that "in the middle of the fifth chapter of the book the entranceways, the alienations . . . suddenly disappear: the repetitions [of the post horn and such] stop. For perhaps thirty pages Oedipa receives no immediate signs of the Trystero, nothing more than some historical documents and second-hand reports."[20] In order to pursue the historical data on the Tristero, Oedipa must turn away from the concrete, living data that have always been around her (but that may or may not point to Tristero), and this necessary turning away is symptomatic.

The *Courier's Tragedy,* since it is a courier's tragedy, concerns the transfer of communication, but it is itself implicated in this transfer. It is a kind of metaphor, a carrying across, that "turns and taxies across the sea" from centuries-old Europe to current American life (119). Oedipa chooses not to see it as a metaphor but rather as revelation: as a historical origin that explains the present and determines it rather than as an analogy that, in part, she herself makes and in part is provided by fragments of evidence. Unlike the dead men in the play's Lago di Pieta, the GIs in the historical Lago di Pieta have already been moved to another place; such meaning as they had has been transferred and in the process altered, as they have been carried across the sea. The symbolic meaning of the dead is thus already caught up in the circulation of signs.

Although anything is possible and one could construct a model whereby the Trystero conspiracy posited by the Scurvhamite play continues to the present day (obviously that is what Oedipa does, so it can be done), there is no compelling reason within the evidence itself to do so, despite some striking analogical similarities. This, I suggest, is why Driblette's walk into the Pacific, clearly a gesture comparable to that of Niccolo at the end of the play, has such an opposite result, yielding not some authorizing revelation of origin and end but simply more words, words, words.

If this is the case, the question remains: Why, without compelling internal evidence, does Oedipa feel obliged in the first place to pursue the Tristero conspiracy as if it continued to elaborate the destiny depicted within a Jacobean revenge play? What about Oedipa's own assumptions makes this such a seductive possibility to carry forward? What impels her to literalize the metaphor, to treat this play as governing her interpretation of historical events and history as a form of revelatory theater?

Ones and Zeroes: The American Way and Its Double

In seeking a reason for Oedipa's embrace of the "Tristero" solution to these historical puzzles and the feel of plausibility inhering in them despite their objective limitations, we should return for a moment to consider the administered world whose tower the reader, like Oedipa, too easily assumes to have left. What I sketched in the first section was only a partial description of consumer society in postwar America: the secular aspect, we might say. Underwriting this world is also a kind of civil religion of American destiny, whose *arché* and *telos* guarantee and authorize the transactions of the commercial arena; this authorization unfolds the destiny of the unitary state and its favored citizens. Thus do the purely private endeavors of entrepreneurs and buyers participate in an authorized public historical narrative. One thinks in this connection of the dual connotations of the term *American way of life:* at once a commercial meaning (home ownership, prosperity, the "dream") and a state meaning (those freedoms that must be defended against the Other, the Adversary).

The partnership of government and business of which Yoyodyne, "San Narcisco's big source of employment" (25), is an emblem is a pervasive theme here, going all the way back to the Post Office, set up chiefly as a public means of assisting private commerce. Beyond that, the activity of consumption as such is given the imprimatur of civic duty in the struggle against the Soviet Union. This adversary, perhaps by virtue of the same "ritual reluctance" that forbids the name of Trystero to be announced before the close of the *Courier's Tragedy,* is not named and scarcely alluded to; but the Scurvhamite pretext, the strategy of exclusion based on elect and preterite that has been such a Pynchon theme here and elsewhere, draws particular force from that confrontation of light and darkness that has prevailed since the Second World War.

It is with this background that Oedipa's nostalgic reflections on the fifties, whose child she is above all, are best understood: "For she had undergone her own educating at a time of nerves, blandness and retreat among not only her fellow students but also most of the visible structure around and ahead of them, this having been a national reflex to certain pathologies in high places only death had the power to cure. . . . Where were Secretaries James and Foster and Senator Joseph, those dear daft numina who'd mothered over Oedipa's so temperate youth? In another world" (103–4). The "dear daft numina" in question are quite likely John Foster Dulles, secretary of state under Eisenhower and chief promoter of the civil religion of anticommunist brinksmanship; James Hagerty, Eishenhower's press secretary; and Senator Joseph McCarthy, now notorious anticommunist crusader. A numen is a guardian deity, and these figures are said to have "mothered over" Oedipa's youth. Although "daft" conveys a telling condescension to their crusading zeal, "dear" is surely not too wide of the mark for this Young Republican of yesteryear. It is one of the few explicit mentionings of formative forces in Oedipa's past, so it may have a certain strength.

Beyond accounting for Oedipa's feeling of isolation walking across Berkeley's mid-sixties campus, this passage tells us something of the available categories of America's civil religion in her time of maturation. The enemy had been clearly defined and marked with a teleology and cultural values the opposite of our own, whose victory would inevitably mean our defeat. It was not merely outside the pale but in active contestation of the American way of life: if it won, lie would extinguish truth. But since the principle from which this enemy operated was not godly, there was no question of its victory. Oedipa's youth had been mothered by this form of thinking, with its world of truth and lie, good and evil, and national destiny. The possibility that the nation had no unitary destiny to begin with— that this was an abstraction needed by the numina of Cold War civil religion—has not been considered. Consequently, when Oedipa sets out to find a box for the nameless oddities she encounters in San Francisco, she most conveniently finds the Tristero conspiracy as an organizing principle.

The paradox of Tristero is that it has the effect of taking Oedipa out of the administered cocoon, yet in a fashion that ensures she will never fully appreciate or understand what she has discovered on the other side.[21] During her "dark night of the soul" in San Francisco, Oedipa wanders amid the human wreckage of consumer society, those unassimilable for various reasons to its imperatives and its values. It becomes evident that were it not for their imputed connection to the Tristero narrative, their existences would have been quite simply waste, meaningless (and for Oedipa to be the waste of the official society is to be meaningless). The starkest instance of this may be the encounter between Oedipa and the children in Golden Gate Park who claim to be dreaming their gathering: "The night was empty of all terror for them, they had inside their circle an imaginary fire, and needed nothing but their own unpenetrated sense of community" (118). When she corrects their nursery rhyme to make it accord with her research into the Thurn and Taxis mail system, they tell her they have not heard of that: "Oedipa, to retaliate, stopped believing in them" (119). This episode dramatizes two things about Oedipa's quest: it ignores specific, socially evolving processes of meaning formation in favor of subjecting these to one all-encompassing narrative (in this case the counternarrative of Tristero), and it sets off from the assumption that the reality encountered is a brute given, a revelation either of God or the devil to be credited or dismissed, believed or disbelieved.

What this approach leads to is, of course, the famous passage toward the end of the novel, with its stark binary choices, its ones and zeroes all in a row. By pursuing the Tristero quest, Oedipa has both come to comprehend an ever larger swath of history and also become ever more isolated. Her state, finally, is close to that of the paranoid, as she declares to herself: "Either you have stumbled indeed . . . onto a network by which X number of Americans are truly communicating whilst preserving their lies . . . for the official government delivery system. . . . Or you are hallucinating it. . . . Or a plot has been mounted against you. . . . Or you are fantasying some such plot, in which case you are a nut, Oedipa, out of your skull" (170–71).

The problem with this formulation, which Oedipa herself remembers as her reflections continue, is that it does not complete the possibilities at all. Although she has "heard about excluded middles" and what "bad shit" they are, this does not stop her from excluding a number of other possibilities from her consideration (181). There is, for example, the obvious possibility that Tristero is a sort of joke (and not necessarily Pierce's, either), or a fad, or a genuine network for X number of Americans but not for all Americans who may have withdrawn from the "official life of the Republic," as is elsewhere implied. This last detail is critical, because much of Oedipa's interest in the Tristero conspiracy arises from the conviction that the detritus of society can be redeemed only through an overarching narrative: "either a transcendent meaning, or only the earth" (181). The unassimilable marginalia of consumer society, like the dead themselves, are only earth if they cannot be made part of a larger paradigm of transcendent meaning: meaning that here assumes the aspect of a double for the meaning of the official culture as such.[22]

Caught within her self-imposed matrix of ones and zeroes, Oedipa has returned to her tower of chapter 1 with a vengeance. The process that has led her thinking to this place can be traced to the quasi-religious justification of the American way that has been the guiding feature of those numina of her youth mentioned above. Elsewhere, of course, Pynchon follows the course of theories of national destiny back to the founding fathers and the Calvinist Puritans.[23] Here, the chief touchstone is a postwar cultural and political reality, insofar as Oedipa is its carrier. Her reduction of "diversity" to these binary choices makes sense when the sacred narrative of the American way forms the assumption behind so much of her thinking.

It was shown initially how the consumer society takes over the meaning process of socially active people, detaches the meanings from their social context, and presents them to potential consumers as fixed, the resultant social identity as conferred. This "secular" aspect to the American way is now seen to be complemented by a "sacred" aspect of official national destiny. This grand narrative allows the individual to take his or her place within it, and so also, like the administered world of consumerism, confers an identity and a meaning. Since for her people cannot participate in a "calculated withdrawal, from the life of the Republic, from its machinery [the two are here conveniently conflated]" without going "into a vacuum (could they?), there had to exist the separate, silent, unsuspected world" (124–25).

The chance that these various groups are as different from one another as they all are from mainstream, upscale consumers such as herself never really occurs to Oedipa; the thought they might evolve according to their own interactions and the pressure of events, rather than a timetable of public destiny, is also far from her mind. Furthermore, the way Oedipa has constructed the two realms of official and alternative America, there is inevitably between the two of them the same sort of unrelenting hostility one associates with the superpowers, the only difference being that these two competing historical narratives coexist within one country. There can be between these two narratives, the implication is, no fruitful interaction; the twain may meet, but never to learn from each other, only to kill. (The Tristero, not without reason, are always figured as angels of death.)

Musing on the conspiracy she thinks to have uncovered, Oedipa asks herself: "how had it ever happened here, with the chances once so good for diversity?" (181). This may be among the most ironical lines in the novel, for in her "dark night" of wandering Oedipa in fact encountered a great deal of diversity: more, arguably, than she could deal with at the time. Perhaps the sacred narrative with its revelation safely postponed until the point of death was a way of shielding the witness from the more direct impact of what she saw.

Whether or not such psychologizing befits a character such as Oedipa, what we can affirm is that these competing narratives, as they evolve, have the effect of further buffering, insulating her from the world she encounters. In fact, what the grand schemes do, both to her and probably to most readers, is to cause them to overlook the very tragic realities they have the potential to confront in Oedipa's midnight journey: "she might have found the Tristero anywhere in her Republic . . . if only she'd looked. . . . If only she'd looked" (179). Between the first lament on the part of Oedipa ("if only she'd looked") and its repetition, perhaps by Oedipa or another narrative voice, falls the shadow of a certain irony. She wishes she had picked up her clues to Tristero earlier—but there is also the possibility that even this time she has not really looked.   Hite argues that Oedipa does not understand that what she thinks of as waste—and what may in fact be waste—does not need some larger narrative in which to have meaning conferred on it: "The pathos and even tragedy that redeem Oedipa's world from banality emerge as a by-product of the quest—as the residue or waste generated by her being-toward transcendence."[24]

There are three major reasons why the waste Oedipa observes as she pursues her project becomes more central than what she is after. First of all, the "wastes" of subcultures encountered by Oedipa in San Francisco actually have their own forms of significance, which are mutually created and sustained by community: not reducible to features of the administered culture with which Oedipa is chiefly familiar. Only when meaning is thought of as a noun rather than as a gerund does this process seem insignificant. It is in this sense that the postal system provides a clue to the existences of these subcultures. It is, after all, the only two-way communications medium that figures prominently in this novel; and something like that two-way communication is intrinsic to the formation of values and meanings within any culture, no matter whether they can be fully assimilated to the larger, dominant culture or not.

Second, as mentioned at the outset, the values and meaning generated by these marginal cultures are in fact not strictly speaking opposed to those of the administered culture. Rather, it is precisely the genius of the administered culture and its Maxwell's Demons to take what can be used from those cultures and plug them into the system of circulation of goods whose emblem within the text is Oedipa's dead lover. It is in this sense that the dead GIs in Fangoso Lagoon are the proper occasion for Oedipa's journey. They are the dead—that community of outcasts—who have been used three times: as sacrifice in war, as commodities, and as advertisement. Having first "used up" the servicemen in war, the system resulting from the war can then use their remains twice more. What is scandalous is not that the dead GIs are waste—this is precisely why they would be honored—but that they are used by the postwar system of Pierce Inverarity. Through this central mystery, whose solution is not some Tristero conspiracy but the more banal workings of contemporary capitalism, there is dramatized the complicity between the "American way of life" whose child Oedipa Maas is and various outcast groups, the dead being the most extreme example. The relation between the dominant culture and its machinery and its marginal or outcast others, then, is not one of contestation but colonization.

Finally, and most importantly, the fact of waste itself becomes a crucial fact. The resonance of this is strongest of all in the sequence wherein Oedipa comforts a dying sailor. Edward Mendelson's famous article has alerted us to the sacred as a theme in this text; but what is less immediately obvious is the nature of that sacred. It is not a sacred of the sort established by some sort of teleology or founding national myth, whether of "America" or "Tristero." Rather, the sacred is confronted in "a time differential, a vanishingly small instant in which change had to be confronted at last for what it was, where it could no longer disguise itself as something innocuous like an average rate" (129). The moment of this sailor's death is indeed sacred, but in the sense that Georges Bataille has defined it: as a privileged instant.[25] This privileged instant is also an instant of loss, of waste.

Simultaneously, this is an instant of metaphor, of the transfer of meaning. As David Cowart points out, "*Metaphor*, the word itself, also has a suggestive etymology; it comes from the Greek *pherein* (to bear) and *meta* (across, beyond), and indeed it bears us into the beyond along with Oedipa's old sailor."[26] The real transfer of meaning here is founded, ironically, on the loss of substance, on death. The moment of the mattress burning is one in which Oedipa feels "as if she had just discovered the irreversible process" (128), and does "not know where she was" (129). These moments of loss and bewilderment constitute the closest thing to revelation of a genuine kind in the entire novel, because it is only here that change is at least obliquely encountered for what it is. That the old man is a sailor and that she holds him in a fashion reminiscent of the pietà has been observed before, and there is a clear thematic lineage from the incident in the Lago di Pieta. But above all, there is the fact of death, of loss, in all of its irreversibility: not as a part of a mystery story to be solved on the final page, or some grand narrative of national destiny—or for that matter of anarchist destiny, as Jesus Arrabal hopes for. It is only feeling that keen edge of suffering and loss that Oedipa enters fully into the interactive process by which meaning really is created. Metaphor, the carrying across of meaning, is here part of the same process that carries Oedipa across the Styx with her boatman. Rather than seeing it as either "a thrust at truth" or a "lie, depending where you were: inside, safe, or outside, lost" (129), Oedipa is better off seeing the metaphor here as a between space where meaning is communicated and distorted at the same time, always at once inside and outside. It is not because Oedipa has died that this meaning is hers, but because she has almost died—has witnessed death and been altered by it herself.

The transfer of meaning has taken place not because of being inside or outside, but because of a proximity, one registered by touch: "She was overcome all at once by a need to touch him, as if she could not believe in him, or would not remember him without it. Exhausted, hardly knowing what she was doing, she came the last three steps and sat, took the man in her arms, actually held him, gazing out of her smudged eyes down the stairs, back into the morning" (126). The vocabulary of the sacred registers itself in this passage: Oedipa needs to "believe in" this sailor, just as Mucho Maas needs to believe in his rock groups, we might say. But the facetious tone with which other such aspirations are mentioned is lacking here, and this tonal shift, characteristic of the entire passage concerning the sailor, accompanies one of the few instances in which the heroine touches another person, leaves the insulation of her tower. What would otherwise be a potential source of satire on the topic of the heroine's need for belief is in fact, then, more of a counterpoint to the forms of sacredness in the text that derive from some obsessional teleological system. What is communicated by this scene is not assimilated into any sign system (including, of course, that of the narrative itself); however, one might say that such moments as these in fact are central to what Baudrillard at least would call the symbolic exchange. The fact that the sailor gives Oedipa a message, unknown to her, to deliver to a trash bin is itself evocative of the dead letter office in Melville's "Bartleby the Scrivener," and his mattress constitutes little more than a "memory bank to a computer of the lost" (126). Perhaps Oedipa's desire to remember the sailor in her turn, like her sense that the dead should persist, is part of her own ambition to become that computer as well. But the "data" she receives is hardly retrievable by computer—in fact, irretrievability, disinheritance, waste are the essence of what is communicated. The fact that a man is dying and nothing can be done about it—the fact that as Oedipa says, "I can't help," even though she wishes to—that is above all what is conveyed, the meaning that is transferred.

The meaning of this sailor's fate, and by extension the fates of those other GIs, is the tragedy of the fate itself. This, and not some solution to the mystery or clue to national identity, is what Oedipa must learn. Such a meaning would be hard to assimilate to her administered world not only because it concerns an element that world prefers to ignore but also because the sorry lack of meaning—the senselessness—of the fate is its primary sense. What is communicated by such meaning is this, then: the loss of reassuring, fixed, and rational meaning itself—a loss against which the administered world in both its secular and its quasi-religious forms struggles (not without reason).

It is small wonder that, given Oedipa's immersion in that world's reassuring sign-system, she recovers as quickly as possible from this traumatic moment and happily resumes her detective ways. Emblematically, instead of reading the clear message on the place where she deposits the sailor's letter—"WASTE"—she decides (no doubt with relief) to interpret this message as some other message with its own teleology, albeit a reverse one to the official destiny: "We Await Silent Tristero's Empire." This turn to teleology (or counterteleology) is an index of what the entire novel works to depict, both in Oedipa's trajectory and in that of the reader whose chief access to the narrative is through Oedipa; this is so because in recuperating the loss of this sailor by situating his fate within a narrative of destiny, she is not (as some critics have seemed to believe) approaching the sacred but in fact is in flight from it. After this brief, flaming exception to the "detective story" rule of the novel, both Oedipa and the reader flee to the familiar promise of full meaning presented by both sacred and secular narratives, ignoring the tragic possibility that it is the loss of meaning, the waste of a life that constitutes those words "you never wanted to hear." At the same time, this moment of loss is properly speaking sacred, because surely this moment is one of the few of any emotional resonance in the book.

Oedipa was wise enough to intuit regions of experience that were unassimilable to the administered world of her background; but in positing all that did not fit into this world as a "mystery" in need of solving by its own narrative, she only duplicates the meaning processes at work in the dominant culture, then inverts them. The truest gauge of the mystery at work among the disinherited was available to her in her encounter with the sailor, if only she'd noticed. That it is almost inadvertent to the design of Oedipa's quest, and that it is (despite Oedipa's desire) so easily forgotten, attests to the miracle, the inverse rarity, of such moments—attests as well to the valiant and altogether sensible efforts of cultures, heroines, and readers to forestall such moments and, if they should occur, to forget that they ever did. Such willful amnesia in the face of absolute loss may be the case for all cultures, including those marginal cultures sketched by Pynchon; however, their very lack of material resources forces those within the marginal cultures more often to confront realities such as the one Oedipa briefly encounters here.

The incident pierces the narrative just as the tower of Oedipa's solitude is pierced, but briefly. Soon, mercifully, the barriers are erected again, and the narrative that provides the tower's tapestry resumes its course; the reader, after this interlude, follows the unfolding story comforted by the promise of full meaning. No doubt by the time that meaning is withheld, the reader is scarcely aware that the dilemmas presented by Oedipa lost amid her binary ones and zeroes are quite tame compared to the glimpse of the abyss that she and the reader have fled many pages ago.

chapter eight

From Tombstone to Tabloid: Authority Figured in *White Noise*

Although the setting for Don DeLillo's novel *White Noise* is a small midwestern college town, there are surprisingly few countryside descriptions. There is, certainly, "the most photographed barn in the world," well known chiefly for being well known; there is the countryside glimpsed as the residents of Farmington and Blacksmith flee the airborne toxic event; there is, at the novel's conclusion, the spectacular sunset on view near the highway, courtesy of the local sky's chemical recomposition. Such scenes are scarcely bucolic, however, having as much to do with the acids of modernity as with the sort of rootedness one is expected to feel in the country. But there is one exception: "the old burying ground."[1] Here the novel's hero, J. A. K. (Jack) Gladney, visits the ancestral dead, and no tourists, refugees, or sightseers get in his way. Three small American flags are "the only sign that someone had preceded me to this place in this century" as Gladney tries to decipher the "Barely legible" headstones with their "great strong simple names, suggesting a moral rigor." He listens to the dead: "The power of the dead is that we think they see us all the time. The dead have a presence" (97–98). Yet the dead "are also in the ground, of course, asleep and crumbling. Perhaps we are what they dream" (98). Whether or not that is true, the dead, along with death itself, are what Gladney dreams.

This caesura in the story line, so reminiscent of the famous graveyard scene opening in Dickens's *Great Expectations,* figures as that scene did a quest for identity through the reading of tombstone names. But the names of Gladney's own parents do not appear, either on these tombstones or indeed anywhere else in the novel; and since the town where he lives is itself only the latest in a series for him, there is no reason to impute a search for personal roots to his visit. Its ancestor worship is of a vaguer sort. It is as if Gladney's homage is not to his personal forebears but to the very idea of the past as a source of authority for the present. For it was always the dead who offered the surest claim to authority for the living, and the surest means of defeating death itself. One respected those who had died, hoping perhaps superstitiously that death for oneself would mean accession to a dynasty and not mere extinction.

Gladney's life has been in severe drift for many years, but his malaise may best be seen as a crisis of authority. His life is falling apart because it needs several registers of traditional authority in order to stay together. And all of them are coming under attack in the America of DeLillo's text: not from revolution, of course, but simply from those acids of modernity.

When We Dead Awaken: Gladney's Transmission Lines

White Noise dramatizes through the Gladney family and the Gladney career the current fate of several traditional forms of cultural transmission. Each harnesses the living to the dead in its own fashion, and thus each has its own version of immortality. This immortality is assured by means of a certain narrative that figures, each in its own form, the way an individual's present life is bonded to the past: a bonding that in recompense grants the individual a role in that narrative's version of the future.[2]

There are roughly speaking four master narratives of cultural transmission in Jack Gladney's universe: the familial, the civic, the humanist, and the religious. The familial relates people to their forebears through the blood tie; the civic to their community, its tradition and duties; the humanist to that patrimony of Western learning held in trust by the university; and the religious to that larger lineage from the ancestral dead. Despite the tensions among these narratives, it is fair to say that in their tendency they are all broadly speaking religious, since loyalty to the ancestral dead (with its consequent hope for immorality) finally grounds them all. Fittingly, Gladney relies on all of these legitimating lines: lines that are tangled, if not cut, by the world presented in this text.[3]

For a start, the narrative of Gladney's family line is an errant one, with offspring from each of four marriages to its credit. One suspects its family tree would have many branches but no trunk. The parent figures ("parents" seems not to indicate the role properly) are Jack and his wife, Babette, but they do none of the passing on of wisdom that is supposed to be the older generation's portion. Instead, the television seems to be the chief source of information and even guidance; its urgent messages frequently interrupt the narrative of *White Noise,* but they seem more like that from which any other learning is the interruption.

Heinrich, Gladney's son from a previous marriage, is the closest thing the family has to a repository of learning, because he is "plugged in" to things scientific. It is important that nobody knows whether Heinrich is generally right or not: he is merely the possessor of scientific discourse, and that is enough to unseat the parents as sources of moral authority. When he insists at the dinner table that the "radiation that surrounds us every day" is "the real issue," the adults try to denigrate the matter, but they worry he is right (174).[4] When they try to regain the field by throwing out remembered fragments from old history and civics classes ("how a bill becomes a law," "Angles, Saxons and Jutes," and so forth), they conjure up only "a confused rush of schoolroom images" (176). Such Gradgrind-like touchstones are all they can come up with. It is only when Babette appears on TV teaching her posture class that her family pays her the reverential attention customarily accorded the wise, but it is clear that her appearance on that medium is the chief reason for everyone's newfound respect. With this exception that proves the rule, the people in charge in the Gladney household tend to be the children. After all, Jack's ultimate threat in trying to force Babette to reveal her secret life is the wrath of her daughter Denise, who has figured out her lies. "I will unleash your little girl," Jack swears, reversing the cliché, "Wait till your father comes home." Babette has been "bad," and Denise will punish her for it.[5]

Heinrich's own moment of apotheosis, oddly reminiscent of Jesus' appearance in the temple, occurs with the onset of the airborne toxic event, which finds him "at the center of things, speaking in his new-found voice" to a growing crowd "impressed by the boy's knowledgeability and wit" (130–31). In this hour of crisis, Heinrich's sort of knowledge, however spurious, is evidently what people feel is needed. The scene has its exact analogue in the same section when Gladney himself awaits information on his exposure to the event from the much younger keyboard operator for SIMUVAC: "I wanted this man on my side. He had access to data. I was prepared to be servile and fawning if it would keep him from dropping casually shattering remarks about my degree of exposure and chances for survival" (139). In addition to the superstitious undercurrent of thought here, this passage also indicates how the moral authority subtly shifts. The sort of experience transmitted from older generation to younger—with his four marriages, for instance, Gladney has in once sense a great deal of experience, though it does not add up to much—yields to "access to data," the sort of wisdom this young keyboard operator can give or withhold.

Admittedly, Gladney almost implies he would rather the data be withheld than given; but either way, the authority has passed to the younger generation in this encounter.[6]

As for the narrative of community, the small town of Blacksmith, despite the "moral rigor" suggested by its "simple name," is largely a backdrop for the careers of the professors at the College-on-the-Hill, the phony establishment where Gladney works. The town's poor upkeep and general shabbiness are noted in passing: "Some of the houses in town were showing signs of neglect. The park benches needed repair, the broken streets needed resurfacing. Signs of the times" (170). Such signs are little noticed nor long remembered by the host of "New York Émigrés," even by one so otherwise sensitive to signs as media medium Murray Jay Siskind, an adjunct professor in the department of American Environments. Murray and his colleagues claim to have come to the Midwest in search of "American magic and dread" but in reality are grateful just to have a peaceful night's sleep (19). By and large they get it, too, because Blacksmith is almost as sleepy as the old burying ground. With the airborne toxic event that occupies the center of the novel, the town bids fair to become an old burying ground itself.

Granted, the event and its aftermath provide a certain renewal of civic spirit in Blacksmith. The SIMUVAC mock-up of a toxic event, with townspeople including the Gladneys' young girl Steffie playing victims, or the spectacular sunsets the townspeople view, probably made possible by residue of the airborne event—these are the venues wherein community enacts itself. In both instances, what the community enacts is the death of the community. Significantly, the one point during the airborne toxic event when the townspeople evince any solidarity in outrage occurs when they discover that their plight did not make the newscast: "What exactly has to happen before they stick microphones in our faces and hound us to the doorsteps of our homes, camping out on our lawns, creating the usual media circus? . . . Our fear is enormous. Even if there hasn't been great loss of life, don't we deserve some attention for our suffering, our human worry, our terror? Isn't fear news?" (162) Apparently, this community sees its victimhood as the only way to present itself to itself or others. The possibility of mounting some political opposition to the conditions that produce the event in the first place is not even considered here. Were the residents of Blacksmith, under the aegis of SIMUVAC, obligingly to play victims, it is an expression of citizenship in its most perverse form. For in playing victims, they would in reality only be playing themselves. In a similar pattern to that where parents become authorities at such time as they appear on TV, the residents of Blacksmith ("citizens" seems too strong a term) are willing to enact the death of their city in order to achieve media recognition for it. The exercise is justified by the idea that enacting it makes it less likely to happen, but this odd notion is just as likely a cover for the feeling that somehow a media apotheosis assures immortality more readily than commitment to a community and loyalty to its fate. (In any case even this projected event is canceled for lack of interest.)

As for spiritual lineage, the one religious venue mentioned in the novel is the Congregational Church basement now used for Babette's posture class. Jack says of her students that he is "always surprised at their acceptance and trust, the sweetness of their belief. Nothing is too doubtful to be of use to them as they seek to redeem their bodies from a lifetime of bad posture. It is the end of skepticism" (27). The childhood faith in the redemption of souls is here transferred to the body, along with the hope of triumphing over death. The one religious figure in the novel is a nun who materializes in a hospital in Iron City, and although she deigns to treat Gladney for his gunshot wounds, she is hardly out of *Going My Way:* "It is our task in the world to believe things no one else takes seriously. . . . If we did not pretend to believe these things, the world would collapse" (318). She proceeds to insist that even though Gladney wants her to believe in the "old muddles and quirks . . . great old human gullibilities," it is all a pretense: "Those who have abandoned belief must still believe in us. They are sure that they are right not to believe but they know belief must not fade completely. . . . We surrender our lives to make your nonbelief possible" (319).

When Gladney encounters this nun, the scene has particular force because she mirrors in her profession the sort of bad faith he feels in his. Gladney's career is a living mockery of every ideal of liberal humanism. His world-historical concerns have been boiled down in convenient kitsch form to something he has christened "Hitler studies." As part of this new career move, he has changed his name from Jack to "J. A. K. Gladney, a tag I wore like a borrowed suit" (16). To round out the Inspector Clouseau effect, he has added some weight, "an air of unhealthy excess, . . . hulking massiveness," as if physical girth could somehow confound itself with intellectual solidity. (17) Finally, a pair of dark glasses, along with the ceremonial robes that all faculty of College-on-the-Hill are, preposterously, required to wear, complete the donnish getup, which converges in some sinister fashion on the Hitler persona. Gladney adds as an afterthought that he is himself "the false character that follows the name around" (17).

The protagonist's self-awareness is precisely what makes this fakery especially painful. When he calls neurologist Winnie Richards brilliant, she replies that everyone in the academy calls everyone else that. But he demurs:

"No one calls me brilliant. They call me shrewd. They say I latched on to something big" (188). He is a charlatan, in brief, and unfortunate enough to realize it. He does not even know German, though he tries to learn a smidgen for the conference over which he presides. Furthermore, all of the figures with whom he interacts have the same con artist aura about them: Murray, Alfonse (Fast Food) Stompanato—indeed, all of the self-styled media analysts who inhabit the American Environments.

Gladney is never presented in Socratic dialogue with his classes, but his flights of rhetorical exuberance in lecture have little to do with the Third Reich and everything to do with his own neuroses and obsessions: "I found myself saying . . . 'All plots tend to move deathward. Political plots, terrorist plots, lovers' plots, narrative plots, plots that are part of children's games. We edge nearer to death every time we plot. . . .' Is this true? Why did I say it? What does it mean?" (26) In addition to being significant of the deathward plot of the novel, this passage suggests the vague nature of Gladney's instruction: why did he not ask himself these questions before finding himself saying these things? Perhaps because authority, at least in the world of this text, is above and before all positional; the words uttered by Jack become portentous rather than silly by virtue of their utterance by him. The professors, like the media idols they study and strive to emulate, gain authority not from any innate ability or credential but from personal magnetism or, failing that, the mere fact of having the enunciating role. One suspects that in the world of *White Noise,* these students never think to wonder whether what Gladney, Siskind, and the others have to say is true, or even serious. The mantralike words Siskind uses to seal so many of his pronouncements are a symptom of this self-referential authority. If his interlocutor seems at all skeptical of some outrageous formula of his, he will simply retort, "It's obvious." And why is it obvious? Nowhere in the book do his interlocutors ever think to ask this.

There is for both Gladney and Siskind an additional source of precious professorial authority: charisma by association. Both are making their careers by attaching themselves, as critics are wont to do, to some eminent figure whose glory they parasitically procure. Thus Gladney, who did for Hitler what it is Murray's ambition to do for Elvis (or is Elvis doing it for Murray?), enters Murray's class and begins a running colloquy wherein the personal, *National Enquirer*–like tidbits about Elvis are contrapuntally answered by similar data about Hitler's life. Gladney senses the debt in which he is placing Siskind: "His eyes showed a deep gratitude. I had been generous with the power and madness at my disposal, allowing my subject to be associated with an infinitely lesser figure, a fellow who sat in

La-Z-Boy chairs and shot out TVs. It was not a small matter. We all had an aura to maintain, and in sharing mine with a friend I was risking the very things that made me untouchable" (73–74).

This reflection establishes two essential features of Gladney's moral authority: that it is based on aura rather than intellect (the aura alone is what makes him untouchable, and not any scholarly eminence), and that the aura in turn arises from the association of the professor with some legendary figure (so that to link Elvis to Hitler is to share Gladney's power with Siskind). Small wonder that when Gladney, minus his gown and sunglasses, happens upon one of his colleagues from the college in the department store, he is told with brutal relish that he is a "big, harmless, aging, indistinct sort of guy" (83). (It puts the newly infuriated Gladney "in the mood to shop" and so to illustrate what one could call DeLillo's Law of Consumption: that people expend money in direct proportion to their fear of death or dishonor.)

Perhaps Jack's laying on of hands also indicates a passing of the humanist's baton from world-historical interests, even if sensational ones, to the simulacra of the mass media. The phony theme park aura of the College-on-the-Hill, its professors forced to wear silly gowns (and, to judge by Gladney, loving it), depicts American humanistic learning at its most compromised and meretricious. Even Murray himself is a bit embarrassed by its character: "there are full professors in this place who read nothing but cereal boxes" (10). Whatever can be said in denigration of Hitler Studies, there remains an irreducible consequentiality to that event in world history, whereas the consequences of the Elvis "event" are chiefly, perhaps solely, symbolical ones. Gladney's gracious gesture has the effect of debasing the liberal humanist lineage even further than his Hitler studies program has already done.

Thus Gladney, whose role in cultural transmission is short-circuited in his own family and community, plays a dubious role even in the culture he claims to hand down as a humanist. In such fashion, all of the forms of cultural transmission, with their attendant stories, are one by one failing Gladney, in part because he is failing them—and in part because the modern situation is such that nobody can any longer properly honor them.

Better Things for Better Dying: Science and Salvation

The void left by the traditional narratives prompts the desire for other stories, other lineages by which to ensure immortality. As Heinrich's fifteen minutes of fame imply, the discourse of science could be one such story, but its results in the narrative are not encouraging. It is true that science produces, with the airborne toxic event, a new form of death, which Murray rightly describes as "growing in prestige and dimension" and possessed of "a sweep it never had before" (150). (In other words, he describes it, characteristically but in this case saliently, as in essence a media event: a TV miniseries, say.) But the toxic event can ennoble only the spectacle of death itself, not the fate of any person who may die.

When it comes to rationalizing the event it has brought forth, science fares little better. Though "a death made in the laboratory," the event is regarded in a "simple and primitive way, as some seasonal perversity of the earth, . . . something not subject to control" (127). Even were it accessible to the generality, a merely scientific explanation is anyway not enough to transfigure the process of death, to sublate it as earlier narratives of cultural transmission were able to do. Science by its nature cannot provide the promise of immortality that earlier stories, always implicitly religious regardless of their specific lineages, were once able to render.

Instead it is the rumors spawned by the event that transfigure the specter of death more than the possible rationales of scientific discourse. The many rumors and far-fetched explanations resurrect a kind of folk culture, since the "toxic event had released a spirit of imagination. People spun tales, others listened spellbound. . . . We began to marvel at our own ability to manufacture awe" (153). This is awe of a highly self-referential sort, with a consequent tinge of falsity, but awe nonetheless. Among the things marveled at are items from the various tabloids on hand in the shelter—many of which, to speak of manufactured awe, feature some twist whereby an oncoming disaster is rendered magically harmless or salubrious, much in the manner of *Close Encounters of the Third Kind,* a popular film when *White Noise* was written. To be sure, Heinrich is listened to with awe as well, but his story is not received as if it were different in kind from those in the tabloids.[7]

The flourishing rumor mill revives, however briefly and freakily, the spirit of community in Blacksmith. But at least as crucial is the lack those stories are vainly pressed to fill. For it becomes evident in the airborne toxic event that science, while it has evolved new and sweeping means of wreaking death, has not found a way of ennobling or explaining it. The result is that superstition and rumor must begin anew their time-honored task: "The genius of the primitive mind is that it can render human helplessness in noble and beautiful ways" (140).

Perhaps scientific discourse renders this helplessness in noble ways as well. Still, it is fair to say that neither ghoulish Heinrich nor reclusive misanthrope Winnie Richards are sterling exemplars of the spiritual uplift on offer from scientific discourse.

If anything, the scientific advance chiefly on display in this world—the event itself, with its attendant SIMUVAC teams and medical studies—reduces the people further to infantilism, primitive fantasy, and dependence on the system as if on a deity. Indeed, DeLillo charts throughout the novel a recursive movement whereby the large, impersonal forces of technology first produce death-dealing consequences and then offer themselves as palliatives to the fear of death they have themselves aroused. TV and radio may produce deformed babies, and they certainly thrive on the specter of death; but that fact does not keep anyone, including Dylar dealer Willie Mink, from using these very media to annul their fears. Gladney himself, a mess beneath his outsize costume of gravitas, becomes almost tearful when an automated teller machine shows his checking account balanced: "The system had blessed my life" (46). Such a blessing, as Gladney soon finds when confronting his SIMUVAC technician, is a conditional gesture, always capable of retraction.

The first two sections of this three-part novel relate the process by which Gladney comes to realize that his favored means of immortality will no longer do. Since early on DeLillo has linked the fear of death to the relationship between Babette and Jack—"which of us will die first?" is a perpetual fear on the part of both—it is by a natural passage that he comes to associate her initial stealthy drug taking (in the cause of reducing her fear of death) with some deeper unfaithfulness. Typical for this novel where the children frequently assume parental functions is the fact that his daughter Denise, a close reader of the *Physicians Desk Reference,* is "on to" her mother long before he himself is convinced, but soon the incriminating Dylar vial is uncovered. This in turn leads him to extort from his wife the confession that she has indeed slept with her distributor to obtain the illegal drug.[8]

Gladney's subsequent rage at his wife's infidelity is doubled by his revulsion at the scientific rationale behind the notion that a drug "specifically interacts with neurotransmitters in the brain to make its own inhibitors" (200). His reply to the thought of being "the sum of [one's] chemical impulses" is to wonder what "happens to good and evil in this system? Passion, envy and hate? Do they become a tangle of neurons? . . . Are we being asked to regard these things nostalgically?" And most prophetically for the novel's climax: "What about murderous rage?" (200) In the context of the novel, Gladney's decision to fell his wife's lover, as deranged as it is, springs also from the need to see the deeper impulses not as the things of nostalgia but as forces with a mythic vigor. Rather than chemical reactions to be suppressed with neurological nostrums, "passion, envy and hate" are to Gladney fundamental things. The Dylar drug Babette takes to ward off the fear of death does not really work, although it appears to be addictive anyway. Science, it seems, can no more end the fear of death than it can redeem the fact of death: Babette's Dylar is as powerless as was that good posture which was her other means of curing a spiritual ill by bodily means. However, it must be added that Gladney's counterattack also employs the magic bullet that preceded Dylar and is, in its own way, just as mechanistic a solution: the pistol. Fittingly, the pistol is a gift from his father-in-law, representative of an earlier, less sophisticated generation. Going after her supplier thus strikes a blow in two directions: it reasserts Jack's traditional role as husband in the most old-fashioned of ways, to be sure, but it also defeats, by implication, a proffered scientific solution to a moral problem.

But the moral simplicity of Jack's retribution is complicated by the fact that he believes he himself may be dying and that by killing someone else his own death is somehow less likely. If Babette's father provides the practical means, then, it is—again fittingly—Murray Jay Siskind who gives the casuistical theory that justifies the gun's use: "it's a way of controlling death. A way of gaining the ultimate upper hand. Be the killer for a change. Let someone else be the dier. Let him replace you, theoretically, in that role. You can't die if he does. He dies, you live" (291). Such a theory, it is clear, is wholly symbolical—or, if you prefer, superstitious. Indeed, Murray himself draws an analogy to burial rites. In affirming the morally human against the inhumanly technological, then, Gladney has recourse only to the earlier, more primitive technologies of his father-in-law's generation and to earlier magical forms of rationale. In a paradox that goes to the heart of the complicity between advanced technology and primitive superstition, it is postmodern Murray who delivers the most primitive argument of all, invoking "some prehistoric period" when "to kill was to live" (292).

In trying to reassert his former authority as head of his household and as spokesman for humanist values, Gladney entrusts himself to superstition in its most regressive form. Making as if to assert his ascendancy, he in fact succumbs to a "prehistoric" mode of action. His crime of passion is already an ancient enough sort of activity: his reasons for it, as propounded by Murray, are even more primitive than that. And Murray's argument dramatizes the true nature of his analyses of mass culture's waves and radiation. His cult of the child, that prime target of TV demography, and his resultant desire to transcend the rational in some McLuhanesque way take on an especially sinister character here.

Gladney inhabits a world in which advanced technology cohabits with the most primitive of superstitions—wherein, indeed, the former encourages the latter. His plan to go to Iron City and shoot Willie Mink partakes of his briefer journey to the old burying ground, as an attempt to revisit an earlier, more straightforward time. He nurses the additional hope that by enacting this particular old-fashioned narrative, he can create the conditions under which the other abandoned or decaying narratives can compel belief once again. For in attacking Willie Mink, he is after larger game, too, especially in the symbolic terms of this novel.

It is Willie Mink who has convinced Babette that the fear of death can be overcome by a pill, and it is not without point, surely, that his speech is a word salad of phrases from that other ubiquitous modern drug, TV: "Did you ever wonder why, out of thirty-two teeth, these four cause so much trouble? I'll be back with the answer in a minute" (312). Living stateless in a motel, watching TV and downing Dylar pills, answerable it seems to none of the traditional narratives, Mink appears the perfect candidate for a comeuppance: "Transient pleasures, drastic measures" (304). With death imminent, he will pay for his freedom from those narratives by the stark terror with which he will be forced to greet his own demise. His constant popping of Dylar pills, in this respect, is to Gladney a hopeful sign.

But finally, this primitive solution does not work. Despite the archaic symbolism of the revolver bequeathed from his father-in-law and the immemorial character of his crime of passion, Gladney cannot make his own narratives live by making Willie Mink die. He is himself too much a part of the world of Willie Mink to be a proper antagonist in the first place. He freely admits he is as terrified of death as is his wife, and in succumbing to a magical solution, his own superstition seems no alternative to the sort rampant throughout the book.

The revenge narrative itself takes the form of that purveyor of folklore, the tabloid story. This form is emphasized by Gladney's plan to leave his car in the driveway of blind Old Man Treadwell who lives for the tabloids. It is his attempt to gain back by sheer brute force the moral authority that he is otherwise losing, but since his plan combines superstition, tabloid aggression, and faith in technology, it represents the collapse of his authority more than a regaining of it. He is, finally, too good to follow through on his plan: "I looked at him. Alive. His lap a puddle of blood. . . . I felt I was seeing him for the first time as a person. The old human muddles and quirks were set flowing again. Compassion, remorse, mercy" (313). The precivilization scenario of which Americans are so enamored, that mano a mano fight between two antagonists, cannot be the moment of truth for

Gladney. And in the ensuing hospital scene, with its cynical nun, it becomes clear that what holds for the old Adam will also be true of the tale of redemption.

When Gladney seeks the ancient story of vengeance, he rejects the sheltering stories of family, polis, and learning: all the approved forms of cultural transmission. However, he has not stepped outside religious or mystical narrative one bit. Even the formula Murray confers like a benediction—"He dies, you live"—resonates as a bargain uncannily like that offered by Christ. So it is that his journey into the elemental emotions of passion, envy, and hate confronts him with the religious subtext underlying all of the other narratives, including Gladney's crime of passion, for the first time in the text. The nun understands his crying need to believe, to submit to authority in order to save his hopes of immortality. But she is less than sympathetic, telling him scornfully, "You would come in from the street dragging a body by the foot and talk about angels who live in the sky" (320).

Elvis Lives: Celebrity's Heavenly Stars

In the absence of a straightforward, old-fashioned solution to modernity's muddle, what is left of the old narratives that provides a source of authority, a reservoir of legend and story, and the hope of immortality? What is left is, quite simply, celebrity. In an ironic fashion, the picture Gladney espies on the wall, "of [John F.] Kennedy and the Pope in heaven," provides the clue (317). But the heaven they are really in is that reserved for media idols: the Parnassus of the famous. Believing in heaven may be hard, even (or perhaps especially) for the designated believers such as Gladney's German nun. But belief in personality, and in the perpetual renewal of personality by the mass media, is still possible.

Indeed, the celebrity is time and again the object of what cultic power is left in the world of *White Noise*. Relevant here is the lengthy discussion among the faculty of American Environments, in which Alfonse Stompanato the chairman rounds on other participants, asking them where they were when James Dean died, as if challenging their bona fides (68–69). There may be few things that unite Elvis Presley and Adolf Hitler, but star status in film is surely one of them. Orestes, Heinrich's friend, wants to get into the *Guinness Book of World Records* in the worst way, and Heinrich's mass murderer pen pal *has* gotten famous in the worst way. In the familial reverence that greets Babette (when on TV) or the reaction of Gladney's daughter Bee to the fact that passengers in the near crash of an

airplane will not be on TV ("They went through all that for nothing?"
[92]), we see that being on television is apotheosis to those who otherwise
merely watch it.

The technology that brings them into the home may be as alien and
inscrutable as that of Dylar or the airborne toxic event, but the celebrities
themselves, at least, are people, only with that charismatic glow that contact with mass media lends. The honored dead in the society of this novel
are not those named on illegible tombstones in the old burying ground, but
those whose visages have been fixed in the media constellation. With the
waning of the old stories of lineage and immortality, the best guarantor of
immortality is now not written, let alone discursive; it is iconographic: the
televised image, the radio voice. This, and not the old burying ground, is
the postmodern dynasty of the dead.

The religious narrative in this new world is thus preserved but applied
to human celebrity rather than angels or gods. The near crash of the airplane demonstrates how the elaboration of technical means has the paradoxical effect of rendering people more and not less infantilized, dependent
on reassurance from images of authority (their grateful response to such
reassurance at this point is to assume the fetal position). The thaumaturgic
figure of the chief steward as he comes down the aisle after the plane averts
disaster is itself proof enough that faith in authority is being rewarded
(90–92). Thus does the iconography of authority outlive its legitimating
stories.

The significance of the fact that it is not European history that Gladney
teaches but, precisely, Hitler studies becomes clearer as a result. Hitler,
after all, was a figure who took unto himself the authority of death, and
the reports of his death, like Elvis's, were long thought greatly exaggerated.
Given what Gladney says about him in the only glimpse the reader has of
his teaching, his approach to his topic is biographical, anecdotal, and psychoanalytic—in short, an academic variant of the approach taken by
tabloids and fan magazines toward their celebrities. Celebrity, a hit parade
of historical personalities and great men, hence becomes his way of defining the liberal humanist heritage.

And as for the family, it too is retained, but now the purpose is not to
change children into adults (the traditional function of the family) but
rather to ensure that adults remain children (the consumer paradigm). The
childlike faith in celebrity transfers nicely to the products that in many
ways the celebrities resemble. The barn in Farmington stands as the
emblem of this transformation of the country's past into a theme park culture: it is called "the most photographed barn in America."

It is a commonplace to view *White Noise* as a critique of American materialism, and this is true to a degree. But that too easy term must be defined and explained. DeLillo is most conscious of how the more elaborate forms of spirituality that preceded consumer culture still inhere, in a degraded and superstitious form, within consumer culture itself. If the materialism in DeLillo's universe can be given a spiritual inflection, then, it would be a certain kind of Manichaeanism: one in which spiritual status is marked off by association with the right food and clothing, or proximity to holy ones.

Similarly, the Americans of *White Noise* pursue the right consumer items and try to connect with celebrities, or with celebrity itself, in the hope that proof of spiritual election will follow. Gladney's frantic accretion of weight, wives, and consumer items comes increasingly to be seen as symptomatic of his fear of death, his desire for a talisman to ward it off. (In this regard, it is only when Gladney has convinced himself that he is dying that he begins to throw out the things he has bought, with the same mania with which he acquired them.)[9]

In the twilight of the earlier narratives of immortality, there is no rational paradigm that presents itself to Gladney and the others, least of all that of science or technology. Instead, the products of modern technology became themselves fetish objects: the miracle drugs, the Promethean airplanes, the electronic temple of modern media. Indeed it is a corollary of the Manichaean emphasis on personhood, on the physical as prerequisite for spiritual authority, that the mere fact of one's positioning by the mass media is itself the sign of election. The moral dimension to publicity—whether this is achieved through mass murder, in the case of Heinrich's pen pal, or good deeds—becomes secondary to the fact of election itself.[10]

Similarly, the collective worship of these gods produces a community of a sort, but not one that bears much relation to the old story of citizenship. Rather, the result is a community of spectators who enact and view their own possible demise. Such is this way of defining the residents of Blacksmith that even their airborne pollution becomes an opportunity to "go to the overpass all the time" and sit in lawn chars "watch[ing] the setting sun," now enhanced by toxicity. "The sky takes on content, feeling, an exalted narrative life," Jack tells the reader. But as with TV, the crowd comes to look, not converse: "We find little to say to each other" (324). The glow of the sunset, like that of TV, is the source both of fascination and anxiety; like moths to a flame, the people of Blacksmith go to bask in the glow of the very thing that could do them the most harm.

By novel's end, Gladney has himself assumed the passivity that is characteristic of the other townspeople. Gladney has been doubly victimized by

modernity now: his exposure to the airborne event has increased his awareness of his own mortality, and the hegemony of science's story, whose audience numbers his own wife, has weakened the traditional narratives that
were his refuge. The weary irony with which Gladney narrates the closing
supermarket scene indicates that what the preceding events have taught
him is only the exhaustion of previous narrative promises of immortality,
not any bright new hope.[11] It is now only as that quintessentially passive
figure, the consumer, that Gladney has what faint glimpse of immortality
is now allowed him.

In that spirit he revisits the supermarket, a virtual omphalos for so many
White Noise episodes. Here, it is not only through the "holographic scan-
ners" installed in the checkout counters that "the dead speak to the living"
(326). The bread of life is available, to be sure, but so are the lineage to the
ancestral dead, the celebrities, and the attendant hope of immortality.
These spiritual essences are embodied in the only discursive form remaining in Gladney's world: the tabloids. Through their liturgy, the customer
may participate in the American celebrity cult while also consuming
American products. Here the profane consumer items in one's cart mingle
with the viaticum promised by the sacred image and text of the tabloids.

If the supermarket is indeed the point of intersection between profane
consumption and sacred celebrity, it is the tabloids that make it so. The
things of the body are cared for, as always, by the supermarket—but so are
the things of the spirit. Denied the ability to touch the saints of the mass
media directly, the consumer may instead read these devotional tracts. All
of Gladney's protective irony cannot conceal the fact that, with the failure
of his other narratives, he has no recourse but to look to the tabloids for
support, just as all the others do. He can no longer read his own immorality in the old stories, so instead of the inscriptions on the tombstones of the
old burying ground, Jack Gladney is last seen reading the covers of the
tabloids: "Everything we need that is not food or love is here in the tabloid
racks. The tales of the supernatural and the extraterrestrial. The miracle
vitamins, the cures for cancer, the remedies for obesity. The cults of the
famous and the dead" (326).

chapter nine

Mao II: A Portrait of the Artist in the Age of Mechanical Reproduction

W*hite Noise* can fairly be said to be Don DeLillo's full depiction of the electronic world that surrounds literary artists, to say nothing of everyone else. Still, it cannot be claimed that J. A. K. Gladney is a full or even partial depiction of an artist. The fact that he is at once a humanist academic and a bit of a fraud indicates his liminal status—both diagnostician and symptom of contemporary malaise. His flawed attempt to reverse the tide of history by playing Humbert to Willie Mink's Quilty only underlines the extent to which the commercial culture's products have informed his thinking. The failure of his project is dramatized in a way Humbert's never is, since for one thing it is never implied that this incident is a precondition for Gladney's becoming narrator. Thus, even though DeLillo renders as complete an inscription of the cultural dilemmas of postmodern life as is possible, the intriguing question of what a man of letters is to do in response to such dilemmas remains.

In *Mao II,* one has a kind of answer. The career and life of Bill Gray, modernist novelist in a postmodern universe, comes as close to a straightforward portrait of the artist as DeLillo has given us. But as will become clear, the path between description and prescription, and the synecdoche that authorizes such exemplary status for DeLillo's protagonist in the first place, must both be negotiated in a text that guards its ironies almost as carefully as Nabokov's.

That having been said, this novel is a rich source of analysis of the serious writer in American culture, which analysis yields a plight at least as desperate as those to which Henry James's artists and writers have been subjected. In fact, with *Mao II,* we return with an uncanny sense of familiarity to the concerns first dramatized in those Jamesian tales of the nineties. DeLillo's version, being of the 1990s, is naturally somewhat different, but thematically it has striking affinities with the fiction considered at the outset of this study.

The title refers to the famous Andy Warhol portrait of Mao Tse-tung that reproduces his picture in a multitude of colors. This pregnant marker of the celebrity machine, geopolitical power, and the artwork as reproduction also unites to all of these motifs another that proves to be DeLillo's most obsessive: the conflict and convergence of individual identity and mass awareness. DeLillo has remarked in fact that the twin inspirations for *Mao II* were the Ayatollah Khomeini's fatwa, or death sentence, against Salman Rushdie in the late eighties and a photograph of the enraged, would-be reclusive author J. D. Salinger. What both incidents point to is the inability of a writer to escape the machinery of publicity (the book often compares cameras to weapons) or the tides of political and cultural history. Curiously, in a paradox that recalls "Death of the Lion," the same process that forces an author into a certain form of notoriety willy-nilly also works more and more to marginalize the literary life as a vocation. The classic ambition of the modernist artist—to flee from personality in order to affect people through the impact of one's art—is curiously inverted, as the needs of personality, or rather the need for personalities, is served at the expense of the work itself. Rushdie, after all, achieved true worldwide fame by being singled out by Khomeini for death, and only secondarily from his novels.

It is DeLillo's ambition to paint the portrait of a kind of absolute individualist, a recognizably American type of the writer as a man resolutely refusing to succumb to the machinery of mass publicity, which DeLillo artfully confounds with the totalitarianism of the despot in subtle ways offensive to some in the West, for whom there is no connection between the tendencies of tyrants and the free play of the consumer-friendly market. Bill Gray—and his creator—seem to see a considerable connection, almost a collusion. *Mao II* is a polemical reply, in effect, to the work of Andy Warhol, which forms its sinister obbligato throughout.

Thus in the face of overwhelming postmodern force from the dread world of consumer society and its evil twin of tribalism, DeLillo constructs with Bill Gray a figure to respond to these tendencies with a great refusal. But this ambition gives rise to its own very special dilemmas, chief among them: how does one in fact paint a figure defined by absolute individualism, by his work as an artist rather than by his life—a figure who lives the barest minimum of life, in fact? I leave aside the grand philosophical question about whether absolute singularity could be fictionalized to begin with, except to note that I have already referred the character of Bill Gray to preexisting literary models such as Rushdie and Salinger, and perhaps most centrally Samuel Beckett. (What we are dealing with here is clearly a type of the individualist, in a sense, rather than an individual.) More than that, the status of this construct is such that characterization is hard to achieve: the irony is that the more irreducibly singular the author is posited as being, the more adumbrative, the more shadowy his persona must be made. The strange duplicity of Bill Gray is such that there are only the most fugitive glimpses of what one would call his personal life (typically taking the form of ex-wives' complaints about him), at the same time that his selfhood, his radical individuality, is a given of the narrative. Why?

His story must be both told and left untold because DeLillo wishes the reader to understand that his sensibility is somehow under siege by the forces of publicity and personality—the subtext of this narrative can be read as the losing battle of selfhood against personality—and yet cannot himself directly represent the complexity of the life so under attack. There is the dramatic question of how to render such singularity in any detail without it seeming like everyone else's "singularity." (Indeed, this happens several times anyway, as Gray's daily ablutions and bodily excrescences are invoked, for instance.) But additionally, it is as if DeLillo, in his most Jamesian novel since *The Names* (1982), works to present a phenomenon that, like a supernova, only shows forth as it goes away. With the reticence about the life goes the total pledge of silence surrounding the justification for all the artist's crankiness: the work of art itself. We get, so far as I could determine, not so much as a sentence from the great work, nor even the barest idea what the subject of the work might be. Of course, this sort of thing does not matter since it is by the style alone, by the perfection of the prose, that the work will ever be justified. (We do learn at one point that it is not remotely autobiographical, scarcely a surprise.) The dramatic advantage of such a shield is obvious, since any direct gaze on the magnum opus would yield only disappointment: he destroyed his life and those of his loved ones for this? But there is also, one suspects, a further rationale that explains much of the obscurity of the narrative as well.

What at first appears only to be a polarity of opposition within the text of *Mao II*—that between cultic activity, whether of tribes or adoring fans, and literary culture as the pursuit of free-thinking individuals—is reproduced at an obscurer level as a similarity. The curious notion that the literary text survives without attaching any sort of aura to itself, in the mode of the despot or of the celebrity, is undermined throughout the book. DeLillo first of all presents the hermitage of the author himself, somewhat satirically, as furthering the very fame he hoped to elude by absconding. The book

itself grows in weight and status as its debut is further delayed; its author
gains mystique as he hides from the world. Added to this is the necessarily
fetishistic character of art—or, if you prefer, its magical aspect. The irreducible singularity of the individual transfers itself by degrees to the artwork, but in each case profundity is gained at the expense of obscurity.

In the disenchanted time of modernity, the earlier mysteries, those
shared incomprehensions of the age of faith, are not as reliable a shelter. In
their stead, what remain are secrets: the sole purview of the aura that survives. This is one reason secrecy, and its more benign bourgeois liberal
cousin "privacy," are so zealously preserved as values in this otherwise val-
ues-challenged time. Bill Gray, like his famously elusive author, understands the value of secrecy, of the silence that for James Joyce accompanied
exile and cunning. It is his desire to preserve the aura of the work he is writing by sacrificing the cult of personality, and his creator allows him to do
this by a like reticence about what Gray is writing. But of course essential
to literary culture, even nowadays, is publication; and it is this opening to
publicity, this final unveiling, that Gray becomes incapable of imagining or
bringing about. The opposition between the surface of publicity, where
one's picture comes out "flat as birdshit on a Buick," and the depth of literary complexity with which this text plays is apparently solely formalist.[1]
But it is not: rather, this obscurity, this complexity, are posited also because
it is a post-Enlightenment approximation of priestly mystery.

Given the respect DeLillo chooses to maintain for his hero's privacy, his
obscurity as a character as well as an author, there is little of the overt conflict with which psychological realism generally invests its characters.
Indeed, Gray's status becomes almost wholly allegorical. Apart from the
required activities and as much human contact as allows him to continue
his reclusive ways, Gray scarcely has human dimensions at all. He has
become a modernist writer in his flight from personality, above all, but he
has ceased to participate much in the human cycle of reproduction. His
narrative is framed by marriages, one mass wedding in Yankee Stadium
under the regime of the Moonies and another in Beirut witnessed by Brita
the photographer. But Gray is not present in either chapter.

DeLillo's novel, then, is a Beckettian treatment of an author who resembles a Beckett character and whose work appears modeled in part on
Beckett's art. It is Gray's belief that "Beckett is the last writer to shape the
way we think and see" (157). This ability so to shape the way people think,
Bill Gray believes, has passed, lamentably, to terrorists. But since Bill Gray
himself can, by his nature, supply little of the conflict of the book, that role
has to be filled by the larger social surround against which he is posed—and

indeed, the larger social surround is a far more active, though seemingly separate, presence than is the author who is the book's apparent center.

The paradox is hard to escape that in order to dramatize the quandary of the artist in the modern, or postmodern, universe, DeLillo is forced to concentrate on the forces arrayed against Gray more than on Gray's interior struggle. The reader gets a few hints, more than a few hints, that Gray is getting old and weary and doubtful of his book's merits and his abilities as an author. Beyond that, there is little in the way of insight into the depths of Gray's soul. What DeLillo implicitly directs us to is the contest, and to the side that is winning while Gray is losing.

Passion and Death of the Author

It might almost be said that in addition to allegory, DeLillo is after apotheosis for his author: at first Bill Gray's exemplary—and undefined—life looks like the life of a literary saint. The forces threatening to destroy him and, more importantly, his secret (which is his novel), and the heroic gesture he makes of substituting himself for another writer, suggest a kind of altruistic, Christlike grandeur. The strange pain in his side (which leads to his ultimate death, it is implied) recalls the stab wound of the crucified savior. But Gray's life saves nobody, least of all himself. The world is not redeemed by his new book, and his intervention does not rescue his writer, kidnapped by Beiruti terrorists. But there is an allegorical logic that compels DeLillo's hero to see this extreme pilgrimage as the best solution, and it is the logic that he tries to set forth by means of the evocation of Karen's Moonie wedding and Brita's photography. For these are the two characters with whom the book begins and ends, respectively.

The Moonie wedding ceremony combines the two themes of crowd and image from the outset. As Karen is getting married, she wonders whether she ever imagined she would be "in a stadium in New York, photographed by thousands of people? There may be as many people taking pictures as there are brides and grooms. One of them for every one of us" (10). Even though they participate in a mass wedding, each of the people getting married has family members who faithfully take pictures as if it were a private wedding ceremony in which their loved one could be seen. It is her father, Rodge, who "watches and muses. When the Old God leaves the world, what happens to all the unexpended faith?" (6–7) The taking of pictures along with the mass wedding ceremony itself are both expressions of a faith, and at the same time, they both express tribal solidarity and the potential for violence that accompanies it. The terrorists at the novel's end wear pictures of dead friends and family members—as memorials and also as incitement to further vengeance. Indeed, Brita, with whom the novel ends, is treated as a violative force, an aggressive presence who manages to get inside Gray's wilderness compound and shoot him.

Theirs is an agon not only because Gray usually shuns publicity but because, one is given to understand, insofar as her world wins, his loses. Brita's hobby is to photograph famous writers, arguing that their personality, as expressed in their faces, governs all that they write. One need not have memorized T. S. Eliot's famous line about the flight from personality to imagine what Gray thinks of such an idea. Although on the surface, Brita's hobby would seem leagues apart from Karen's credulous activities for the Moonies, the kind of cult of personality implied by this picture taking does for the mass society of the West what posters of Mao did for China. Like the Warhol paintings frequently alluded to, Brita's photos reduce their subjects to surface dimensions. What aura they superadd is of the sort that would appeal to the crowd, which desires to worship a new icon rather than absorb a complex, obscure personal vision. In this passion she recalls figures such as Mrs. Weeks Wimbush in James's "Death of the Lion," who was so interested in bagging the author that she never got what he was writing.

The link between worship of celebrity in advanced society and the more evident retrogression involved in cults will be familiar to those who have read *White Noise*. The aggressivity of both tendencies, especially the latter, is more starkly drawn here, however. For one thing, the use of the image as part of charisma is essential to any dictator, as Scott recalls when he thinks of "great leaders who regenerate their power by dropping out of sight and then staging messianic returns," such as "a photograph of Mao taken in the course of his famous nine-mile swim" in the Yangtze River (141). But while Scott makes a link from Mao to Bill Gray, who has allowed Brita to take a picture of him, the chief point seems to be contrastive: the image may be life to a manipulator of crowds but death to a writer such as Gray. "Bill had his picture taken," we are told, "because he wanted to hide more deeply. . . . Bill's picture was a death notice" (140–41). The postmodern worship of the image, always ironic of course, has perils for the writer every bit as hazardous as those of tribalism's crowds, and although the crowd in the advanced world is usually lonely, the perils in some fashion are of a similar sort as well.

According to DeLillo, it turns out that Walter Benjamin was probably wrong after all in his essay "The Work of Art in the Age of Mechanical Reproduction," in which he argues that the decline of the unique work of art or of craft heralds the waning of a work of art's aura as well. On the contrary, the rise of mass reproduction for both visual and aural image has ensured that a new kind of aura, akin to the "manufactured awe" DeLillo speaks of in *White Noise,* will accompany the growth of these phenomena. One thinks here of those audiocassettes of the ayatollah's voice that became sacred objects of the coming Muslim revolution in Iran: the imam's chaotic funeral, so unlike Bill Gray's own unmourned and unnoticed demise toward the novel's end, provides one of the book's vignettes. The book dramatizes two reasons for this perverse fact.

First of all, the very process of revelation through imagery—the photo of Mao swimming, for instance—relies also on a dance of concealment. Every politician—indeed, every performer—knows the danger of overexposure. Gray's own stature as a writer, growing as his public persona fades, attests to this need to retain mystery (or at least its modern cousin, secrecy) in the figures revealed by those images. Second, the publicity mechanism itself becomes another proof of the power of the aura, though of an opposing sort to that of the singular object. One way to think of it is as a process whereby extension replaces depth. The artisanal object was, and still is, revered largely because of the inward reaches of its rich elaboration, the fact that it has perfections that nobody can see, not even in principle. By contrast, the aura prized by the age of postmodern celebrity, and the electronic version of tribal power as well, resides in the sheer extension, the profusion of representation. That a person can be so widely known and not be exhausted in being known—that the primal fear that an image of one will steals one's life goes unrealized—is central to this second kind of awe. The apparatus of spectacle itself promotes this awe, which rests on the direct relation to masses of people: to fame that is more than *Fama,* or rumor.

It is fair to say that Bill Gray's phobia about publicity is more than a modernist Great Refusal, then. Noting the first reason why aura is retained in the age of spectacle, one could argue that Gray doubts his own ability to show forth properly. The concealment may be his only way of keeping his aura intact; revelation could bring an end to his enchantment in a "shitpile of hopeless prose" (159). He is the victim of an electronic leveling, no doubt, but equally he is prey to self-doubt. The reader, be it said, has no notion whether this self-doubt is justified, since the work itself is never cited—just that he has it. His objection to the age of media hype is hard to fault: it is, at least in America, the ultimate way of contrasting the deep to the superficial, as I have noted throughout. However, his motives seem complicated, and not solely heroic, for going into exile.

How much does Gray will his own demise? DeLillo plays with this possibility, never giving the reader enough leeway to decide the issue very closely. But Gray himself is hit by a car in Athens (something one can indeed have done without much deliberation), and then, having more or less diagnosed the severity of his injury, declines to have it treated. We will revisit the scene of diagnosis, since it is the most pregnant scene of Gray's story. For the moment, let us observe just these facts and how they suggest Gray's complicity in his own victimhood. The only remaining issue is whether these gestures are intended to suggest Gray's further complicity in the larger writerly predicament that gives rise to this endgame.

One register of this complicity, curiously enough, occurs with one of the few instances of personal reminiscence, deep memory returning to the childhood world of the author, before he became an author. As his deathward delirium proceeds, Gray thinks back to something he always used to see as a child in a haberdasher's store he frequented with his father: "Measure your head before ordering" (216). There are several suggestive valences for this phrase, given Gray's own self-doubts: his possible feeling that he should have better measured his own head, or spiritual capacities, before ordering his career as he has, for instance. At the same time, the fact that what he most vividly remembers is already a written instruction solidifies Gray's identity as someone who thinks in literary terms (quite literally). But in another sense, his memory underscores the inseparability of individual sensibility from the mass-cultural past. This phrase, arising from the impersonal world of commerce, calls back an era now lost—an era when men wore hats, to be exact, but by synecdoche a much richer association with a bygone postwar landscape. The interchangeability of hat styles prefigures that loss of individuality Gray undergoes in death, as his very passport is taken to be someone else's substitute identity. But more than prophecy, this final memory is also a straightforward coming to terms with the humble sources of artistic inspiration, modernist or otherwise. Not only artistic image but even artistic endeavor depends intimately on the already commodified surround of impressions and clichés that are its raw material: Gray's irreplaceable head unavoidably confounded with infinitely replaceable hat sizes.

Thus does Bill Gray's final gesture invite a double reading. As he goes beyond his previous obscurity by opting for oblivion, the manner of his going implies a heroic self-abnegation, on the order of Ambrose Bierce's famous disappearance. Like Bierce, he chooses to open himself to hazard in the cause of helping another writer wrong-footed by tribal politics. But it also suggests an act of evasion, a retreat more profound than the one he has already embarked on in upstate New York. He wishes to escape the unbearable lightness of being postmodern, which kills writers with the kindness of celebrity, along with the unbearable weight of ancient tribal disputes, wherein writers may be killed without kindness (as witness the Rushdie affair that provides part of *Mao II*'s inspiration). The gesture of leave-taking has the effect of convincing us that the writer for whom Gray is a sort of synecdoche is being victimized by these forces and so is simply their enemy. Yet as the vigil kept by Scott and Karen indicates, a writer can attract a cult following just as Mao and Moon do; it just happens to be smaller. The cult of the writerly is arguably more fragile than those based on the apparatus of entertainment celebrity or the loyalty of the tribe. Yet cult it is, and a writer's desire for exquisite sentences may not be all that different from the shaman's desire for the most powerful incantation. Further, the writer must be actively complicit with the machinery of publicity and the aura of priesthood both if he or she is to flourish as a writer, and it is a complicity the writer acknowledges, however unwillingly. Bill Gray, after all, consents to have his picture taken, although it is close to his last official act.

Above and beyond all of that is the interior doubt of the author himself. Whether because of the aforementioned complicity or because of sheer limitation, Gray clearly sees himself as at the end of his potential as a writer. Under those circumstances, his decision to embark on his vanishing act in the Middle East can be seen both as heroism, whereby the author sacrifices himself in the knowledge that he is no longer of artistic use, and as cowardice, whereby the author prefers, like Jean Renoir's aristocrat in "La grande illusion," the "bonne solution" of death to a life of continuing, losing battle with his text. Paul Valéry's remark that a poem is "never finished, it is only abandoned" applies here with special force; in abandoning his text, to which he has given so much of himself, the author sees no alternative to abandoning his life, which his text has perforce become.

The Author as a Character

Considering the crowning gesture of Bill Gray's literary career—which is to say his very life—thus leads to an inevitable impasse. There is no way to interpret his death as fully willed, a Hemingway-like suicide, since it needs a random incident, the car accident in Athens, to happen. Further, even if the death is accorded the status of a conscious gesture, which it arguably becomes, every attempt to assign a moral valence, whether of heroism or of cowardice, to this gesture comes up against its contradiction. But of course, the only basis on which any of these issues arise comes not from Gray himself, strictly speaking, but from an audience of people he meets on the way to Lebanon. The diagnosis on which he relies is not self-devised—Gray in fact "authors" very few aspects of his nonwritten life, it seems—but is granted him by one of his listeners.

This scene of diagnosis detains us, for it is also a scene of storytelling: the only glimpse one has into Gray as the maker of a fiction. Moreover, his audience is an ideal listenership, supplying just the interpretation the narrative demands. This almost perfect sphere enclosing storyteller and listeners is as secure as anything created by Charlie Marlow aboard the *Nellie*, and it serves as the last contact Gray will have with the world as a maker of fictions. The appearance of perfect communication is, however, only partial, for the audience thinks Gray has made a fiction (and he has), but does not know that this fiction also refers in some measure to Gray himself.

He insists that he is constructing a fictional problem that requires the advice of the other passengers on board with him: "'I'm doing a passage, see, where no amount of digging through books can substitute for half a minute's chat with an expert'" (206). He then proceeds to describe what has in fact happened to him in Athens in order to glean a diagnosis from one of their number: "'The only plausible recourse is a doctor'" (209). All agree that sending this character on a cruise is "totally implausible," as he is likely to die: probably of a lacerated liver, in one strong reading. But what has actually happened is that the other passengers are collaborating with Gray in constructing this scenario of injury and death; he has given them elements for the story and they have molded it on that basis. His chief reason for doing it appears to be pragmatic: he wants to decide whether to go for a doctor. (He never does carry out that decision, although he thinks of doing it a couple of times.) What is important here is that, given his reticence about the autobiographical in all of its forms, Gray chooses even here to present his malady as that of a character he has made up. The author has revealed himself as indeed an author, albeit not the sort one sees on TV; but this is done only to assign his own quandary to a fictional character. As with assenting to the photograph, Gray reveals himself only to conceal himself more thoroughly in the end.

It is as if Gray has sought solace, as he is dying, in becoming a fictional character. His ideal audience assists him in this illusion. And, of course, it is tempting to see *Mao II* itself as DeLillo's attempt to render his own dilemmas as a writer by creating a fictional persona that, like the one Gray creates, is actually a means of diagnosing his own malady. This is, I think, a temptation to refuse for several reasons. First of all, and least compelling, is the fact that DeLillo's own life does not much resemble Gray's in what detail we know of it. He does shun publicity, but not to the pathological degree that his character does; a life in Westchester County with an investment banker hardly constitutes seclusion, at least no more than suburban life in general does. But more than that, the figure of Gray, already pseudonymous within the novel and blatantly allegorical in any event, is best seen less as the writer's version of his own role than as the public's version of a certain sort of writer's role.

With this point we return to the representational question that began this chapter: to what degree can the artist paint his or her own portrait in the age of mechanical reproduction? DeLillo may have answered that question very indirectly, by sidestepping it. The artist figure who is the character in *Mao II* is more a contemporary dream of the modernist author: the cantankerous and rectitudinous hermit guarding his idiosyncratic sensibility from the intrusive publicity apparatus. The doubts, obsessions, and self-pity that plague Gray may well plague DeLillo also—indeed, may plague any recent writer—but his starkly heroic profile, and the swashbuckling mission on which he embarks only to disappear, suggest how the very form of his being fulfills a now established audience expectation for a certain sort of highbrow or "difficult" writer. The hall of mirrors cannot be penetrated, for Gray is a presence formed by the public's own needs as much as by any psychic gratification of the author. Just as Miss Lonelyhearts falls to dreaming, only to dream his readers' dream of him, so DeLillo, employing various conventions drawn from the lives of Samuel Beckett, Graham Greene, and even Thomas Pynchon (whose admiring blurb graces the hardcover dust jacket, by the way), creates a figure who can serve as the Alienated Artist without our seeing so much as a line of his writing. The significance of his prose never being cited goes in this direction, too.

In one sense we return with this text to the sorts of issues Henry James raised a century before in his artist tales; but there is an important distinction. The portraits James paints are almost certainly those that occurred to him, not those that he draws from the publicly available catalogue of highbrow writers. DeLillo, by contrast, has a hundred years more of exactly the sort of modernist alienation with which we have been dealing. As a result, the stock of clichés for such a role has accreted and entered the awareness of educated people, so that now the individual who opts out of the commodified world of media hype has his or her own image. Within the narrative itself, Scott is fully aware of the fame potential of the author's very reclusion: "after a time [subsequent to Bill's disappearance] he might take the photographs to New York and meet with Brita and choose the pictures that would appear. But the manuscript would sit, and word would travel, and the pictures would appear, a small and deft selection, one time only, and word would build and spread, and the novel would stay right there, collecting aura and force, deepening old Bill's legend, undyingly" (224). Interestingly, Scott sees himself as guardian of a cultic legend quite narrowly, rather than a profiteer from sales. Nevertheless, he understands the degree to which Gray's very escape from the media aggression has given him a profile within the media universe, just as a DeLillo reader knows what an alienated highbrow author should do and say. Since the portrait goes so little beyond those allegorical traits, it is safe to say that Bill Gray does not disappoint in those basic terms. His author escapes into a fiction, just as Gray does. But unlike him, his author has constructed a fiction not to diagnose his own problems so much as to answer a certain demand on the part of his reader, and perhaps to diagnose the reasons behind that demand.

Forming this argument runs the risk of reducing the Bill Gray character to a phantasm of the public, a lieutenant for a certain romantic—or more precisely, modernist—version of the artist whose Joycean silence and exile is not quite matched by cunning. The echo of *White Noise*'s "Mr. Gray" lends indeed further glamour to that temptation, since a simulacral embodiment of stoic modernist refusal would be an appropriately high-cultural bookend to an equally simulacral embodiment of mass culture. But complications have to be respected.

It is safe, for example, to guess that Gray's self-mistrust, his phobia in the face of his own project (anthropomorphized in the Frankensteinian form of a "naked humped creature with filed-down genitals" [92]), his procrastination, even his principled absence from the academic vineyards of Creative Writing—all of these features can legitimately be drawn from what (little) is known about DeLillo's own experience and outlook.[2] Even if they are not, though, I would argue that given the high seriousness and pathos with which the main character is invested, he is presented sympathetically, if not quite from within. There is a resonance to the muted bitterness of Bill Gray's retrospection that is not owing, one feels, to memories of Samuel Beckett alone. The larger point is that the writer in *Mao II*, regardless of intention, has become enmeshed in a public role, just as surely as if he had stayed in the public eye. Hence the iconographic status that so appealed to his agent: a self-exiled writer reading the works of a hostage writer.

Moreover, Gray's choice of this mode of being was already part of the available menu of the late-twentieth-century West. After Joyce and

Beckett, Salinger and Pynchon, William Gaddis and William Burroughs, the game of absent presence is an almost stereotypical modernist gesture. A society of spectacle must have its darkness, some secrecy against which to define itself, just as Western bourgeois democracy needs its terrorism, the successor to Gray's man of letters as society's enemy of choice. (When Frank Lentricchia obligingly calls DeLillo a "bad citizen," taking columnist George Will's accusation as a compliment, he effectively places his writer into company with Bill Gray[3].) It may also help that in each case, the antagonist is sure to fail against overwhelming odds, nobly in the case of the writer, basely in the case of the terrorist. Gray's death in obscurity deeper than had prevailed even during his life satisfies the schadenfreude of a society that has always resented the principled eccentrics it sometimes claims to honor.

There is nothing so conformist, somehow, as American culture's images of rebellion, and Bill Gray's great refusal fits that tradition. DeLillo plays with the heroic potential of that role but ultimately relies, I think, more on the parodic tendencies the role calls forth. Gray's courage is praiseworthy, but his martyrdom itself, owing more to drink and happenstance than to terrorism, has more than a touch of the absurd about it. Gray lets his listeners select the way his fictional character's story will end, and they are prophetic. By contrast, DeLillo constructs for his hero the sort of end, exilic and anonymous, that modernist and postmodernist readers would expect for their doomed hero—but for all of that, there is little danger that author will follow suit after character in this regard. Bill Gray, saint and martyr, sets no example to his author any more than he does to his readers, for the ideal for which he seemingly risks his life is doubly flawed: he cannot have beneficent influence on affairs without being published, and to be published he must truck with the Charlie Eversons of the world; he must be a presence as well, which means he has to let his image go forth. Beyond that, the influence writers strive for is always reminiscent of that formerly reserved for tribal chieftains and shamans: literary remnants of the bardic. For all these reasons, and not solely external practicalities, Gray's integrity, which has its own charm for a certain readership, is doomed to ineffectuality.

But at another level of abstraction, the fascination in *Mao II* is with how the cult of Gray answers certain deep needs of the audience, just as the cults of Mao and of Sun Myung Moon do for their adepts. Gray mentions more than once that the novelist, in his conception, is in eternal competition with the terrorist. They are fighting over the same territory in a way, it is true, because each has been designated as ordinary postmodern life's freelance enemy: individuals against the system. We dishonor terrorists, by and large, and honor serious writers, after our fashion; but in the end, each type fulfills a certain role as places against which to define normality, as guardians in their differing ways of secrecy in the age of publicity. But these very roles, to reiterate, are publicly defined. If a serious writer aspires to the status of absolute individuality, as Gray seems to, such a dilemma has endless frustrations. Perhaps for one in such a position, some variant of his self-sacrifice would be the only way out. But if a writer were fashioning the very allegory of Gray as a way of dramatizing a role the postmodern public prepares and encourages for serious authors, then his is better read as a cautionary tale, one whose outcome only brings to light the deathward trajectory on which the public is just as happy to see its literati pointed. To accept the Manichaean oppositions of Bill Gray—word against image, the deep secret (a much-repeated word in this text) against aggressive publicity, the individual against the mass—is to tempt the fate of Gray as well. The author will not follow the character to that fate because by means of that character he has analyzed too well the popular image, the simulacrum of the great author, that audiences feel compelled so often to fashion. Like Gray on the ship, DeLillo has collaborated with the educated readership in fashioning his dying author. But unlike Gray, and crucially, he has used the story of his dying author to diagnose not himself, but his age, and what his age would literally make of people such as he.

Part Three

Epilogue

chapter ten

Concluding Unsystematic Speculation: Within the Crisis of No Crisis

W ith the vanishing of the enigmatic Bill Gray, the story that starts out with Henry James's beleaguered artist figures comes full circle. Although his literary lion was hunted and bagged by people more interested in capturing the famous man than his obscurer meaning, at least a Neil Paraday escapes in death. It is not clear that Gray will have even that much luck, since DeLillo has already alerted the reader to the publicity value of a writer's demise, with his evocation of those black-bordered newspaper announcements by which publishers announce the decease of their suddenly more valuable authors. In the world publicity built, it appears that disappearance itself has become merely a vanishing act. There is to be no exit from the infernal machine.

The world presented in *Mao II* provides a perverse, paranoid twist on the Warholian dream: here once famous, even an author is hard put to return to anonymity even for fifteen minutes. In the dance of celebrity, as Jackie Kennedy's failed attempts to guard her privacy proved, avoidance is at least as intriguing as approach. And Bill Gray is no Jackie Kennedy. Yet in some ways the most striking, and least probable, aspect of the DeLillo novel is its assumption that a mere author is fit to attain this level of American celebrity in the first place. The Mailer niche is not very wide; even if Mailer were willing to share it, there would not be enough room. Pynchon and J. D. Salinger are practically the only literary authors who would have to work very hard to shun the crowds of the present hour, and they are already of an older generation. Anonymity is more generally the lot even of the "famous" authors of our day.

What may be more symptomatic of the state of letters today, however, lies not in Gray's failing attempts to become a recluse but in his strange desire to reenact the grand gestures of Ernest Hemingway, André Malraux,

171

and George Orwell. It is not clear how much of DeLillo's irony attends Gray on his way, but I find this need to plunge into the destructive element of political intrigue the useful symptom of a literary nostalgia that extends far beyond DeLillo or his hero. That is the nostalgia for a crisis.

Amid the many and varied essays one reads these days deploring the sad estate to which our cultural life has fallen as the century turns, it has yet to be noted that the element that most inspirited literary life in the mid-century—and to be sure much other life as well—was the very sense of world-historical Western crisis that infected the interwar years. Looking back on the kinds of esprit that motivated an F. R. Leavis to call for a renovation of aspirational culture, or even John Crowe Ransom to fashion the American New Criticism, it was easy to take color from the gathering anxiety of Western civilization in that era. This sense of crisis helps a literary culture in two ways: it provides additional urgency to the project of fortifying a culture, as mentioned, and it provides cultural material that must be processed somehow by the literary establishment.[1]

Postwar American critics have on occasion expressed a certain regret that the solidarity of mid-century writers, that sense of an aesthetic mission that was also a more conventional social mission, has long dissipated, to be replaced by the melancholy and backbiting with which we are all familiar.[2] What is not as likely to be enunciated is the backdrop of Western conflict that fused these elements into a sense of mission in the first place.

The speculation to which the title of this chapter refers is roughly this, then: that in the United States (in possible contrast to nations with a more established and commonly accepted role for literature in the public sphere), serious literature is only a major factor in the culture when the educated stratum of the country undergoes a radical disorientation so strong as to jar its customary assumptions. Of course, this happens only occasionally, though it has occurred perhaps three times in the twentieth century, as mentioned. More typically, the literature is decidedly marginal to American life and thus feels its subjection to the market with special keenness.[3] The usual avenues of transmission for literature are two: school (the academy, chiefly, though additionally if decreasingly secondary schools) and "middlebrow" cultural outlets such as book clubs or reviews and other pieces in the higher journalism of the major media.[4] The growth of electronic media in the postwar years has further shelved the literary, whose stock in trade is inevitably words, not images. Some think the computer revolution will eventually prove a boon to books, but according to publishing houses this has yet to happen. It probably has made it easier for enthusiasts of a given author or books in general to congregate: I was surprised when researching

Walker Percy's *Moviegoer* (1960) at how many listservs there were on that author, for instance. But the aggregate help to be expected from the Internet for literature (as opposed to pornography, perhaps) has not been dramatic.

The only times when literate America turns spontaneously to literature for some help in puzzling things out is when the old stories are not enough to sustain belief: dislocations of spiritual assumptions such as war and depression, as at mid-century, or war and breakdown in larger norms, as in the sixties and seventies. Unexpected novels (and much more rarely poetry) suddenly get discovered and elevated to cultic status; people actually address life questions to literary figures (one saw this as late as the seventies, albeit with mixed results). The search for gurus, guides to the perplexed, and cultural horse whisperers commences.

It does not generally commence right when the caesura occurs but after it has worked its way through and down into the culture, though there are some exceptions to this (the Philip Roth of *Portnoy's Complaint* [1967] and after had all but inaugurated the sixties, his most famous satire having been published in the same year as the Summer of Love). Characteristically, it takes the better part of a decade for the literary returns to come in from some major shift. World War I and its answering postwar cultural echo, which George Trow correctly suggests was the most thoroughly "processed" such moment in the preceding century, was responded to by literary culture by the close of the 1920s, mostly by Hemingway and Fitzgerald, but also by Willa Cather and e. e. cummings, Sherwood Anderson, and many others. Although the mid-century war and depression moment was less directly processed by literature, no doubt, it is nonetheless instructive to realize just how many careers in literature seem to have come out of the immediate postwar period: Norman Mailer and Gore Vidal both wrote directly of the war, but John Cheever did also; Malcolm Lowry, Paul Bowles, Ralph Ellison, and William Burroughs all owe to the war and its aftermath for their formation, as does John Hawkes. The sixties can boast Roth, Thomas Pynchon and Don DeLillo, Tim O'Brien and Robert Coover, Donald Barthelme and Kurt Vonnegut, whose most serious book, *Slaughterhouse Five,* also treats World War II.[5]

In times of tranquility, it is as useless for literary people to complain of their dependence on the marketplace and its promotional capacities as it is for soldiers in peacetime to bemoan their status as wards of the state. When received wisdom or the routines of the culture seem suddenly inadequate to the events that have overtaken the society, educated people may turn to writers in conscious or instinctive desperation. We have seen how uncannily Trow's caesurae will yield up the inception of brilliant literary careers. (Even William Faulkner, whom we probably associate more with the thirties, wrote his first novels in the postwar era and was himself profoundly affected by that war and its aftermath.)

In the absence of a crisis within the culture, something obvious and shattering to the spirit, the marketplace mechanisms are all that there is. America, unlike its European and even English-speaking cousins, has little that endures in its tradition outside of the workings of the market, and certainly no deference to the needs of artistic elites in any form.[6] The cultural patrimony is scarcely of interest even to the upper-middle classes and the rich, who would in another society be its likeliest champions. (Oddly, one will often find more respect for these matters among the "lower orders," perhaps in the mistaken belief that familiarity with their workings is a mark of the well off.) And when the prosperous folk wish to proclaim their lavish largesse, it is not the literary field they tend to patronize but the visual arts.

What this means for serious writers is that in order to flourish, literature usually has to be "sold" as part of the middlebrow market, which entails accepting the terms of that market rather than expecting readers to come to one on one's own terms. The fear of the middlebrow that analysts such as Dwight Macdonald express comes down to a fear of the inevitable kowtowing to the needs of the marketplace of readers, for whom the love of literature is decidedly not what impels them to pick up a novel. It is an understandable fear, because these analysts realize that as long as imaginative writers spend their time answering to the machine, they are to that degree less able to form an esprit of their own, which Macdonald for one felt was essential to establishing the basis for first-rate art.[7] Without this esprit, however, writers must sell themselves to the readership in guises other than the strictly literary.

One of the standard ways to sell literature to a readership not undergoing a big national crisis of some sort is as helpmeet in individual crises. Hence the very popular idea of literature as in effect a thirteenth step: a kind of therapy. This idea appalls the literary community itself quite often but is one of the few ways and means to get ordinary literate people to actually buy and maybe even read serious fiction. It is also, more narrowly, a way to market fiction to its most likely gender demographic, which is female.

Oprah's Gravitas

This leads with a certain inevitability to Oprah Winfrey's book club. It is now late and lamented, especially among publishing houses, for which a recommendation by her was a godsend. But while it endured, the books it publicized enjoyed sales of a magnitude rarely seen by the high of brow. Admittedly, not all of her selections qualified as highbrow in the first place, though a striking number of them were, in common parlance, quite hard.[8] Her experiment was probably the first such ambitious attempt to use a mass forum to elevate taste since the days of Clifton Fadiman. But it is fair to say that central to her approach was a certain view of what fiction should be for, in both senses: the right positions to take and also the right effect to have on the reader's psyche. Literature under the Oprah regime may not have been reduced to chicken soup for the soul, but for some people it came uncomfortably close to that formula.[9]

It is in this milieu that poor Jonathan Franzen landed with a plop in 2001, when his book *The Corrections* was selected for Oprah's book club and the author invited to appear on the talk show Winfrey hosts. Then he let slip some ungallant remarks about how the prospect made him feel (being a writer, he was of course ambivalent). When Winfrey got wind of this ambivalence, she reacted unambivalently: she canceled his appearance, though she allowed the selection itself to stand. (Oprah may have known just enough about literary people not to allow them to say that she had changed her judgment of a book's quality because of a falling-out with its author.) This flap got a surprising amount of publicity, particularly considering it was going on during the period of the September 11 attacks. In a way, I suppose it should be encouraging that there was so much interest in what was, at least on one side, a literary feud of sorts.

What was not so encouraging was the response of most literary people, and particularly publishers, to the controversy: they sided completely with the enraged monarch Oprah. To some degree, this was an easy call on the surface. By accepting her invitation and then voicing misgivings about her show, Franzen was violating an obvious law of hospitality, and on those terms he is clearly in the wrong. What was discouraging was the refusal to engage the larger issues the controversy raises. Franzen after all was only saying out loud what not a few of Oprah's bookish guests have surely said behind her back; there are problems with marketing fiction as a form of therapy (the chief problem being that it isn't). But the publishing houses are so eager to avoid offending Oprah Winfrey as to suggest a disproportionate dependency on her good graces, almost as if they need her sufferance to continue to survive. And this was the other thing that was discouraging about the furious reaction in favor of Oprah.[10]

The glaring gender divide in the controversy—pale male DeLillo protégé Franzen versus feminist multicultural heroine Winfrey—cannot fail to call forth the inevitable comparisons to Andreas Huyssen's famous discussion of the modernists' tendency to render their hated alter ego of mass culture and kitsch in female form.[11] Franzen, it was darkly suggested, was not just a snob but a retrograde male as well. This may well be, and it is even possible that his nervous anticipation of his *Oprah* experience was as much about fear that he would lose some male readers (which could have been the assumed base for his book) as it was about any vulgarization of his work or persona.[12] I would not want to assume that Franzen could not possibly have a misogynistic streak. But my suspicion is that his fear of the feminine is actually a subtler fear of what, for good or ill, has come to be meant by the feminine in literary circles: fiction as therapy.

If it takes a major break in the culture to force a distracted and complacent citizenry to take a second look, or indeed a first one, at matters literary, then the obvious question is how literature that aspires to any complication or awareness of life's problems may make its way in ordinary times. And one provisional answer would be as therapy, as a kind of ministry to the reading wounded. If Oprahphobia means anything among highbrows, it is this distaste for the attitude that takes up a novel in the same spirit as one would a self-help manual or a celebrity's up-from-under memoir about cocaine addiction. There is of course nothing wrong with taking serious literature in this vein, just as there is nothing wrong with analyzing *South Park* as if it were *Paradise Lost*. But among people who still see intrinsic value for the literary as such, it will inevitably be seen as a coarsening, or at least as the addition of an external utilitarian goal to a process that insists above all on itself.[13] How to maintain that distance which lends enchantment in the age of television, whose images are usable and also disposable?[14] Franzen's pudency in the face of Oprah's seduction was awkward and ill mannered, but the predicament he was in is positively Jamesian.[15] Having said that, one has to add that it is a predicament many novelists wish were afflicting them, which accounts for the perversely pro-Oprah reaction in the literary world.[16]

The Oprah flap demonstrates something else that may connect to a larger fact making the present era a more formidable antagonist to the serious writer—indeed, to the serious as such—than was the case in the past. Some have seen Winfrey's book club as only the latest in a long line of high vulgarization, the ongoing process by which guides to the written word bring the larger public into the sacred precincts of art. With apologies to Jacques Barzun, one could almost see Oprah Winfrey as being in the tradition of Clifton Fadiman himself—or more precisely, as having been, as one gathers she has recently suspended the book club.[17]

There is, of course, another, possibly more significant aspect to this controversy, one that will open my discussion out to some final considerations of the situation in which fiction writers find themselves. The reason for Oprah's immense sway, and the explanation for the way publishers and not a few writers united with her in casting out her ingrate author, is something that very much separates her from the middlebrow conduits of a gentler time: she is on television.

What makes the nostalgia for a crisis seem vain and fruitless is not so much that the culture is incapable of undergoing one: if history is any guide, it is likely to sooner rather than later, regardless of the obviously complicated question of whether September 11, for instance, qualifies as a cultural crisis or as an unprecedentedly horrific media event. The deeper issue is whether the United States will be in a position to even know of a literary establishment to turn to should it feel the need to sort things out in any future crisis of culture. After all, in the three caesurae that Trow speaks of, the only one fully processed by the "literary elite" would have been World War I; "the sixties" have been almost completely colonized by electronic media (and in the view of some, were made possible largely through those same media in the first place). Increasingly, people who wished to "make sense" of Vietnam went to *Apocalypse Now* (or for those of another persuasion maybe *Rambo*) rather than opening Michael Herr or Tim O'Brien. As we all now live in the house that electronic media built, the literary realm has faded from view in recent decades. It could be that the vast public relations "pseudo-environments" with which the last century ended are enough to process whatever shocks the cultural system may have to endure; or else the white noise of our fictional media and PR universe is so all-pervasive as to produce its own effect of reality, or rather unreality, regardless of what trauma may try to thrust through the scrim of fantasy. If so, the culminating achievement of the age of TV could well be the creation of a near-total second skin of vivid illusion, an almost impermeable security blanket with just a few holes in it for History to be glimpsed, shuddered at, and once again abjured.

It is of course a matter of opinion and conjecture whether or how much we have become addled or our ethical judgment impaired by the way the publicity machine has elaborated itself since the Second World War. It is also true that one can level almost any charge against television and people will be predisposed to believe it. Just as forms of culture require a place and a name, so TV is needed to give the new regime of publicity that place, that name. But where is that place? And what does that name really signify?

Staring into the Intense Inane

A thick description of the role TV plays in our lives would stray well beyond the confines of this speculative conclusion. Still, it is hard to ignore such a full embodiment of mass publicity, one so powerful in its influence over our lives. With each year, we hear of political rituals and contests shaped with the medium in mind; most of the games we are shown, both professional and amateur, have altered their rules to conform to the informal but stringent requirements of broadcast. Even computerization and the World Wide Web, a supposed rebuke to passive spectatorship and a return to reading, are compromise formations, co-existing with all of the streaming, graphics, and CD elements that render the computer more of a screen than a library. But in what way does this medium with which Americans spend an approximate half dozen hours a day of their waking lives infringe upon the audience and expectations for, say, the great American novel, assuming the will to write it persists?

The shortest way to state the harm it does is to say that TV does two things simultaneously, and these things paradoxically reinforce each other: it represents the culmination and continuation of the ongoing Western technological project of rendering the objects of perception with heightened effect of reality, and it also blurs the line between truth and illusion. On the former, suffice it to say that people still imagine that something seen on the screen is "realer" than the same thing rendered in words. I have taught several adaptations courses in which, when asked whether film or text was better, the students invariably opted for film, because the ambiguities of the written format were solved and the result directly presented for the viewer's delectation. The latter, which is the accompanying derealization, takes slightly longer to explain. I will confine myself to two major things that TV does to the elements of serious literary narrative. The substitution of image for word, as already mentioned, does in much of the cachet of the "literary" itself. What of the "narrative" and the "serious?"

To take up the narrative question first, I note a couple of important observations made by John Ellis, who is a British media critic and veteran of TV. He points out that, unlike even the cinema, TV has essentially a brief assumed attention span for its viewer: the short sequence of less than ten-minutes' length, known as a segment, is its basic unit. Although the narrative for a given show does provide a kind of enchainment for the segments of that given program, the more important thing for television is the repetition and novelty of formula across shows within a series. The point is that the short-term unit (i.e., the segment) and the long-term (i.e., the series) are neither of them primarily concerned with the "story" as an organic whole in the way a novel or a movie would be. Presumably this is due mostly to advertising necessity, which involves getting the viewer to return after the commercials (and ideally to see the commercials while waiting to return) and then to return after the intervening week (to see the program's next round of commercials).[18] The phenomenology of the series format, or for that matter of the brief segment, is not that of a three-act play, for instance, which is still the template for most motion pictures. If a series, whose ultimate form is the serial or soap opera, resembles any other narrative at all, it may be the roman-fleuve more than anything else: "closure and finality is [sic] not a central feature of TV narration. . . . Repetition in the TV narrative occurs at the level of the series: formats are repeated, situations recur week after week."[19]

There is little room in this form of narrative—an extraordinarily weak form, it would appear—for the sort of tension and resolution, to say nothing of the heavy symbolic scumbling and thematic undertow, to which serious writers like to subject their material. The story for a given night is a string on which the beads that are its segments are to be arrayed. This strategy militates against extreme emotional investment in any narrative by the viewer, as does the requirement that the commercials must be held supreme in the viewer's attention.[20] Such a form of narration makes for a strange venue in which to make more than the crudest attempts at continuity and helps to explain why the typical one-hour teleplay format in the United States, the *West Wing* or even *Sopranos* drama, tends to have not one thread of plot but three or more. It also explains why the occasional shows that are designated as cathartic are so often set aside as "very special" episodes of *Friends*. In sum, though, the relative slackness in the continuity of story within any given episode of TV was obvious years ago to movie director Alfred Hitchcock, who gave the game away by saying, "Unlike cinema, . . . with television there is no time for *suspense,* you can only have *surprise.*"[21]

The reason the effects of years of TV viewing might be to dull the sensibility for novel reading is that this form of storytelling is based largely on surprise, or better yet shocks to the viewer's system: small enough not to offend, but big enough to keep interest and wonder, if not suspense. This is not generally the way a novel or film works; a viewership ill suited to narrative would seem to result from six hours a day of watching this parade of little segments, even when loosely bundled into an episode.[22]

But the above detail about the centrality of the commercials leads to the other main effect of the emphasis on television: its dethronement of seriousness. Ellis notes this fact in a number of registers. First of all, the traditional

Western distinction between fictional and nonfictional modes of narration is one he claims inappropriate to TV, where the "distinctive regime of fictional narration . . . owes much to its non-fictional modes."[23] Although it is probably specious to assume that the factual is more "serious" than the fictional, what is conveyed by this convergence of modes (not to mention the fact that both are found to be coming from the same source in the house) is that neither form is all that worthy of keeping separate from the other. Put simply, both fiction and nonfiction are chiefly branded as guests in TV's house and in the viewer's home.

This guest status means that nothing on TV is allowed to have too much consequence. Just as the visual field of TV is more flimsy and unfurnished than that of film, designed for "the look and the glance rather than the gaze," so the use of sound to "drag viewers back to looking at the set" presumes a viewer already treating the medium "casually rather than concentratedly."[24] The faint aura of the disreputable that still clings to TV (which it nowadays wears like a badge of honor, with sleazy and sordid reality programs and celebrity boxing) has always meant that it must constantly tug at the viewer to stay tuned: "Broadcast TV does not habitually offer incentives to start watching TV; instead, it offers them to people already watching TV: trailers, promotion material, announcements. The incitement to watch is part of TV's own internal activity."[25] In addition to advertisements, then, and channels such as MTV whose building blocks of programming consist in promotional material known as music videos, one confronts numerous forays into self-promotion by the station or network itself. Everything on TV seems to be there to promote something else, to be ancillary or utilitarian to some other goal. The incitement to watch that Ellis speaks of suggests the well-earned insecurity of the medium: it knows it does not speak for itself—or rather, that it has to. But it also points to TV's deepest function, which is to cajole and pander. This very promotional imperative means that it is publicity in its purest form, publicity that to do its work must not be overwhelmed by any merely internal content.[26] Ellis is blunt about the half trance in which TV is generally viewed and the care taken by programmers to avoid extremes of emotion. The famous irony dished out by so many television "personalities" such as David Letterman is as attributable to the needs of the form as to their own individual talents.[27]

The mood that TV tends to require is a mild receptivity, a spun-out fascination of sorts, without any high-stakes involvement or overinvestment in any particular event or story presented on the medium. The medium above all promotes itself and the goods and services of its advertisers, but promotion is the goal overriding viewer satisfaction. How often, after all, does TV even deliver on its promise of entertainment? If we think about it, a fully satisfying encounter with an episode or broadcast is actually threatening, since the viewer may feel sated and turn to something else. As a purveyor of pure publicity, TV is the medium most of all where the sizzle is the steak.[28] Surely one of the reasons why films are still seen as artistically superior to broadcasts, even though much that is on TV seems at least as worthy as most of the Hollywood product in theaters, is that there is a relative transactional purity to the film event. The viewer there pays money directly for that showing, and in exchange receives the movie. At least on commercial TV, by contrast, one is always aware that the real point of the show one is watching are the commercials that punctuate it. This contributes a meretricious air to even the most aspirational program.

Let us say that this description of the general attitude the viewer adopts in receiving television has validity. What import would this have for the literary arts? The briefest way of describing it is to say that when most of one's compatriots spend hours a day absorbing their stories in this form, it has to affect how they treat other narratives, and indeed the things of culture generally. If renting eyeballs to advertisers is the reason for presenting what we see on TV on any given day, and if in fact excessive seriousness as such is as great a threat to the televisual project as utter indifference would be, then it should not surprise that cultural forms that require seriousness are met increasingly with indifference.[29] On the one hand, TV demands not to be taken too seriously and is reluctant to take anything else too seriously either; on the other hand, the open-ended temporality of its series (with soap operas only the most extreme instance) lends its characters and situations some of the illusory ongoingness of life itself. Even if TV is seldom lifelike, it is ever more like life (and vice versa).

The sort of fiction that resists the easy read or gets at some underlying truth of life will find its audience harder and harder to come by in a symbolic universe governed by the (ever larger) small screen. The publicity machine is now actually represented by a machine, and it has taken over much of the landscape of culture in the United States. Is it a stretch to see a cultural landscape governed by the assumptions of mass broadcasting as a kind of vast wasteland?

Plutopia: The Value(s) of Money

The other, possibly related phenomenon that relegates serious fiction to the sidelines is that the market itself, once only one of many competing realms of public life, has in the last decade or so become truly the measure of all

things. So all-encompassing has this takeover been that the organs of publishing themselves no longer distinguish their activities from those of Proctor
and Gamble, or for that matter WorldCom. An earlier generation of publisher would be typified by Roger Straus of Farrar, Straus and Giroux, still
alive as of this writing. But his brand of edification is in short supply among
most of his coevals in the profession.[30] If book publishing houses of yore may
have regarded themselves as philanthropic foundations that also tried to
make some money, the contemporary publishing house is more likely to have
the profile of a go-go corporation that also markets books—or, in the current
idiom, "provides content." A powerful weapon in the corporate takeover of
publishing throughout the 1980s and 1990s has been that reliable howitzer
of "elitism." Whenever it has been suggested that publishing houses ought to
try to publish books that would elevate taste and knowledge, rather than
Dick Morris's memoirs or Madonna's *Sex* book, say, somebody is always on
hand to denounce any such suggestion as a sign of retrograde elitism. Who
are we, after all, to impose our judgment on others? is the characteristic
refrain. This ignores the obvious fact that inferior product that is easier to
move—what the public "really wants"—is also imposed, and that the reign
of the greatest number actually limits rather than expands the choices available to book buyers.[31] The willingness to take a chance even on adventure-
some nonfiction texts, particularly leftist ones, to say nothing of avant-garde
fiction, has diminished apace with the growth of corporate ownership of
Random House, Simon and Schuster, and other major houses.[32]

It is hard to see the paramount role of mass commercial media in dis-
tributing—and above all in presenting (i.e., selling)—such common culture as we have as less than vital in making this shift to the "values" of the
market possible. A second, little-noted factor in the collapse of aspirational
culture in the last quarter century has been the eclipse of the eastern establishment, which at mid-century still exerted considerable sway over the
self-definition of educated people. It now has very little cultural influence,
having lost ground to California and the Sunbelt, with their rather more
relaxed standards of cultivation. And since Reagan, the eastern elites themselves have begun to get out of the business of elevating taste through
patronizing the arts (except for buying the occasional Old Master). The
irony is that as the rich have waned as a source of cultural aspiration, they
have waxed in riches: they are more than ever a power elite, but more than
ever it is only power—not any ideal to accompany that power—that they
possess or are admired for having.[33]

Above all, the phenomenon that arose at century's end to validate the
ascendancy of the market was the bull market itself. Despite the occasion-

al warnings that definitions of democracy such as Thomas Friedman's "one dollar one vote" were really defining plutocracy, the general mood of the decade was that the national fate was in the hands of the stock market, and that if we were good to it (as we generally were, especially on the regulatory side), it would in turn be good to us. The magic number was "401(k)," and the fact that so many Americans possessed them was taken not as a sign that our employers were more inclined to risk our money for our retirement than to contribute theirs, but rather as a token of our decision to vote with our dollars.

This confusion of marketplace decisions with the exercise of considered popular wisdom is called "market populism" by Thomas Frank.[34] Everywhere in the nineties, the tenets, stated or implied, of market populism were employed to rule out of court any concern that the things of culture could not be reduced to the status of commodities, that the scabrous inanities of reality TV, say, were not inherently better than Marcel Proust just because more people voted with their dollars, or their minutes, for the former than the latter.[35] The language of populism is shrewdly turned to favor the most concentrated forces of mass media the country has even known. There is nothing populist about Fox TV or the *New York Post,* not to mention their owner; but the burden of proof was suddenly on the critics of such venues to prove why they were any worse than the elite media.

A superficial identification with the public, on the condition that it put up with whatever the merchants of entertainment were purveying, was used as a new way of enforcing the rule of the market: the very force that was widening the gap between rich and poor and making democracy harder rather than easier as a matter of practice. Suddenly the enemies of the people were no longer corporations, which served people as consumers: they may not have served them as citizens, but in the nineties who cared? Instead, the enemies of choice were the malefactors of great intellect, or snooty writers such as Franzen. What the romantic era, and every era since, had seen as an artist's essential obligation, to be true to an authentic vision, was now pronounced the merest self-indulgence. That artist should get a job, was the feeling—and that job is entertaining.[36]

Depriving Arnoldian high culture of its onetime status as a source of authentic cultural capital has not resulted in a postmodern unconcern about the question: in this regard, the reception of Jean Baudrillard in the United States, for example, is quite mistaken. Just as the greater the truth, the greater the libel so the greater the authenticity quotient, the better the fake. In a fascinating dialectic, it can be argued that as the mechanisms of simulation grow in scope and quality, so do the frantic searches for "authenticity" to apply to its cultural products. This authenticity does occasionally still hail from high culture, as in the automobile advertisements whose musical cues derive from Bach or Ravel, but more typically the sources are down-home and folksy. Being "down with" the music or sports of the masses has become the marker of progressiveness more than adopting a mere sociopolitical position.[37] Identifying with a literary figure is unfashionable enough as it is in the best of times, but now it is unheard of. For one thing, culture is more and more seen as a matter of direct self-adornment and activities. What is the use of defining oneself by reading, which is done in private and garners no direct praise from others?[38] If the market was the measure of all things, the amazing thing was not that publishers did not exert themselves more on behalf of their midlist writers, but that they still carried midlist writers, those supercilious freeloaders, at all.

American writers have reason to sense their marginality, and for that matter the marginality of serious discourse in general.[39] Small wonder that some may yearn for the very crisis the rest of us fear.

Don DeLillo did not delight in the crisis that arrived. His article in *Harper's* on the September 11 attack on New York and the Pentagon strikes the right note of anguish and disbelief. Still, in its assumption that the new reality created in the wake of this attack changes everything—specifically the culture of money he refers to in his first paragraph—DeLillo's treatment of the aftermath of this national trauma is strangely hopeful, or in any case premature.[40] In what does the hope reside? Perhaps as with so many other commentaries during the period after the attacks, it resides in the belief that the sheer enormity of the events would be enough to shock us back into the serious. The question of whether this hope has yet been borne out is too soon to assess, though early returns are not greatly encouraging to this observer.[41] But in any case, the likelihood is that a culture so inured to silliness—and in recent years to coarsening and degradation as well—does not suddenly become sicklied o'er with the pale cast of thought with one event, as disturbing as it is. After all, if the sixties, our last great national nervous breakdown, did not prompt much processing by serious culture among the educated classes, then relying on another crisis to prompt a new round of reflection is as uncertain as it is churlish.

Marketplace as Muse: De Bulgari Eloquentia

The authors studied in this volume have generally been thought to be depicting characters in whose thematics they had little direct stake *as* authors. I hope my readings have thrown that assumption into some doubt. The governing contradiction that makes possible the connection I was trying to draw—which is that between the author's desire to be a prominent contributor to the public sphere, if not rich, and the equally strong desire to be true to an inner aesthetic or perspective that might be unpopular—seems to be fading from view. Failing the sort of soul-searching reaction to crisis invoked by Don DeLillo, one sees the age-old conflict between the muse and the machine gradually giving way. In this regard, the way forward could be pointed by Fay Weldon, whose *Bulgari Connection* constitutes the first known instance in which a work of literature, or fiction anyway, is expressly designed as an advertisement. If crassness is a Platonic essence, and to deny one to it would be elitist, then surely Weldon is its embodiment.

But in fairness, she may only be drawing conclusions and acting accordingly. The highest form of contemporary creativity, and certainly the only reason most of us continue to watch the Super Bowl, may finally be the advertisement. In the age when public relations pseudo-events dot the landscape, its upfront cynicism may even seem somehow more honest than only exploitative. To boot, the sort of "historical inevitability" arguments being forever rolled out by the proponents of the new omnipresent marketplace tell that there is no alternative. (Until high-technology companies started going south, the Internet was of course the favored carrier of this historical inevitability of the private sector. The facts that it was developed by the Defense Department and that the World Wide Web was actually designed by a European socialist were conveniently forgotten, impossible to process.) Though Weldon is English, there seems something very American about this venture of hers.

The genius of Weldon's concept is that the selling itself forms the essence of the initial inspiration. The process whereby the pipeline preforms its own material, begun years before in the cinema and radio and now perfected on television, achieves its own kind of paradigmatic status in publishing as well with this act. As with conceptual art, the Warholian point can be "read" instantly, without any inspection of the book itself or adjudging of its literary or aesthetic effect. The publicity that the gesture itself garners for Bulgari, and perhaps also for Weldon, the outrage of the real and imagined literary "old guard," are themselves what assures that the gesture has succeeded. If people also read the book, that may be a nice bonus. But the publicity play is the thing, not the play of the story itself.

Jonathan Franzen's prickly hesitancy to get into the mass media swim was ill mannered and may itself have been prompted by some of the very demographic concerns he would disparage. But the fact that he objected to any aspect of marketing at all strikes one as something soon fit for nostalgia, for there will be ever fewer occasions when a serious writer will be able to make any gesture, nice or otherwise, in public, and fewer writers of any sort who will be able to even conceive of themselves as contesting public space with the products of mass publicity. For that matter, Oprah Winfrey's project of cultural ambassadorship, with its overtones of pedagogy and betterment, may itself soon recede into the mists with its middlebrow predecessors. Following Fay Weldon's example, we will learn to stop worrying and love the market, and then nobody will sell out or compromise with the organs of publicity again. First will be publicity, then the content provided for it.

The stance of literary purity, as I hope I have shown in this study, was always illusory, compromise always inevitable. But if the very source of artistic inspiration is itself publicity, if every novel can be a version of Mailer's *Advertisements for Myself* from the very start, then compromise is not an issue, for the market, like Shrike, has already written the first line. Absent a major crisis of a scale hard to conceive of now, it will soon become the case that mass publicity, like the business culture from which now more than ever it comes, will be impossible to denounce because, in Thomas Frank's words, "we will no longer have a life, a history, a consciousness apart from it. . . . [Indeed, even now it is] putting itself beyond our power of imagining because it has *become* our imagination, it has *become* our power to envision, and describe, and theorize, and resist."[42]

Notes

Notes to Chapter 1

1. Jürgen Habermas, in his *Structural Transformation of the Public Sphere*, remarks the importance of this shift in the arts from excrescences of privilege within the aristocracy to in effect self-standing spheres of the modern institutional hierarchy. He notes as well the centrality of the eighteenth-century version of the coterie, or salon, to this development: "in the first half of the eighteenth century the *amateurs éclairées* formed the inner circle of the new art public" (40).

2. See Bourdieu's *The Rules of Art*, which demonstrates the way the postromantic conception of sensibility as the ultimate justification for artistic endeavor (a justification embodied famously in Emile Zola's remark that a work of art is finally "a corner of creation seen through a temperament") is made possible by the development of a literary field that becomes a world apart from bourgeois society (139).

3. Mary Poovey, in *The Proper Lady and the Woman Writer*, is particularly interested in the implications for women's autonomy of this newfound distance of writer from reader: "the rapid demise of literary patronage after 1740 meant that a woman *could* publish anonymously, without having either to solicit the interest of a patron (nearly all of whom would have been male) or even to acknowledge her own sex" (36–37). Beyond that, in a point Poovey will develop with her specific authors, "To write is to earn attention without directly claiming it; sometimes the text can even serve as a surrogate in the activity one would 'personally' never undertake" (41–42). Although she speaks "in its broadest sense" of women writers' "style" as a response to specific forms of internalized ideological pressure, the fact is that sensibility and style, in exactly their broadest sense, are what the new dispensation of authorship at the turn of the nineteenth century is all about for both genders (46).

4. Colin Campbell, in his *Romantic Ethic and the Spirit of Modern Consumerism*, makes much of this facet of the romantic poetic sensibility, allying it to the rise of modern consumerism in general. Citing and explicating the relevant invocations of "pleasure" in Wordsworth's preface to the *Lyrical Ballads*, Campbell eventually defines the romantic self-concept: "the Romantic was someone who had an ideal sensitivity to pleasure, and indicated this fact by the spontaneity and intensity of his emotions. By the same token, he was an individual who could give pleasure to others, not to much directly through his person or his actions, but indirectly, through his embodied imaginings, a pleasure which served to spiritually renew and enlighten them, as it had him" (193). I merely note that this indirect form of "spontaneity" is remarkably similar to that indirect form of praise seeking Poovey attributes to her women writers.

5. I would again refer the reader to Bourdieu, especially his discussion of Charles Baudelaire and Gustave Flaubert in "The Conquest of Autonomy" (47–112).

6. Elizabeth L. Eisenstein, in *The Printing Revolution in Early Modern Europe*, puts it well: "Anxiety about getting attention and holding it was . . . built into the trade of the new professional author. . . . Alone with his quill pen, . . . the professional author . . . was himself an alienated man who worked hard to promote leisure, fought for a commercial success that he despised" (105).

7. McKeon, *The Origins of the English Novel*, 248.

8. As Allon White has shown in his *Uses of Obscurity*, the case of George Meredith was a pivotal one in the literary nineteenth century in England: all the attributes of prose style that previous critics had denounced as obscure and pointlessly arcane were trumpeted as proof that Meredith was a first-class writer. In other words, the coterie audience was publicly declaring its independence from the larger audience during the decades before the First World War, and "the reciprocity of values which is understood to guarantee the exchange process underlying publication is thrown into jeopardy by the author's separation from the realm of his addressee, the 'public'" (31).

9. Colin Campbell in fact links the two quite tightly: "Bohemia is the social embodiment of Romanticism, with Bohemianism the attempt to make life conform to Romantic principles; therefore it is here that the most obvious and clear-cut illustrations of the Romantic ideal of character are to be found in modern society" (195). He goes on to enumerate these as the elevation of pleasure above utility and an overall contempt for Philistine society. He also points out, intriguingly, that the reason Paris was the first city to develop a Bohemia in the 1840s "was probably because it was in France, in the aftermath of the Revolution, that the triumph of the bourgeoisie seemed so complete." Perhaps. But has it not occurred to the English author that Paris may simply have been the most compelling of major cities in that era? Bourdieu also gives *la bohème* its due (54–57).

10. Walter J. Ong, in his *Rhetoric, Romance, and Technology*, adds another reason why the romantics came to champion the originality of the poetic conception over the ability of literature to reproduce topoi of opinion. In the chapter "Romantic Difference and the Poetics of Technology" (255–83), he points out that by the time of romanticism, print had been around long enough that a complete encyclopedia was being undertaken by Diderot, for example. Since "in the absence of writing the major noetic effort of a society must be not to seek new knowledge but to retain what is known," oral cultures favor "standardization and fixity," the better to retrieve things from memory (261). With the advent of mass printing, the older sense of writing's role as merely an aide-mémoire transcribing rhetorical commonplaces was now archaic, and poets could feel free, even obligated, to be startling and fresh in their expression rather than derivative. Ong stresses Wordsworth and Coleridge's irritation with the prefabricated phrases of the traditional *gradus ad Parnassum*, as in a sonnet of Gray's that Wordsworth dissects. Ong shrewdly notes: "All the lines Wordsworth likes . . . focus explicitly on subjective feelings, the lines he dislikes more on the exterior world as processed or interpreted through standard epithets. Romantic subjectivism exists here not in contrast with an 'objectivism' built on observation but rather in contrast with adherence to formulary expression" (272–73). By linking in this fashion the growth of poetic individualism with the rise of print technology, Ong shows yet another way in which "Romanticism and technology . . . are mirror images of each other" (264).

11. Martha Woodmansee, *The Author, Art, and the Market*, 50.

12. Ibid., 42.

13. Woodmansee does acknowledge that the post-Renaissance notion of the author was "an unstable marriage of two distinct concepts," one the traditional craftsman who works with "traditional materials in order to achieve the effects prescribed," and the other an unaccountably "inspired" figure who introduces something previously unthought. As Woodmansee notes, though, in contrast to postromantic conceptions of the author, "in neither of these conceptions is the writer regarded as distinctly and personally responsible for his creation" (36). The former role owes the honor chiefly to the tradition, the latter to God.

14. McKeon also notes the paradox that the ability to "claim" as one's unique product a piece of writing prompts the need to have it officially recognized by the act of giving it to the

public: "once ideas can be owned, their value lies in disowning them by making them public—not only in the economic sense of the creation of surplus value, but also in the sense that the very meaning of conceptual ownership depends upon the knowledge of others of your ownership, upon their capacity to know your ideas without also being able to extract material profit from them" (123–24). Thus, to paraphrase the old song, when it comes to ideas, ownership is only really ownership when it is given away.

15. Woodmansee 38. Woodmansee goes on to cite Wordsworth's claim that the author's "task" is "of *creating* the taste by which he is to be enjoyed" and notes that since "his immediate audience is inevitably attuned to the products of the past, the great writer who produces something original is doomed to be misunderstood."

16. And the marketplace is itself getting ever more of a mass character. The rather smaller circle of the eighteenth-century readership was expanding in the succeeding century, but its materials were also coarsening somewhat. Henry-Jean Martin's *History and Power of Writing* puts it succinctly: "The eighteenth century had been the age of the book; the nineteenth was the age of the newspaper" (414). Journalism increasingly became the master paradigm for all that was printed, as in some sense television may now be taken as the master paradigm for contemporary American entertainment product.

17. A marvelous early guide to this overlay of community upon what at heart is a lonely pursuit is Honoré de Balzac's *Illusions perdues*. In fact, this underrated novel is as thorough a map of the literary life of its time as one is ever likely to find. Its materialism is at least as honest as George Gissing's later *New Grub Street*, extending even to taking the reader on a tour of a printing plant. (Seldom is a reader made more aware of the gap separating the symbolic cultural material he or she reads and the insensate machine that delivers it!)

18. Actually, according to Charvat in *The Profession of Authorship in America,* the patronage may have gone the other way, on balance: "It was one of the discouraging facts about American authorship that few of our writers before 1850 escaped loss through the bankruptcy of a publisher" (34). See "Conditions of Authorship in 1820" (29–48).

19. Melville's "Telling the Truth" is discussed by Gilmore in his *American Romanticism and the Marketplace* as an instance of this desire that the work be "'orphaned'" because "only if it has been severed from its parent or producer, can it provide a secure medium for truth-telling'" (60). Gilmore interprets this desire for anonymous authorship as "a revelation of Melville's own divergent impulses toward deception and transparency as ways of relating to the book-buying public" (61). More than that, though, it implies that if he tells the truth in his own person the public will flee—or else come to get him, perhaps. He notes elsewhere that Hawthorne himself actually published his own early tales anonymously, in the tradition of the gentlemanly writer (81).

20. Joan Shelley Rubin's *Making of Middlebrow Culture* discusses shrewdly the seeming contradictions in which Emerson could deal. His "announcement, in 'Self-Reliance,' that 'nothing is at last sacred but the integrity of your own mind' summarized his rejection of the idea that readers owed allegiance to the judgments of a 'literary moral elite.'" (10) Yet he still saw "the 'scholars'" as a kind of "'knighthood of virtue' comprised of the 'few superior and attractive men' equipped to 'calm and guide' the people." People needed "tutelage," it turns out, even (or perhaps especially) in the greater interests of their self-culture and ultimate self-reliance. What perplexes Emerson sooner or later comes to perplex educated Americans in general, and this uneasy relation to cultural authority is certainly no exception.

21. Ronald J. Zboray treats exactly this turn and its consequences for technical advance in his "Antebellum Reading and the Ironies of Technological Innovation." One such irony concerns the laying of the national rail track, which while facilitating the "shift from a local to a national print culture," could still only distribute materials along its main routes, thus

"creat[ing] geographical biases in literary distribution" and at first actually *increasing* the sway of New England and Northeast culture, rather than diluting it as would be assumed (192–93). He also notes that publishers, even in using technical innovations, retained "an artisan ideology" all the while (181).

22. Michael Gilmore treats the ambivalence of a generation of literary figures toward the marketplace: from Thoreau and Emerson to Nathaniel Hawthorne and Herman Melville. Especially interesting is how Gilmore manages to ally the reflections on the perils of the market from these writers' essays and letters with themes in their own fiction. Hawthorne's *Seven Gables* heroine Hepzibah Pyncheon, for instance, is convincingly argued to be a semblable of the author himself: "Although she herself is not an artist figure, she resembles her creator both in her history of isolation and her need to earn a living" (100).

23. See Charvat: "most scholars assume that literary history can be adequately represented by a line—with the writer at one end and the reader at the other. Actually, instead of being merely linear, the pattern is triangular. Opposite both the writer and the reader stands the whole complex organism of the book and magazine trade. . . . In this triangle, cultural force or influence runs in both directions" (284).

24. According to Charvat, this process had actually already gotten under way by the time of the Civil War. See his "James T. Fields and the Beginnings of Book Promotion, 1840–1855" (168–89), which shows how the nationalization of the potential market for books made publishing less local, less a matter of patronage, and more a business of the type we assume it to be today. One amusing sidelight of this chapter is the revelation that the term *puff* for a piece of publicity-friendly journalism goes back to 1847, from a citation from Horace Greeley (175).

25. Christopher P. Wilson's *Labor of Words*, 41. Whereas *Century* editor Richard Watson Gilder is recalled as trying to include one article of "spiritual significance" in each issue, by contrast *Post* editor George Horace Lorimer, "when . . . told his magazine was attracting 'thoughtful' readers, . . . quipped that he would try to correct the error" (41–42).

26. Especially interesting in its treatment of the turn of the twentieth century in magazine journalism is Richard Ohmann's *Selling Culture*. See in particular chapter 10, entitled "Fiction's Inadvertent Love Song" (287–337), which treats some of the literary effects of periodicals such as *McClure's*. Ohmann's larger thesis throughout the book seems to be that the early testing grounds for most of the advertising of this period, when the national American market was said to be forming, was not "the masses" in any real sense so much as the professional-managerial classes (or PMC), which was the first large-gauge class to move toward relative leisure at this period.

27. Ann Douglas cites such a figure in her *Terrible Honesty*, 64, noting that after 1929 those figures are "not to be reached again until after World War II." I assume these are constant dollars, though Douglas does not specify.

28. Douglas might fit this brief intellectual's love affair with advertising into her larger thesis about the twenties as the era of "terrible honesty" by pointing out that ads increasingly appealed openly to desires previously suppressed under the dreaded regime of Victorian America. Strangely, though, as far as I can see she does not. On the other hand, she does note an interesting reason why writers of the twenties such as Marianne Moore and F. Scott Fitzgerald may not have seen the publicity machine in quite the stark way it tends to be viewed by their counterparts today: "Today's . . . celebrity authors are formed as performers in good part by the media in which they appear, fully formed media that long antedated their appearance. The comparable people in the 1920s began their careers as the mass media were being invented, when they were still plastic and receptive to influence. Formed by an older tradition of live performance and broad but limited and cohesive audiences, the early media stars had a vivid

cultural identity that antedated any identity the media could bestow" (71–72). In other words, there was greater porousness between the realms of high art and mass entertainment because the latter was still getting its conventions and institutional protocols in order. By the 1930s, and certainly the 1950s, this was no longer the case.

29. The air may have been leaking out of the twenties balloon before the crash itself, though. Douglas notes that West, whom she defines as "chronicler of the media's impact on American life, [began] his first novel, *Miss Lonelyhearts* . . . in the late 1920s" (467). The journalist George W. S. Trow's *Within the Context of No Context* underscores *Miss Lonelyhearts's* depiction of "the world of journalism of the 1920s," with particular emphasis on the "goat and adding machine ritual" clipping carried reverently around by editor Shrike as his presumed ideal of good reporting (14–15). Given that Trow, like Douglas, sees the tabloid sensibility that forms so much contemporary culture as having been formed in the twenties, it is not surprising that his reflections grant pride of place to West.

30. As if Americans have some ancestral memory of the coterie function, though, they have always elaborated other, usually more market-driven simulations thereof. Rubin offers a balanced view of the various appurtenances of middlebrow culture, the literary guilds and five-foot shelves of yesteryear, in chapters 3 and 4. Even Oprah Winfrey's periodic programs on novels, those now-defunct shows watched by scattered viewers in their homes, were dubbed a "book club." And now whole cities, to jump-start civil society, are experimenting with reading the same novel at once. Whether these really are coteries with the germinal function of salons or not, what is interesting is the continual desire to evoke that status all the same.

31. Gilmore argues that Hawthorne's and Melville's "most strongly held values conflict," defining those values as "democracy and capitalism" on the one hand and their devotion to their art on the other (57). He even argues that "Rappaccini's Daughter" is Hawthorne's covert cri de coeur against the audience and its dragging knuckles: "It exposes the ideal of a free people as enlightened patron of the arts as a myth" (69). By the time Melville writes his *Confidence-Man* in 1857, he has abandoned his onetime "democratic enthusiasm" and produces a book whose "multiple con men . . . are versions of the artist who tell stories to obtain money and use language, not to communicate truth, but to obfuscate their motives and ingratiate themselves with listeners" (150).

32. In some ways, one could argue that the vast American system of libraries—the municipal and university systems both—were and are the closest facsimile of a coterie the United States has outside the Northeast, Chicago, and the Bay Area. One of the symptoms—and causes—of the current malaise in literary circles and in humanities departments is the declining funding for libraries, which could in the past be relied on to buy "midlist" books that the great public would not immediately flock to read. André Schiffrin recalls in his *Business of Books* that Victor Gollancz, for whom he once worked, would routinely "order the same number of copies of a book from Pantheon—1,800," and upon being asked why replied that he could "count on orders for 1,600 copies from Britain's libraries" (105). He generalizes this point to note that "public library purchases were once large enough to cover most of the costs of publishing meaningful works of fiction and nonfiction." That "once" is the problem, as much for imaginative writing as for its scholastic cousin.

33. Trow captures the poignancy of this great divide by speaking of the two grids remaining when what he calls the "middle distance" fell away: "The grid of two hundred million and the grid of intimacy. Everything else fell into disuse. There was a national life—a *shimmer* of national life—and intimate life. The distance between these two grids was very great. The distance was very frightening" (*Within the Context of No Context* 47). If this distance is frightening for the mass-culture consumer, and no doubt it is, think how the eternal silence of those vast spaces must terrify the creative artist!

34. I use the F. R. Leavis formula because it is easily recognized, but I would rather speak of "group culture" in the sense that T. S. Eliot gives it in his *Notes towards the Definition of Culture*. Like Leavis, he understands the importance of an inner core of culturally interested people for the flourishing of creative endeavor (what Eliot terms *the elite*). It is, if you will, the alternative or at any rate supplemental form of mediation to that of *the media*. Unlike Leavis, though, he realizes how thoroughly the cultural activity of the elite and the larger realm of cultural consumption of the group both depend on the relation to the underlying culture of the society as a whole: a possible clue to why he chose early on to leave the United States for England.

35. One of the exquisite pleasures of Francine Prose's *Blue Angel* is its detailed inspection of the agonies of the creative writing "workshop" class.

36. In this regard, perhaps the only sustained narrative excellence in Martin Amis's recent novel *The Information* concerns Richard Tull's disastrous American book tour. One inevitably wonders how much of the horrific material in this rendition came from Amis's experience flogging his own books in the United States.

37. In his *Oeuvres complètes* Flaubert notes they even say it together ("puis, enfin, [ils] se la communiquent simultanément" [2: 301]), so that neither one can even claim authorship of the *idea* of copying!

38. I am not speaking here, be it emphasized, of quality in some strictly aesthetic sense. There is such a thing as well-done "trash" or thoroughly commercial product, and there is also terrible "art." Functionally, though, people have always made (if not always admitted to making) a distinction between market-driven fiction written to order and writing that tries to explore and clarify some spiritual quandary or historical paradigm shift, or is prompted by a profound desire to share one's viewpoint with someone else. Everyone is amused by the prim way Graham Greene sorted his "entertainments" from his serious novels, but few pretend not to understand the general thing he means by the categories—and indeed, one would wager not many people who follow literary matters would disagree a great deal about which books went where!

39. One of the earliest successes—and this a poet—was George, Lord Byron. Dwight Macdonald mentions him as one of the first writers to become in effect a "celebrity," or mass-culture icon. See *Against the American Grain,* which argues (against my grain as well) that romanticism, "a new creed whose emphasis on subjective feeling as against traditional form was suitable to the democratization of taste that was taking place," worked quite well as a sort of marketing strategy for Byron (I think inadvertently, though). He takes Byron's double to be Sir Walter Scott: "Each represented an aspect of Masscult [his nickname for mass culture], Scott the production line, Byron the emphasis on the artist himself. Antithetical but also complementary: the more literature became a branch of industry, the more the craving for the other extreme—individuality. Or rather, a somewhat coarser commodity, Personality" (21).

40. It is, by the way, fascinating how often portraits of the literary life drawn by literary people seem to need this doublet, this pseudo-couple. James's penniless genius Ray Limbert needs the contrastive example of Jane Highmore, who turns out triple-decker novels as efficiently as she does children (and, it is implied, because of those children); the noble failure of Gissing's New Grub Street, Harold Biffen, takes additional depth by setting off the base success of the glib Jasper Milvain; even in our own day the recriminative modernist writer Richard Tull has his perfect foil in the down-market charisma of the lower-middlebrow novelist and media darling Gwyn Barry in Martin Amis's *The Information*. Admittedly the last is a twist on the traditional morality play: the reader is made almost to want Tull to "lose" the implied competition with Barry, partly because his integrity resolutely lacks merely personal charm, and partly because he so obviously is on the way to losing anyway. But again and again, on those rela-

tively few occasions when writers of literary ambition depict the careers and circumstances of their coevals, they have recourse to some demagogic charlatan as a counterexample.

41. It may have been as consumer even more than as producer that the New Woman was most resented, however, since her tastes had an impact on what writers could produce. Ohmann points out that with the new manufacturing capacity of the postbellum United States, the woman became less significant as contributor to production and, as if in compensation, "she entered the money economy as a purchaser and manager of commodities" (76). To the extent that authors were among these commodities, their resentment of this power could border on misogyny.

Notes to Chapter 2

1. In fact, James biographer Fred Kaplan, in *Henry James: The Imagination of Genius,* sees the turn, with the nineties, to almost exclusive short-story writing as the indirect "result of the gradual transformation of the nature of magazines and of the relationship between magazines and their readers from the high-Victorian concentration on serial fiction to the shorter economic and literary attention span of late-Victorian readers" (367). As always, though, James tried to square this economic necessity with an aesthetic one.

2. In Leon Edel's account of this debacle, he describes something approaching a prolonged battle between approval and contempt when James "came forward shyly, expectantly," to acknowledge what he thought would be applause: "Jeers, hisses, catcalls were followed by great waves of applause from that part of the audience which esteemed James and had recognized the better qualities of the play. The two audiences had declared war. The intellectual and artistic elite answered the howls of derision; the howls grew strong in defiance. This was an unusual kind of passion in an English theatre, where feelings were so seldom expressed" (*The Treacherous Years,* 78). James, not surprisingly, stopped his attempts to conquer the stage with this disaster, and fell into a creative funk afterward. In his *The Jameses,* R. W. B. Lewis helpfully adds to the record of humiliation the information that the competition between approbation and hostility lasted about a quarter of an hour, the author standing the whole time helpless before the melee (505).

3. Lewis describes the way James saw his theatrical ventures, which started with an adaptation for the stage of his early novel *The American* (1876), as *at first* motivated by "economic need" (his novels had already ceased earning out their advances by the late 1880s), but *subsequently* undertaken as if art was also at stake. After the success of this adaptation, he wrote to Robert L. Stevenson that he felt "'as if I had at last *found* my form—my real one—that for which fiction is an ineffectual substitute'" (445–46).

4. Kaplan, 335.

5. Michael Anesko's *Friction with the Market* may be the most systematic argument for the position that James was always intensely concerned with popular success and money. He even, perhaps with strained effect, chooses to read James's late turn to modernist difficulty as a strategy to make "being *un*popular, unsaleable at any price . . . [into] a cachet of its own" (143). This sits ill with Anesko's admission that James continued to write what he thought of as potboilers, such as *Turn of the Screw.*

6. The fact that "The Death of the Lion," among others, was first published in *The Yellow Book* shows James's adoption of aestheticism to be all the more bound up with his desire for friendly outlets. See Jonathan Friedman, *Professions of Taste,* 177. Friedman's larger point about aestheticism, that it is an "effective strategy for advertising commodities that would at once glorify and efface the act of consumption itself by grounding even the most mundane acquisitive choices in the nonmaterial realm of transcendent value designated by the aesthetic,"

certainly has resonance with James (109). One thinks, of the stories here discussed, in particular of "The Lesson of the Master."

7. Marcia Jacobson in her *Henry James and the Mass Market* invokes the names of Max Beerbohm's "Enoch Soames," Rudyard Kipling's *Light That Failed,* Frederick Wedmore's *Renunciations* (a 1893 book whose title may have anticipated James's tale collections *Terminations* and *Embarrassments*), and Ernest Dowson's *Dilemmas,* among others. She also pays due respect to the forerunner of so many of these dour portraits of the literary life, George Gissing's *New Grub Street* (98–99).

8. Anesko asserts this: "The temptation to read these tales [of the literary life] autobiographically is almost overwhelming—many critics have fallen into the trap—but, unlike his doomed protagonists, James had no intention of being martyred by the marketplace" (143).

9. *The Complete Notebooks of Henry James,* 43–44.

10. *The Complete Tales of Henry James,* 7:282. Subsequent page references are given in the body of the text.

11. That light comedy also puts the patented Jamesian ambiguity to work in undercutting some of the effect of Henry St. George's *l'art pour l'art* speeches, as Edel points out in his *Henry James: The Middle Years:* "the Master does not follow his own counsel. One wonders at the end of the tale what this ironic 'lesson' really is. Admirable though James's statement may be, on behalf of the sanctity of art and the danger of worldliness, the reader—and the young idealist—feel rather 'sold'" (240).

12. James, *Notebooks,* 87. The neglected manuscript is prefigured in James's "question of whether any one (in the crowd of lionizers) does know, really, when it comes to the point, the first word of the work the hero's reputation for having produced which is the very basis of their agitation" (86).

13. In James's later tale "The Birthplace" (1903), another critique of the cult of writerly personality he saw emerging, even in death the author does not escape being turned into a personality. James's bizarre but for him logical solution: the caretaker begins fabricating his own stories about the dead writer, thus freeing his works from any connection to an actual life.

14. "The world might ignore him; but Henry [James] knew that so long as certain readers experienced his work as profoundly as this his personal *gloire* was assured" (Edel, *The Middle Years,* 314).

15. Paraday may himself also be at fault for his susceptibility to Society's flattery. Sara S. Chapman's *Henry James's Portrait of the Writer as Hero* actually links "Lion" to "Lesson" by means of this quasi-female weakness: "In his failure to resist them, he reveals a weakness before the demands of others, especially strong-willed women, that James had already portrayed in Mark Ambient ('The Author of Beltraffio') and Henry St. George" (64).

16. Susanne Kappeler's *Writing and Reading in Henry James* also notes the extent to which the actual wife in this symbolic economy is sacrificed to the "Muse [who] is really the only full member of that tribe" of art and its practitioners (90). This is true in part because the wife usually represents the sort of domestic obligations that send Henry St. George into his penitential room to exploit his writing talent.

17. Although the narrator pledges to a dying Paraday that he will "print it as it stands—beautifully," the narrator does subsequently report that "the manuscript has not been recovered." He remains devoted, however, to ferreting it out, as does the woman he has fallen in love with (117–18). Their devotion to the sacred text is almost enough to live on, even if the manuscript is never recovered.

18. *The Complete Tales of Henry James,* 9:74.

19. Roslyn Jolly's *Henry James: History, Narrative, Fiction* puts the matter pretty well: "The tales [of the literary life] clearly draw the lines between the custodians of culture and the ene-

mies of literature, all the more forcefully because they frequently do so in terms of gender. Devoted, male readers try to protect vulnerable, male writers who are 'heroes' and martyrs of 'the artistic ideal'" (84).

20. Posnock does try, though. His *Trial of Curiosity* asserts for James an "aesthetic androgyny" that he also gradually came to see as some sort of ideal for women. Though Posnock admits James's "skepticism toward the separatist feminism of *The Bostonians*," for instance, as a violation of the androgyny ideal, he notes: "By 1914 James welcomed women's 'effective annexation of the male identity' as the 'consummation awaiting us' and applauded their 'repudiation of the *distinctive*,' by which he meant the rejection of fixed gender roles" (200). Regardless of whether this is really what James "meant" in this case, the fact that James died shortly after writing this qualifies it almost for the status of deathbed conversion. The alternative view in Alfred Habegger's *Henry James and the "Woman Business,"* overstated and modish though it be, may be closer to the truth—or at least the common consensus, whether fair or not—on James's relationship to "women's issues," which was not very supportive.

21. Edel, *The Middle Years*, 382. Bruce Henrickson's "Functions of Women in the Art Tales of Henry James" has pointed out that in many ways James pays women a greater compliment than the traditional passive muse role assigned by "patriarchal myth," as he terms it. James's women are "often aggressive," particularly gatekeepers such as Weeks Wimbush, whereas his "artists are often maternal" (83). This role reversal is a compliment in reverse, though, because such greater activism on the part of women is part of what makes them more fearsome to James.

22. In a sense, "Figure" is a radicalization of the sort of aggressiveness James has attributed to critics in "The Aspern Papers," for instance, because here it is implied not merely that using the texts to surmise about the author but even trying to get to the bottom of those texts' intrinsic meanings—in short, really to "read" them, one could say—is seen as almost as aggressive, or at least as a game that the author would somehow lose were the reader to win. Such a problematic has no doubt caused more than one critic of James's later, gamier style to nod knowingly.

23. James, *Complete Tales*, 9:232. Subsequent page references are given in the body of the text.

24. Edel, *The Middle Years*, 385. James's *Complete Notebooks* show that the only apparent reason James decided to make the altar a literal rather than merely mental entity is that "I probably can't get an adequate action [into the tale] unless I enlarge this idea" (98). One idly wonders just what sort of short story one would have ended up with had Stransom's altar remained completely interior to his own mind!

25. So, for what it may be worth, seems James to view it. His *Notebooks* refer to Stransom's "noble and beautiful religion," and make no discernible nod to aesthetics or *poesis* whatever (98).

26. It has occurred to me more than once that if James's story was prompted by Fenimore's suicide, this setup is the perfect way to neutralize the suspicion that James may have felt guilty for abandoning her. Whatever Stransom's motive is for enshrining Mary Antrim or Kate Creston, it is not guilt over what he failed to do but a kind of pique at what the others have failed to do. His only omission in honoring the dead, his exclusion of Acton Hague, flows not from indifference or self-preoccupation but rather from in a way caring too much. Stransom, at least, is off that hook, whether or not his creator is.

27. Daniel Won-gu Kim has argued in his "Shining Page" that she is his hollow in other ways as well, particularly in the way her altar recalls the kitsch of mass culture: "The woman's altar, composed of 'simple things,' stands in bathetic contrast to Stransom's oeuvre. 'Photographs and watercolors, scraps of writing framed and ghosts of flowers embalmed'—to

Stransom's bourgeois sense of art, these indicate a 'common meaning' where 'common' has the double sense of . . . unification around the memory of Hague and the supposedly undiscriminating tastes of the masses" (111).

28. In fact, this revelation has the curious effect of multiplying secrecy rather than banishing it. The mystery of Acton Hague only deepens at this point. She does not share the nature of his effect on her with Stransom; he does not tell her the nature of Hague's insult to him—and needless to say the reader remains uninformed of the details of either catastrophe. Furthermore, Hague clearly never informed her of his relations with Stransom, whom he had betrayed earlier in his life: "There were passages it was quite conceivable that even in moments of the tenderest expansion he should have withheld. Of many facts in the career of a man so in the eye of the world there was of course a common knowledge; but this lady lived apart from public affairs, and the only period perfectly clear to her would have been the period following the dawn of her own drama. A man, in her place, would have 'looked up' the past—would even have consulted old newspapers. It remained singular indeed that in her long contact with the partner of her retrospect no accident had lighted a train; but there was no arguing about that" (259).

29. However, as Leon Edel has noted, both Stransom and the woman are afflicted with the sin of pride, even though hers is closer to "the pride that suffers" than to "the pride that stiffens the heart." Each of them pursues, privately, a form of response to the wound each suffered at the hands of the same public man: a wound that replicates itself in the implied contest between the two of them, "mirror-images of power."

30. If Stransom's "altar of the dead" can be conscripted to represent any religion other than his secret cult of absent friends, it would be the religion of art that claims its deepest allegiance. Edwin Fussell's *Catholic Side of Henry James* sounds a baffled note in reading "Altar"'s last chapter in good part for failing to appreciate the unconventionality of Stransom's project to begin with, and the essentially opportunistic use he makes of Catholic premises for it. Viewing it as James's attempt to render the "Catholic view of death," Fussell feels it "too remote from that faith to figure it convincingly at the point where it most called for figuration" (109). I read the choice of a Catholic church, particularly in Protestant England, as part of Stransom's desire to have a palpable embodiment of his piety before his dead in a place that would be suitably private, nobody much ever going there. This also accounts for the fact that the chapel is free and open to use.

31. Edel describes how Stransom succumbs in the most melodramatic terms: "One day he dies before the invaded altar. She is contrite at the last moment; but she may well be. For, finally, he has yielded, and she has her triumph. *She* has been unyielding" (383). Such a reading, in addition to exaggerating, implies that Stransom does not yield of his own accord to including Acton Hague's candle, which quite clearly he does. But the tone is also misleading, as if he would be better off continuing to hate Hague, and that she spoils things by causing him to repent of his coldness toward his dead friend.

32. Allon White's *Uses of Obscurity* is the most compact treatment of what the author finds a trend away from author-as-sage toward something very like the author-as-suspect. He attributes this shift, which occurs roughly between the 1880s and the First World War, to "the author's separation from the realm of his addressee, the 'public'" (31), though he also mentions Lombroso, Nordau, and the like. Owing to this rift, fiction is read—and reviewed—almost as a way of psychoanalyzing the writer more than examining the subject. Indeed, in this "symptomatic reading," the assumption resides of a sort of "inner blindness on the part of the writer, whereby what he wrote about, and what the work was 'really' about, were two separate things" (43, 48). With attention to "the unconscious origins from which [his work] sprang," reviewers searched more and more for clues from the literature to "the mental disposition of the

writer" (48, 43). In such an atmosphere it does not surprise that, in some circles, obscurity as such starts to be prized: White argues that George Meredith started this trend, though it is hard to not to think of Henry James when reading White's chronicle of the ways of the fin de siècle literary world.

33. James, *Notebooks,* 137.

34. Ibid., 143.

35. See his edition of James's *"The Figure in the Carpet" and Other Stories.* Kermode specifically says, however, that it seems to be more marriage than sex per se that is the point of comparison: "Vereker's secret . . . is not, we infer, the sort of thing the celibate and impotent may look for when they speculate about sex. It is a triumph of patience, a quality pervading the life of the subject, like marriage. It is not the subject but the treatment, which is why it is a suffusing presence in all of Vereker's work, and not a nugget hidden here and there" (28). Yet its close proximity to the salacious thing the public often has in mind when sexuality looms makes for understandable confusion, and the power of art is traditionally rendered in masculine, not to say phallic, terms.

36. Another critic who makes this relay is Chapman, who notes that in "Lesson" James leaves the question whether "Marian's love for St. George will ultimately restore his failed artistic power . . . in ambiguity. . . . James would return specifically to the possibility of a connection between sexuality and artistic creativity in both 'The Figure in the Carpet' and *The Sacred Fount*" (42).

37. See Tzvetan Todorov's *Poetics of Prose,* especially his chapter on "The Figure in the Carpet."

38. James, *Complete Tales,* 9:288.

39. Ibid., 9:292.

40. Kermode, in James, *"The Figure in the Carpet,"* 27.

41. Ibid., 28.

42. James, quoted in Edel, *The Middle Years,* 385–86. His further reflections on Minnie Temple are worth citing, among them that upon receiving "news of the extinction of this bright young flame, he [James] had rejoiced that she lived on as a 'steady unfaltering luminary in the mind.' Her image would 'preside in my intellect.' It had been 'almost as if she had passed away—as far as I am concerned—from having served her purpose'" (385). The strangely utilitarian emphasis of this tribute makes it, in my view, not so much touching as unsettling.

43. I have somewhat arbitrarily confined my James tales to the early and mid-nineties; but if one travels a bit further, to that strange novel *The Sacred Fount* (1900), one finds a version of fiction that emphasizes the violence novelists do not to just their subjects but also their readers, at least in the intriguing argument of Roslyn Jolly: "Like James's earlier tales about the artistic life, *The Sacred Fount* illustrates a fundamental opposition of interests between producers and consumers of fiction; the difference is that, as we have seen, it shifts much of the blame for this on to the producer, whose activity is seen to be morally as well as epistemologically questionable" (122).

44. Allon White, 43.

Notes to Chapter 3

1. Bourdieu, 217. Bourdieu says that cultural production defined as art "is founded, as in the game of *loser take all,* on an inversion of the fundamental principles of the field of power and of the economic field. It excludes the quest for profit and it guarantees no correspondence of any kind between monetary investments and revenues; it condemns the pursuit of honours and temporal standing."

2. William Leach has detailed this process superbly in his *Land of Desire*. Especially interesting is the way he treats the publicity apparatus—and in the case of the Metropolitan Museum, even the "high-culture" apparatus—as being increasingly used to promote the emerging national marketplace more or less forcibly installed around the turn of the century by captains of industry.

3. The people who did resist, perhaps predictably, were scions of old eastern families who recoiled from the dawning vulgarity of the age. The standard book on this backlash, which not surprisingly includes Henry James's brother William, is T. J. Jackson Lears's *No Place of Grace*.

4. Of all the authors I treat, Pynchon comes closest to making this process part of his explicit theme, though West in his *Day of the Locust* also broaches this idea.

5. Ohmann has a fascinating chapter of *Selling Culture* that focuses on "The Discourse of Advertising" (175–218) emergent during the century's turn. He stresses that despite our assumption of cynicism, naturally many of the advertisers themselves felt the pull of the American dream they were selling to others. After showing how some of these implicit appeals to rising middle-class ideology actually worked, Ohmann adds: "There is no reason to suspect [the advertisers] of cynically promoting a social ideal they saw as hollow. The unreal 'you' of their discourse was also, for them, a 'we.' Through it they said 'I love you' to their own class" (213–14). Of course, since upward mobility was such a huge part of this "social ideal," one could argue that at best the new discourse was a relatively sincere articulation of a cynical ideology.

6. The literature on this derealization of public life is by now extensive, but I would mention just two characteristic works: *The Unreality Industry* by Ian I. Mitroff and Warren Bennis, which focuses on television, and *Amusing Ourselves to Death* by Neil Postman, which treats the effects of the entertainment culture's confounding of truth and falsity upon realms (e.g., religion, politics, and education) that purportedly deal with real life.

7. Habermas also awards the prize for inventing public relations, a "practice [which], like the term itself, hails from the United States," to Lee and points to the operational deception inherent in PR: "The sender of the message hides his business intentions in the role of someone interested in the public welfare." By this means PR "goes beyond advertising; it invades the process of 'public opinion' by systematically creating news events or exploiting events that attract attention" (193).

8. Stuart Ewen's study *PR!* sheds interesting light on this centenarian's personal prejudices in this regard. His view of the masses, and the role expected of them in a Bernays-friendly world, can best be gleaned from an interview Ewen conducted as part of his book, wherein Bernays speaks fondly if contemptuously of his family chauffeur, whose nickname was "Dumb Jack." This pliant member of the lower orders spent the entire day driving various Bernayses hither and yon across New York City for derisory pay, stopping for precious minutes of the day to literally rest his weary head (11–13). Ewen's inference, gleaned not just from this anecdote but other more direct assertions of his subject, is that Bernays's public relations saw the public as Dumb Jack and designed its message in part to keep it in, or return it to, his spirit of long-suffering servitude.

9. For what it is worth, this decade also saw the publication of a significant work by then-guru Walter Lippmann entitled *Public Opinion* (1922), which argues for using the apparatus of illusion now possible at this point to manipulate said opinion through what he actually calls "pseudo-environments." Since the average person is entranced by a "medium of fictions," it follows that this medium could be guided by the wise to channel and use the emotions of the instinctive and gullible in the more sensible interests of the commonweal. Consent, in a word, could be engineered (quoted in Ewen, 150).

10. Nathanael West, *"Miss Lonelyhearts" and "The Day of the Locust,"* 14. Subsequent page references are given in the body of the text.

11. In his *Within the Context of No Context*, Trow discusses in particular a news item about a "goat and adding machine ritual" used to pray for the soul of a condemned man. This grotesque overlay of jaunty novelty on grim sadism is for Trow a tabloid feature set in place in the 1920s: "I always knew that . . . the goat and the adding machine were embedded in the mind that created the text of daily journalism. . . . To put it another way, I always knew that the New America had been created forever in the 1920s" (14–15).

12. Jay Martin's biography *Nathanael West* gives this reason for West's decision to remain under the care of what some of his screenwriter comrades called "Repulsive Studios": "The predictability of the work and salary at Republic was comforting and allowed him to allot time for his novel" (282).

13. In this regard, it should not be a surprise that Jay Martin went on from his biography of Nathanael West to write a book called *Who Am I This Time? Uncovering the Fictive Personality*, whose subject is how we humans require fictions in order to develop satisfactory lives, and how those fictions can nevertheless get out of control if they are inappropriate or disproportionate. He cites West only once in this book, but it is hard not to imagine that working on him helped guide Martin to his future project. Although we do not deal with *The Dream Life of Balso Snell* (1931) and *A Cool Million* (1934), both of these display aspects of the "fictive personality" in their heroes as much as *Lonelyhearts* and *Locust*. The title character of *Snell*, for instance, is literally living a dream in a novella heavily influenced by surrealism, and the protagonist of the latter novel, Lemuel Pitkin, pursues a path rigorously laid out by the Horatio Alger series, a fictional role both disproportionate and, in the thirties anyway, completely inappropriate.

14. Indeed, the noteworthy oddity about *Locust* is that this is a book about failed Hollywood, or not yet successful Hollywood anyway: the Greeners, one accomplished failure and one failure in training; Abe Kusich, Earle Shoop, and Miguel, various *Lumpenproletariat* figures whose natural milieu is a cockfight; and so on. The one moderately successful Hollywood figure in the book is in fact a writer, Claude Estee, almost certainly modeled loosely on West's California colleague and sometime fellow hunter William Faulkner. Estee's character is not heroically framed but seems in any case less grotesque than most of the others. It is possible that one of the reasons West looked up to Faulkner in the film colony, apart from the obvious literary ones, was that though in this world, Faulkner was never really of it. In his West biography Jay Martin writes of "a famous story that Faulkner's producer agreed to let him work 'at home,' only to find, when he called him for a story conference, that Faulkner had returned to Oxford, Mississippi. Faulkner could go home again, for Hollywood was never his home" (355).

15. Vladimir Nabokov, *Lolita*, 158. Subsequent page references are given in the body of the text.

16. Edmund White, "Nabokov's Passion," 216. The doppelgänger reading of Quilty, in fact, leads Elizabeth W. Bruss to argue in "Vladimir Nabokov: Illusions of Reality and the Reality of Illusions" that the killing of Quilty may itself be one of Humbert's fantasies, along with the reconciliation at Coalmont with Lolita herself. Her reasoning is too elaborate to be reproduced here in toto, but essentially it is based on Humbert's early assertion that he has started his memoir "fifty-six days ago," that his death occurs on November 16, 1952, according to John Ray's preface, and that the letter from a now older Lolita that inaugurates reunion with Lolita, her revelation of Quilty as her abductor, and his ultimate confrontation with the evil twin, is "said to have arrived on September 22, 1952," which would put it a day after his composition of the memoir supposedly commenced (46–47). Thus both his tearful coda to his relationship with Dolores Haze and the antiheroic slaying of his antagonist would have been fictional, and Bruss makes her verbally dispatched Quilty into a symbolic alter ego—even for the memoirist

himself, to say nothing of his reader: "If he [Humbert] cannot bear to do it consciously, he has at least subliminally sought and found the source of his defeat and the monster who destroyed Lolita's youth; he has revenged himself upon that monster in himself" (48). Bruss's reading, which I am reluctant to endorse completely, makes the murder of Quilty into a wholly symbolic, or perhaps delusional, episode: a result not inconsistent with my own view, though to my eye overreliant on a trick of dating.

17. On the same page in the novel Humbert makes the rivalry between him and Quilty quite explicitly an aesthetic one; he says to Lolita: "do not pity C. Q. One had to choose between him and H. H., and one wanted H. H. to exist at least a couple of months longer, so as to have him make you live in the minds of later generations." Since Quilty of course neither cared about nor remembered Lolita, this is trivially true, but I suspect that Humbert is also favorably comparing his own fitness for the job to people of Quilty's ilk.

18. The book that most thoroughly treats Pynchon as a purveyor of this literary mode is Theodore D. Kharpertian's *A Hand to Turn the Time.* See especially chapter 1, "Thomas Pynchon and Postmodern American Satire" (20–57).

19. The term *hermeneutic code,* to refer to the central mystery or puzzle inscribed by most prose narratives, was coined by critic Roland Barthes in his *S/Z.*

20. Kharpertian notes "Pynchon's irony . . . that although paranoia constitutes a social ordering activity, its ultimate personal effect may necessarily be disorder and disintegration" (49).

21. The assassination of JFK in *Libra* is actually structured as the reverse echo of Gladney's near miss: Kennedy is not intended to be killed or struck by the attack, as DeLillo construes it.

22. In his book about the increased commercial and technological interest in the phenomenon of human attention, *Suspensions of Perception,* Jonathan Crary has noted the way TV has itself come to embody the process of attention-getting, as round-the-clock American PR: "Television especially . . . emerged as the most pervasive and efficient system for the management of attention," but at the same time "certain kinds of statements about television (for example, about addiction, habit, persuasion, and control) are in a sense unspeakable. . . . To speak of contemporary collective subjects in terms of effects of passivity and influence is still generally anathema" (71). He goes on to note a "tacit a priori conviction [on the part of many who study the media] that television viewers constitute a hypothetical community of rational and volitional subjects. The contrary position, that human subjects have determinate psychophysiological capacities and functions that might be susceptible to technological management, has been the underpinning of institutional strategies and practices . . . for over a hundred years" (72). The ruling assumption of the providers of mass-commercial culture, in other words, was that manipulation was precisely the business they were about. Whether the assurances of John Fiske in *Television Culture* that TV audiences take the cues of the mass media and display their "agency" by reconstituting the elements into other patterns is enough to end Crary's dour manipulation worries is hard to say, but I for one remain skeptical.

23. Lears has some interesting reflections on the paradoxes of a search for more authentic experience, pointing out that the desire has itself in some ways been turned into something to be satisfied by that consumer society which was itself an agent of unreality to begin with: "Antimodern longings for authentic experience, by promoting the self-absorption of the therapeutic world view [another matter Lears treats extensively], provided fertile emotional ground for the growth of the twentieth-century corporate system" (303).

24. Even in the more restricted form it took in the 1930s, however, the apparatus of publicity under description had a way of subsuming the means used to describe it in Nathanael West's novels. Thomas *Strychacz's Modernism, Mass Culture, and Professionalism,* in addition to

linking work of Henry James's such as *The Reverberator* (1888) to the dawning fear of mass culture exhibited later by West, points out that the form of *Miss Lonelyhearts* has the effect of replicating some aspects of the tabloid world it depicts: "It was to be [in West's own words] a 'novel in the form of a comic strip,' as though the only formal principles suitable for describing a pervasive mass culture were to be drawn from its own discursive premises rather than from a literary world elsewhere" (164). Of course, to mime comic strip forms is not to be a comic strip, particularly if there are no pictures, for instance.

25. I inevitably gravitate toward medical metaphors because of W. H. Auden's infamous discussion in "West's Disease," by which he meant the disease West divined in others, which was a sort of down-market variant of *Bovarysme,* or impotent longing, made more virulent by virtue of its existence in a society whose opportunities allegedly extend to everyone. See Rita Barnard's *Great Depression and the Culture of Abundance* for an unsympathetic treatment of what Barnard argues is "idealist [a negative word here] and ultimately reactionary thinking" ill-adapted to West (170). Her rebuttal is not, for my money, a total refutation, but it does serve to emphasize the role played by the confusion of realms between fiction and reality, wherein "wishes and dreams are no longer so easily confined to what Auden chooses to see as the 'harmless' realm of the dream or the unconscious" (172). Whether or not Barnard dispels the power of Auden's analysis, she does have the virtue of underlining the way the world of the movies has itself already undermined the commonsensical distinctions between truth and illusion on which Auden seems complacently to rely.

26. For what it is worth, it appears that West's letters come from letters filched from Beatrice Fairfax's famous lovelorn column of the 1930s, and that apparently none other than Lillian Hellman was his confederate in this ploy (see Martin, *Nathanael West: The Art of His Life*).

27. *Vineland* arguably depicts an ever further encroachment of mediated life into everything else, its characters alluding to old movies and TV shows with their dates helpfully supplied. Even the hippies have been absorbed into the administered world by this point (1984, the time of the story). Critics still try to salvage something more inspirational from it, though. Marcel Cornis-Pope's *Narrative Innovation and Cultural Rewriting in the Cold War and After* sees Zoyd Wheeler's daughter Prairie as a possible way out of the "Tubal" labyrinth, since she is actively trying to piece together her history and because "she is not defined socially," which seems to be seen as a good thing (133). And in *Constructing Postmodernism* Brian McHale has even argued that the saturation of the narrative itself with media imagery and allusions is indicating that in this text "Pynchon has . . . strangely . . . 'redeemed' TV" (141). Whether or not that is the author's intention, one hazards that it will take more than the efforts of even so talented a writer as Pynchon to perform this miracle.

28. The question of when the sheer proliferation of media figments begins to be more significant than any content they may possess, when quantitative changes become qualitative, is one Todd Gitlin explores in *Media Unlimited*. His suspicion of content, reminiscent of Marshall McLuhan, is illustrated by a joke he tells about the man who continually passes a checkpoint driving a huge truck, which is invariably searched for contraband and found clean. Finally the checkpoint guard asks the driver what he could have possibly been smuggling past him all those times, and the driver replies: "Trucks" (3–4).

29. He should not be summarily written off as an elitist, however, particularly in light of his highly bemused reaction to the American mass culture that greeted him when he emigrated here in the forties. See John Burt Foster Jr.'s "Poshlust, Culture Criticism, Adorno, and Malraux," a fragmented tour of Nabokov's reflections on mass culture.

30. Arthur M. Saltzman's "The Figure in the Static: *White Noise*" argues that the nature of mass publicity's hegemony in the novel is its reiteration of the same formulae and rhetoric, which both soothes and infantilizes the populace, or tries to. This argument works nicely as a

way of taking the more usually literary form of objection to mass culture—that it reduces complexity and surprise to the sensibility of cliché—and extends its saliency beyond the intellectual realm. To this rule of cliché he counters that of metaphor: "Whereas metaphor depends upon uniqueness and verbal defamiliarization to earn attention, white noise thwarts distinction, for the proliferation of language, typically through such vulgarized forms as advertisements, tabloid headlines, and bureaucratic euphemisms, submerges difference into the usual cultural murmur. There is always more, but always more of the same" (481). The only quibble with his analysis is the fairly vague notion of "metaphor" he uses, which seems reminiscent of the way Paul de Man used to use "figural." It turns out words and even noises, if they are defamiliarizing enough apparently, can function as metaphors, as resistances to white noise (491).

31. This concern for authenticity in *White Noise* has alerted many critics to the parallels between aspects of Jean Baudrillard's theories of the simulacrum and DeLillo's portrait of publicity culture in that novel. I leave to others most of the task of demonstrating this now familiar relay, and one of those others is John N. Duvall, whose "The (Super)marketplace of Images" is a fairly thorough example of this strain of critique, with particular emphasis on how the threat of fascism that lies just below the surface of DeLillo's novel is inscribed within the peculiar libido afforded us by the apparatus of mass publicity simulation.

32. It is almost quaint to recall that in the 1952 presidential campaign, eyebrows were raised at the fact that Dwight Eisenhower's team had hired a firm to fashion some ads, now considered primitive, for their candidate—or that as late as the sixties, Joe McGinnis could create a scandal by detailing how Richard Nixon's 1968 candidacy was manipulated by political consultants and advertising gurus such as H. R. "Bob" Haldeman of J. Walter Thompson. As I write now, by contrast, pundit America is still recovering from convulsions of laughter over the statement of a recent candidate for the highest office that he will not rely as much on such people or their advice should he run again. The idea that a sophisticated politician would enter the public arena nowadays without a battery of PR people is simply dismissed as, of course, nothing but more PR.

33. See Daniel Boorstin's *The Image: or, What Happened to the American Dream,* an early attempt, together with some of the more popular work of Vance Packard, to describe the growing dominance of appearance over reality in American life. It should not surprise that, despite a naïve-realist philosophical framework to make a post-structuralist scoff, Boorstin's work was an influence on Jean Baudrillard's preliminary work, for example *La société de consommation* (1970).

34. Something like this objection is the one raised by Douglas Robinson's *American Apocalypses,* treating *Miss Lonelyhearts:* "[West's] novel launches a powerful assault on the entire Western tradition of the apocalyptic unveiling of order, but by doing so *verbally,* it partakes in the very tradition that West attacks. . . . By what authority can one destroy all authoritarian images of order?" (215). Robinson's argument essentially takes the one I am making, that using the symbols provided by the commercial apparatus implicates one in what one is critiquing, and turns it up a notch. Saltzman gets at this difficulty well: "For DeLillo himself, the paradox lies at the heart of the writer's profession: he must break the grip of idiom while continuing to exploit its pressures artistically" (480).

Notes to Chapter 4

1. In Robert I. Edenbaum, "To Kill God and Build a Church," 62.

2. Robert Andreach, in his article "Nathanael West's *Miss Lonelyhearts:* Between the Dead Pan and the Unborn Christ," gives this Pan motif about as thorough a treatment as one could want.

3. Edmond L. Volpe has argued in "The Waste Land of Nathanael West" that *Miss Lonelyhearts* constitutes an implicit if not intentional reply to Eliot's poem. Though I would suspect West's first novel, *The Dream Life of Balso Snell*, is a likelier candidate for this honor than *Miss Lonelyhearts*, the intertextual contrast is an illuminating one. Volpe demonstrates that in West's pessimistic vision, the option of mysticism held out by Eliot is foreclosed. It would be of interest to pursue the intercalation of the two works even further than Volpe, since he does not have much to say about either the specific role of cultural reclamation in Eliot's project of spiritual renewal or the way this is satirized by West. One way to approach this would be to argue that for Eliot the great cultural tradition is still a living alternative to the banalizing influence of mass culture, whereas for West, mass culture's reign is harder to question.

4. Strychacz sees West as in a conflicted relation to modernists such as Eliot and Ezra Pound: "Indebted as West might be to modernist ideology, his re-presentation of that ideology within the context of the culture industry could scarcely be countenanced by writers such as Pound and Eliot" (180). If so, it would remain to explain why Pound's distinctly positive review of *Miss Lonelyhearts* is only or partly a misreading.

5. Randall Reid, in his book *The Fiction of Nathanael West*, speaks of the final "hysteria" of Miss Lonelyhearts, though he argues as well that psychological categories should be taken with large grains of salt when studying West (95–96).

6. West himself has spoken of this rendering of hysteria as a goal of *Miss Lonelyhearts*'s style. See Nathanael West, "Some Notes on *Miss L.*"

7. Reid discusses the way West's images reflect not only the inner reality of hysteria as Miss Lonelyhearts may be said to experience it but also the objective conditions that give grounds for that hysteria and desperation (90).

8. Barnard argues that this psychotic decision means that "Miss Lonelyhearts can think of his success only in terms of a transcendental mass culture," with God as the Shrike figure. This is apt, but her conclusion—"For West mass culture is certainly a sham, but so is religion: both gospels are equally mendacious"—seems overdrawn and a bit shallow (205). What Barnard does not understand is that Miss Lonelyhearts's decision is dictated from the start by his very acceptance of the terms offered by the newspaper, both literally and figuratively. To infer some sweeping critique of religion, even relying on West's Jewishness to authenticate an implied dismantling of Christianity, from Miss Lonelyhearts's situation may be hasty. If mass culture provides the form of Miss Lonelyhearts's religiosity, this is easily read as the effects of the tabloid world he is now in on the boyhood faith into which he was born.

Notes to Chapter 5

1. The notion that Tod Hackett is the author's stand-in is of course prevalent. Jay Martin's biography of West gives a detailed account of West's labors in the Republic Studios vineyard (called by its screenwriting proletariat "Repulsive Studios") on 274–89.

2. West, quoted in Richard B. Gehman, Introduction to *Day of the Locust*, ix–x.

3. Richard Sennett has explored this degradation of community in his study *The Fall of Public Man*. Sennett is especially insightful on the cult of the performer as the by-product of the increasing emptying-out of public space as a venue for ritual and expressive role-playing.

4. The "starers" are afflicted by what W. H. Auden calls "West's Disease": "This is a disease of consciousness which renders it incapable of converting wishes into desires. . . . All wishes, whatever their apparent content, have the same and unvarying meaning: 'I refuse to be what I am.' A wish, therefore, is either . . . a kind of play, or . . . a hatred of oneself and every being one holds responsible for oneself" (149–50).

5. This is one point where I take issue with Gerald Locklin's quite perceptive essay "The

Day of the Painter; the Death of the Cock," in which he argues that there are actually "three major groups" in *Day of the Locust*—the "masqueraders," the "starers," and the "performers" (69). It is true that West mentions masqueraders at one point and performers at another, but they are functionally equivalent as against the starers: both groups play exhibitionist to the starers' voyeur.

6. Locklin has noted this similarity (73).

7. Walter Wells in his *Tycoons and Locusts* makes this point (52).

8. This is Stanley Edgar Hyman's remark from his *Nathanael West*, 44.

9. Wells writes: "All that Tod ever does complete of his prophetic painting is a series of preliminary 'cartoons' and some 'rough charcoal strokes'" (62).

10. The complaints of critics such as Hyman and others concerning the point-of-view shifts between Tod and Homer are thus somewhat dubious, as Locklin also asserts (67–68).

11. Critics have looked to Wing Biddlebaum's hands, emblems of thwarted communication in Sherwood Anderson's *Winesburg, Ohio* as prototypes for Homer's. Victor Comerchero, in *Nathanael West*, hints at this line of filiation (6). Reid also remarks these affinities, along with the similarity between the name of Wayneville, Iowa, which is Homer's town of origin, and that of Anderson's mythical town (139).

12. To the extent that the dynamic enacted in West's novel is as I have described and accurate, one strong contention is weakened in Walter Benjamin's famous essay "The Work of Art in the Age of Mechanical Reproduction," in which he makes the case that the tendency of media such as film is precisely to diminish the aura of distance between spectator and artwork.

13. Jonathan Veitch, in his *American Superrealism*, makes a good relay between the arc of frustration West depicts in *Day of the Locust* and the sort of structure of triangulated or mediated desire famously discussed by René Girard in his *Deceit, Desire, and the Novel*. Since the desire is planted in the spectator by "an Other, by ideology," this means that desire must always outdistance any particular object: "Desire thus places the subject in an untenable position: driven by that which it cannot satisfy precisely because that desire never belonged to the subject to begin with. As the distance between the subject and its desired object diminishes, the inadequacy of the object becomes more apparent, comprehension more acute, and self-hatred more intense, until at last the subject is abandoned to 'that disappointment which is called possession'" (122). The only difference: the objects of mass veneration are not liable to be possessed, except in fantasy, which of course carries its own disappointment.

14. Without digressing too far into film theory, I would note in particular in this vein one influential meditation on the medium, Laura Mulvey's "Visual Pleasure and Narrative Cinema." She also stresses the way the female image is projected by the cinema, although she more heavily weighs the male gaze of the protagonist (and implicitly of the audience) as it "commands the stage . . . and creates the action" in a given film (13). Mulvey may rely too much on the illusion of omnipotence she sees in this gaze, too little on the self-abasement before the object of worship that is also implied in many a gaze.

15. See especially Donald T. Torchiana's "The Painter's Eye." It is the most comprehensive treatment of the painterly allusions in *Day of the Locust* I have thus far run across. He is especially interesting on novelistic arrangements taken from Goya's *Caprichos* (252–58). Jay Martin has also dilated on an allusion by Josephine Herbst to James Ensor's paintings to argue that *Les cuirassiers à Waterloo* was a conscious model for the debacle Tod witnesses at National Studios (*Nathanael West: The Art of His Life*, 316).

16. Strychacz has, in this regard, an interesting passage wherein he points up the ambiguity in how West presents Tod's daydream of his mural: "The narrative clues that previously stabilized our understanding of the indicative voice as a representation of an imagined scene now vanish: not 'he imagined that he was standing on a chair' but 'he stood'" (198). He makes

much, arguably rather too much, of the ambiguity here: I don't think many readers construe these passages as meaning that Tod has actually removed to his apartment, since of course the rest of the closing narrative places him with grim certitude in the riot itself. But Strychacz does underline the way in which Tod's devotion to his private vision can become its own kind of denial, its own escape, just as the movies can.

17. Locklin puts the riot into this sensible perspective (78–79).

18. Barnard seems to wish to preserve some sort of revolutionary potential for the rioters, in the absence of much concrete encouragement from the author. This desire results in the following slightly tortuous formula: "if for West, as for Marx, 'the abolition of the illusory happiness of people is a demand for their true happiness,' then the ruinous aspect of the Hollywood dream is not only a sign of decay, but a sign of hope. The destruction of these materialized wishes . . . is the precondition for change, the precondition for an as yet unimaginable redemption" (187). It is true that West implies a vaguely class-based ressentiment as motivating the rioters; but this is only from Tod's point of view, and the inadequacy of his prophetic powers are precisely what the final episode reveals. Still, who doesn't want, in his anarchic soul, something big and horrible to happen to the icons of our show business civilization? On that low level, at least, Barnard's hope may have a purchase. But then, one wonders, would the *National Enquirer*, say, much of whose editorial process relies on the same sort of resentment, also be a "sign of hope"?

Notes to Chapter 6

1. Vladimir Nabokov, *The Annotated Lolita*, 222–23. Subsequent page references are given in the body of the text.

2. If one follows Andreas Huyssen's famous argument in *After the Great Divide* that mass culture for the modernists is defined chiefly in female terms, the anxiety over generic differentiation may parallel that over gender identity in more than solely metaphorical ways. See "Mass Culture as Woman: Modernism's Other" (44–62).

3. One recalls also various extreme reactions to interviewers impertinent enough to raise "public morality" as an issue in discussing his novel: "I don't give a damn about public morality" and so on.

4. Richard Rorty, though a philosopher rather a literary critic strictly speaking, probably best exemplifies this new trend. See *Contingency, Irony, and Solidarity*, especially the chapter entitled "The Barber of Kasbeam: Nabokov on Cruelty" (141–68).

5. Julian Moynahan, *Vladimir Nabokov*, 36.

6. This is Thomas R. Frosch's argument in "Parody and Authenticity in Lolita," 127. At least as important for our purposes is the fact that while Lolita is defined as the object of a romance plot, she is also "an inherently unattainable object" whose "appeal consists partly in her transiency." This is the chief reason, no doubt, why Frosch can later claim that Humbert in seeking Lolita "tries to translate art into life and . . . failed" (136).

7. Michael Bell points out in "Lolita and Pure Art," in Bloom, 69–80, that Nabokov's book bears some resemblance to "the classic bildungsroman," wherein "the hero's emotional and moral growth is inseparable from his growth in the understanding of aesthetic principles. The reason Humbert's story has not the immediate appearance of a bildungsroman is that, apart from flashbacks to his adolescent relationship with Annabel, he is a mature and sophisticated man from the beginning of the story, with considerable literary and artistic experiences. Yet . . . he does not possess this experience in the true spirit. He has knowledge and apparent sophistication but lacks true understanding until the very end of his relationship with Lolita" (75). Bell is exactly and profoundly right here, but the question is what (aside from prison)

accounts for the "true understanding" that I agree we are to attribute to Humbert at "the very end" of this relationship—or as I would see it, after the very end?

8. Martin Green, for instance, speaks of the instability of Humbert Humbert's rhetorical stance and even of his sentences. See "Tolstoy and Nabokov."

9. Some have even argued that the entire story of the trip to Coalmont and subsequent murder of Clare Quilty is Humbert Humbert's figment. Christina Tekiner in "Time in *Lolita*" makes such a claim, insisting that since he claims to have been writing his memoir for fifty-six days, and since this dating would place the project's incipit on the day he says he received both John Farlow's warning letter and Lolita's, therefore "Humbert did not set off at once for Coalmont to murder Richard Schiller, he did not meet with Lolita, he did not subsequently return to Ramsdale, and he did not kill Clare Quilty. Rather, he began to write *Lolita* in a 'psychopathic ward'" (466). This of course assumes the chronology is supposed to be correct. Further, crucial to her argument is the assertion that since Humbert is a bad man and the latter events "tend to exonerate rather than to condemn Humbert [she includes murder in these exonerating events], . . . this in itself is enough to suggest that Humbert has altered or entirely invented them."

10. There is a great deal of criticism in recent years arguing for *Lolita*'s fundamental morality. Lionel Trilling, with his famous early essay ("The Last Lover"), probably inaugurated this trend. His opening paragraph, asserting that *Lolita* is "not about sex . . . [but] about love," does go on to explore the transgressive nature of that passion as defined by Western tradition (5). Still, he credits Nabokov with essential, rather than borrowed, psychological insight. Rorty argues similarly that Nabokov is in the end a moralist; in the chapter "The Barber of Kasbeam: Nabokov on Cruelty" (141–68), he argues, basically, that Nabokov is against it. David Rampton's *Vladimir Nabokov* goes a long way toward allowing critics to read *Lolita* and other of his novels as if ethical questions were not beyond the pale. He asserts that "*Lolita* . . . dramatizes the potential inhumanity of the kind of aesthetic attitude to experience that fails to make [an 'emotional and moral'] commitment" (119). Rampton's "aesthetic attitude" I am rendering as the fictive attitude.

11. Nabokov, quoted in Andrew Field, *VN*, 310.

12. Brian Boyd, *Vladimir Nabokov*, 266–67. Nabokov was not so disturbed, though, as to refuse Girodias for a publisher, but chose as much as he could to deny the nature of the person to whom he was shackling his reputation, once he had agreed, at great length, to sign his name. "'You and I know,' he wrote Girodias, 'that *Lolita* is a serious book with a serious purpose. [An interesting line since Girodias's version of the "serious purpose" appears to have been the hope that pedophilia would become more accepted.] I hope the public will accept it as such. A *succès de scandale* would distress me'" (269). How distressed Nabokov was to be is partly conjectural; but that *Lolita*'s initial *succès* was very much de scandale is scarcely in question.

13. Trilling lauds its "ability to arouse uneasiness, to throw the reader off balance, to require him to change his stance and shift his position and move on" (11). Green notes in admiration that there is never any "vantage point from which to see beyond and around [Humbert]. [This ignores John Ray Jr., though Green announces earlier his intention to "forget" him (17).] He has been beforehand with us in every tone to take about him" (26). This "humiliation" of the reader Green sees as a signally worthy feature of the narrative.

14. In each case it strained the friendships, of course. Wilson, along with a "puzzled" Mary McCarthy, "recoiled at once," despite his own history as a purveyor of obscenity in the brouhaha attendant on his *Memoirs of Hecate County*, announcing to the author that he liked it "'less than anything else of yours I have read.'" Nabokov, irritated at Wilson's dismissal after what he had gathered was a superficial scan of the work, wrote to "prod his friend into reading *Lolita* properly: 'I would like you to read it some day'" (Boyd, 263–64).

15. Indeed, one of the earliest literary figures to so arraign *Lolita* and its creator was a pre-eminent antifeminist, Kingsley Amis, writing in the *Spectator*. While admitting that much of the narrator's cruelty can be explained away as satirical characterization, nevertheless "the many totally incidental cruelties—the bloody car wreck by the roadside that brings into view the kind of shoe Lolita covets, the wounding of a squirrel, apparently just for fun—bring the author into consideration as well, and I really don't care which of them is being wonderfully mature and devastating when Lolita's mother (recently Humbert's wife) is run over and killed. . . . There comes a point where the atrophy of moral sense, evident throughout this book, finally leads to dullness, fatuity and unreality. . . . There is plenty of self-absorption around us, heaven knows, but not enough on this scale [of Humbert's] to be worth writing about at length, just as the mad are much less interesting than the sane" (quoted in Norman Page, *Nabokov*, 105–6).

16. His commentator Alfred Appel Jr., in *Nabokov's Dark Cinema*, loyally maintains the line between Nabokov and "some of the post-*Lolita* Black Humorists with whom he is sometimes loosely grouped" by pointing out his "unsparing . . . criticism" of Joseph Heller, for one, whose *Catch-22* he "indignantly" denounced as "anti-American" (65–66).

17. Lance Olsen, in his survey of *Lolita* and its reception called *Lolita: A Janus Text*, notes: "Much work remains to be done, for instance, from feminist perspectives [on *Lolita*] investigating the role of women in this work, women's responses to it, the complexity of gender issues manifested in its pages," and so forth (25). One reason so much work of that sort "remains to be done" is that, in my experience anyway, a good many women, and almost all strong feminists, find the book itself so hard to take. This is, I hasten to add, no reason not to read and study this important novel, but it does call for a critical stance toward it—more so, I would suggest, than Nabokovians have generally adopted thus far.

18. Boyd, 264.

19. Green insists otherwise: "The moral theory [of Nabokov's] I mean is an application of the doctrine of the immortality of art. . . . The artist is a kind of hero" (29). Green manages by this means to subsume the moral realm under the aesthetic: insofar as Humbert succeeds as an artist (along with his creator), this success justifies whatever previous harm Humbert the person may have done—including, of course, murder.

20. "He [Bishop] found he could not read the novel through: Humbert seemed just too slimy. Offended, Nabokov replied: 'It is the best thing I ever wrote'" (Boyd, 267). Whether Nabokov gainsaid the narrator's "sliminess," though, is not recorded. As it stands, a moral objection is refuted by an aesthetic assertion.

21. Moynahan opines that her "voidness and loneliness [are] only partly created by Humbert's machinations," but rather are "cultural in the first instance, American" (36), and Rampton claims that by the time of her last interview, "Lolita is in the process of becoming another Charlotte, another cipher in mindless America" (115). The ever faithful Appel demurs in *Dark Cinema*: "these pages are easily misunderstood, particularly by those who would read *Lolita* too readily as a 'satire' of America. *Poshlost* observes no geographic boundaries" (65).

22. Appel says in *Dark Cinema*: "Quilty's 'movie picture' *Golden Guts* would clearly have been something less splendid, at best a trivialized version of Humbert's magical vision [of Lolita's tennis]—and at worst the lurid reality of Quilty's cinematic plans" (118). Appel asserts that "Quilty's unkept promise and its pornographic alternative [he does film her, only for dirty movies] at once represent a debasement of . . . the enchantments of art cherished by Nabokov" (116).

23. Indeed, Appel tells us in his edition of *Lolita* that the Quilty doubling plot is "a conscious parody of [E. A. Poe's story] 'William Wilson'" (lxv) and, perhaps more significantly, that the character of Quilty was thought of first as dying, then constructed backward from

that death: "'His death had to be clear in my mind in order to control his earlier appearances,' says Nabokov" (xxxix).

24. Julia Bader's *Crystal Land* makes this case most extensively, arguing that Quilty is "a practitioner of thoroughly conventional art" who "makes use of art in a cold, calculating way [but who] has no creative power; . . . he uses Lolita for a brief scene and then discards her." Because she is explicating Nabokov, however, Bader tries to avoid a moral contrast, obvious though one is. It is as a threat to "the artistic integrity of Humbert's creation" rather than to a live Dolores Haze that Quilty is feared (73). Yet Quilty himself may be another of Humbert's creations, invented in order to be dispatched: "Perhaps Quilty serves partly to dramatize Humbert's ritualistic killing of pseudo-art, which has defiled his own passionately loved art object" (76–77).

25. Appel, *Nabokov's Dark Cinema*, 115. Bader has suggestively remarked, "It is not until Humbert decides to kill Quilty that the playwright actually begins to 'exist'" (77).

26. Characteristic in his ability to follow Nabokovian cues, both regarding irony and altered sympathy, is Appel in *Dark Cinema*, who notes that the "staging of Quilty's death . . . easily outdoes the 'robust atmosphere of incompetent marksmanship' of any previous 'underworlder'" (115); but he also insists that Quilty, "the shadow world's well-paid representative [who] perpetrates *his* mischief at the expense of ladies' lit'ry clubs and movie and theater audiences," is there being "routed" not only by Humbert but also by Humbert's creator (66).

27. Bell claims that Humbert's growing ability to draw on "the latent artist in himself" is shown "in his consciously facing and killing Quilty whom, as the parodic tone of the whole episode indicates, he now sees as his artificially or fictionally contrived double rather than simply as his literal rival" (76). This is a curious argument, using the very parodic elements as proof that Humbert has matured, rather than making the equally plausible point that Humbert is now treating Quilty in exactly the same murderous way he treated Lolita earlier—which would illustrate his continued bondage to a confusion between art and life.

28. This emotional sterility may be one reason why critics seem so ready to believe that Quilty does indeed "tell the melancholy truth" when he claims not to have had sex with Dolly because "I am practically impotent" (300). This sits oddly with Humbert's later remark that when he and Quilty are tussling, the latter is "naked and goatish under his robe" (301). Could this be a Nabokovian hint that Quilty is so dulled of sensibility that, like his mentor Sade, he is only really aroused by violence? In any case, even assuming that Quilty is not lying, the operative word in his revelation would appear to be "practically."

29. The designation "Public" is Bader's , who proceeds briskly to explain it: "he appears in cigarette ads and teenage magazines, and makes pornographic movies" (73). All of Quilty's labors exist to turn words as much as possible into spectacle.

30. See Green: "There is something powerfully disintegrative in Nabokov's sensibility, and, though the novel's form contains and transmutes that something, the total effect of reading it—even on highly trained readers—is not likely to be controlled by the form. *Lolita* is in fact the product and the agent of a corrupt culture. . . . But [unlike Leo Tolstoy] we, presumably, are committed to using primarily aesthetic criteria, and to preferring aesthetically good art. We are committed to judging a novel primarily on its perfect reading, seeing it in perfect sympathy with the author's intentions, understanding it from inside . . . however 'exclusive,' to use Tolstoy's term, the audience for that version of the book" (32–33). Such a view, while admirable for the fearlessness with which it confronts an obvious issue raised by the text, seems to resolve it by resorting to a kind of cultural triage. In this rationale for *Lolita*, the edification of the exclusive, highly trained reader who understands it "from inside" is bought by the further coarsening of those already coarse masses seeing only the titillation of violating a taboo, and presumably the equally coarse outrage of those moralists who see the text only as under-

mining public morality. Green has managed here to gauge his moral measure exactly to Nabokov's, since the most highly moral readers are defined in chaste formalist terms as the closest readers, just as Nabokov always insists on respect for private particularity rather than concern for public morality as the basis for true ethics. I must admit, though, that I see this cavalier renunciation of responsibility for any public harm resulting from a text one enjoys as faintly solipsistic itself. Is defending a clever and sensitive writer against any charge of immorality worth consigning all of his less than perfect readers (which, thus defined, could well be all of his readers *tout court*) to moral debasement? It becomes a strange, though forthright, means of defending a writer.

31. Appel "wonders how many readers, denied further access to Humbert's diary, have unconsciously wished that Quilty *had* narrated *Lolita*, and that his movie [of Lolita giving blow jobs] had formed the body of the narrative, the bodies *in* the narrative" (*Nabokov's Dark Cinema*, 122). Such wonder enlists the fantasied mass readership on the side of Quilty, and Nabokov, in denying them access, on the side of the angels as a result.

32. Bell, 76.

33. I might point out that Quilty's function symbolically (for Humbert and for Nabokov) is roughly equivalent whether he is notional or not, whether the events of Coalmont and Pavor Manor actually occur or not. If actual, then Humbert is freed from enthrallment to the actorly duplicity Quilty has entrapped him in to "go public" with his story by arranging his own arrest (for driving on the wrong side of the road) and thence writing his memoir. If notional, then the staging of these reconciliation and revenge scenes is a metaphor for the narrator's full realization of his own deep love of and sorrow over his use of Lolita. The common thesis that Quilty is the name for Humbert's own unworthy, selfish alter ego works best of all for the latter interpretation, but some version of that thesis works for either contingency.

Notes to Chapter 7

1. In his article "The Crying of Lot 49," Tanner says that while with a detective story "you start with a mystery and move towards a final clarification . . . in Pynchon's novel we move from a state of degree-zero mystery . . . to a condition of increasing mystery and dubiety" (175). Tanner is shrewd to note the crucial distinction between Pynchon's novel and a detective story; I will show, moreover, that paradoxically it is the kind of clarification sought by the particular detective that is Oedipa that results in this "increasing mystery and dubiety."

2. Tanner remarks: "The problem is finally about America. There is the America of San Narciso, but is there perhaps another America?" (188).

3. In addition to Tanner, Edward Mendelson, in "The Sacred, the Profane, and *The Crying of Lot 49*," isolates this feature of the story: "Where the object of a detective story is to reduce a complex and disordered situation to simplicity and clarity, and in doing so to isolate in a named locus the disruptive element in the story's world, *The Crying of Lot 49* starts with a relatively simple situation, and then lets it go out of the heroine's control . . ." (123).

4. Theodor Adorno, for instance, uses this phrase in his *Negative Dialectics*.

5. Jean Baudrillard, *For a Critique of the Political Economy of the Sign*, 32, 65–66.

6. Baudrillard discusses fashion himself, whose "compulsion to innovate signs" and "perpetual production of meaning—a kind of meaning drive—and the logical mystery of its cycle" are all part of "logical processes [that] might be extrapolated to the dimension of 'culture' in general—to all social production of signs, values and relations" (78–79).

7. There is a fine article that takes as part of its gambit the explicit forming of bonds between Pynchon's text and that of Marshall McLuhan's *Understanding Media*. See Thomas

Schaub's "'A Gentle Chill, an Ambiguity.'" Certainly such relays are hard not to make regarding a novel that compares a tract of postwar real estate homes to a radio's circuit card.

8. Thomas Pynchon, *The Crying of Lot 49*, 178. Subsequent page references are given in the body of the text.

9. This point contradicts the drift of Max Horkheimer and Theodor Adorno's argument in *Dialectic of Enlightenment*, 120–67. Whereas they tend to emphasize the "stereotyped appropriation of everything, even the inchoate, for the purposes of mechanical reproduction" (127), the administered world of Pynchon's text draws its sustenance from subcultures and marginal groups while despising them at the same time. Nonetheless, the chief difference between the world presented in Pynchon's text and that presented by Horkheimer and Adorno may be more tonal than substantive.

10. Baudrillard has described this process of use and displacement as the movement from the socially direct, interactive world of symbolic exchange to a system of sign-objects with the social meanings affixed to them in various ways. Baudrillard, ever the anthropologist, links this process to that of fetishism, which he posits as in itself a constant and not necessarily pernicious one: "As a power that is transferred to beings, objects and agencies, it [fetishism] is universal and diffuse, but it crystallizes at strategic points so that its flux can be regulated and diverted by certain groups or individuals for their own benefit" (89). What the ancient priests were accused of doing by William Blake, monopolizing the deities, is roughly what Baudrillard charges consumer society in this century with doing. He points out that *fetish* originally tended to mean fabrication, or artifact. Hence a fetish was the product of artisanal labor and in some measure the result of a conscious "cultural sign labor." Under consumer society, ironically, objects become even more fetishistic than those older fetish objects, at least insofar as they are "given and received everywhere as force dispensers (happiness, health, security, prestige etc.)." The labor of fabrication that was part of the ancient fascination with the fetish is now suppressed, and what replaces it for inspection is some sort of magical force imputed to the object itself (91). Baudrillard's argument effects an elegant reversal whereby the modern-day consumer is actually more prey to a kind of fetishism of the object—the tendency to impute properly internal power to external things—that is more extreme than earlier forms because more isolated from the social process of meaning making. (One thinks irresistibly of Oedipa's flying aerosol can.)

11. Molly Hite, *Ideas of Order in the Novels of Thomas Pynchon*, 90.

12. Baudrillard, 97.

13. Adorno, 50.

14. As Maureen Quilligan says in "Thomas Pynchon and the Language of Allegory," "All of Pynchon's characters are readers, but Oedipa in *The Crying of Lot 49* is the protagonist most consistently as a reader" (200).

15. See ibid., 187.

16. "By becoming the executor of Pierce Inverarity's last will and testament, Oedipa comes close to a kind of sacred discipleship" (ibid., 188).

17. Marie-Claude Profit, in her "The Rhetoric of Death in *The Crying of Lot 49*," makes much of the way metaphor, like death itself, connects two worlds customarily divergent. Citing John Nefastis's statement that entropy constitutes a metaphor because it is a way of connecting the worlds of information flow and energy, she notes: "An important word in Nefastis' remarks: 'it *connects*'" (31).

18. Edward Mendelson makes this relay also: "The logical response to a world where one creates, alone, the only order—where one ignores the *data* of the world—is nihilistic despair. And the logical culmination of an exclusive devotion to the spirit is the sloughing-off of the flesh" (125).

19. Hite puts it this way: "As she [Oedipa] sees it, if her 'project,' the Tristero does not exist, the codes break down. . . . Either the 'residue' of Oedipa's experience means that the Tristero exists, or it does not mean" (77).

20. Mendelson, 132.

21. On this point, see Hite: "She [Oedipa] sees the world behind the tapestry and finds that it is not a void. But she does not understand what she sees because she is looking only for evidence of the Tristero. . . . The Tristero has forced her to see, but she believes she sees only clues to the Tristero" (86–87).

22. Hite remarks that Oedipa's desire for "a definitive message" is what "pushes the narrative forward toward a conclusion so loaded with portents that the attentive reader may recognize that it is unrealizable" (88). With this I concur, although the preceding comment is perhaps the only part of this superb treatment I cannot agree to: "The post horn [of Tristero] is a mark of kinship. It calls attention to the 'wasted' elements of American society and suggests that they compose an alternative society, communicating by different means and relaying different messages." To the extent that Hite goes along with what the post horn "suggests" and reads the clues gathered by Oedipa as indicating this "alternative society," I think this already forecloses the other and likelier possibility that the apparatus of linkage itself is chiefly something that Oedipa brings to her encounters; in other words, the Tristero, even if it is in fact a parallel organization for "X number of Americans" who are alienated from official culture (which is far from demonstrated), is the organization for all the marginal, "'wasted' elements." The mere fact that all the drifters and subcultures Pynchon presents are alienated from mainstream America does by no means show that they are all perforce in league with one another.

23. Louis Mackey, in "Thomas Pynchon and the American Dream," discusses this exploration of Pynchon's with special emphasis on *Gravity's Rainbow* rather than *The Crying of Lot 49*, but it accounts for the sort of Manichaeanism that produces Oedipa's dilemma of narrative and counternarrative.

24. Hite, 88–89. Hite mentions elsewhere in this connection that the "world of shared meanings" encountered by Oedipa "lacks the coherence of a myth that moves toward a projected fulfillment, but it is not incoherent" (81). I take this to mean that socially produced meanings emerge from interactive processes that are not necessarily subject to prior ratification by some official sacred narrative, nor even by official consumer society.

25. In his essay "The Sacred," Bataille says: "The term *privileged instant* is the only one that, with a certain amount of accuracy, accounts for what can be encountered *at random* in the search [for the sacred]; the opposite of a *substance* that withstands the test of time, it is something that flees as soon as it is seen and cannot be grasped" (241).

26. David Coward, *Thomas Pynchon*, 108.

Notes to Chapter 8

1. Don DeLillo, *White Noise*, 97. Subsequent page references are given in the body of the text.

2. The informed reader may see a certain family resemblance between these stories, which are passed down culturally and which in turn are about their own process of being passed down, and those *grands récits* spoken of by Jean-François Lyotard in his *The Postmodern Condition*. Lyotard has indeed inflected much that I present here, but anyone who tries to find any one-to-one corollary between his narratives and those herein described will be disappointed. For one essential thing, his metanarratives have an Enlightenment provenance, whereas mine (the liberal humanist narrative, I would insist, included) antedate that period and its concerns. Even the civic narrative, seemingly drawn from the Revolutionary War, really stems from far

earlier sources such as ancient Greece, at least in DeLillo's text. The closest thing in *White Noise* to an Enlightenment narrative would be the discourse of science, but even those who find it compelling treat it with the sort of veneration accorded magic, not rational inquiry.

3. Cornel Branca's article "Don DeLillo's *White Noise:* The Natural Language of the Species" is one of the few treatments of DeLillo's novel that gives its prominent concern with death, and with the Heideggerian reality of "being towards Death," the kind of consideration it really merits. The general polemic of the piece is that the standard-issue "postmodernist" reading of this text does not account for that death concern. For Branca, at least one kind of white noise "has always been 'the natural language of the species'—death evasion—and which now gets expressed in the argot of consumer society" (466). As part of this argument he con- vincingly suggests that little Steffie's incantation "Toyota Celica" is not mere nonsense but a way of "let[ting her] dread dissolve in the chanting of this media mantra" (469–70). She utters it, after all, in the days following the airborne toxic event.

4. For what it is worth, recent writings of Paul Brodeur on the effects of extremely low fre- quency radiation, of the kind emitted from electrical wires and VDT terminals, suggest Hein- rich may have in fact been on to something. See his *Currents of Death.*

5. Tom LeClair, in his *In the Loop,* has pointed out in this regard that the parents in *White Noise* are in fact much more in need of "what they trust are protective and safe relationships" than are their children. Babette, he notes, sees the children as "'a guarantee of our relative longevity.'" As a result, "the children are more willing to face threats to existence than are their parents," thus becoming "a threat—an inescapable threat, because Babette and Jack have sealed them into the nuclear structure" (216–17).

6. Thomas J. Ferraro's "Whole Families Shopping at Night!" is especially acute on the way in which DeLillo constructs an American mass culture that at once fosters the shredding of the premodern family and offers itself as the means (inadequate, of course) of mending it: "As DeLillo envisions it, television menaces the home with an omnipresent temptation to substi- tute the communal experience of the image for the ties that no longer bind" (24). He has a similar thesis about the shopping center (21–24). Ferraro treats the passage where Jack Glad- ney turns into a munificent gift giver in expansive mood, noting that it ends "abruptly on a discordant note. 'We drove home in silence. We went to our respective rooms, wishing to be alone'" (24). The family is brought together, if superficially, by the spending of money; but once it is spent, the postcoital letdown is undeniable.

7. Nor is this awe the produce of mere stupidity. As LeClair mentions, the "waves and radi- ation" of scientific discourse "are beyond the capability of 'natural' perception: knowledge of them cannot be had without the aid of technological extensions of the nervous system" (225). Or, we might add, without faith.

8. Duvall makes a wordplay connecting this science-fiction element to that very real plug- in drug known as TV: "the title of the third section . . . [is] Dylarama . . . television itself, that means of forgetting death through aestheticization, is Dylar, an imagistic space of consump- tion that one accesses by playing dial-a-rama" (449). It may also be a reference to the "Death- a-rama" joke in Honoré de Balzac's *Père Goriot,* a famous nineteenth-century moment when tragedy is rendered trivial.

9. For more on this link between the accretion of objects and Jack's fear of death, along with the ironic reversal when he starts to throw things out, see LeClair, 214–15.

10. John Frow, in his "Notes on *White Noise,*" discusses the central place of the mass media in this book at length, with much cogency. He attributes the substitution of media simulacrum for "real-life" experience as just one more postmodern feature in the mode described by Bau- drillard, among others. He understands that DeLillo's novel constructs "a new mode of typi- cality" where general representations . . . are then lived as real," yet "so detailed" as not to be

"opposed to the particular" (418). Frow is correct to note the constant *reversio* whereby the media, in purporting to "represent" some aspect of existence, in fact put forth a model to *be* imitated. As he says, "Real moments and TV moments interpenetrate each other" quite a bit in this text (421). But he is too hasty, I suspect, in ascribing this reversal to the sheer profusion of signs in the contemporary world, in forswearing on DeLillo's behalf any "sentimental regret for a lost world of depths" (427). Whether or not Frow feels admitting the palpable undertow of nostalgia in *White Noise* might make it seem insufficiently postmodern, I think he fails to assess the hollows, the felt absences of once viable stories. It is these hollows that role models of celebrity—along with the products they endorse (and that endorse them)—are expected to fill in DeLillo's world.

11. LeClair notes that Gladney draws no conclusion from the miraculous survival of his youngest, Wilder, after the child rides his tricycle across a busy expressway. He sees this as a sign of Gladney's new maturity. This is possible. But its inclusion in the first place suggests to this reader more that Gladney hopes to see it as a "good omen," without retaining by this point any larger narrative frame within which to justify that hope—that, in short, it is another index that Gladney has indeed succumbed to superstition, as well as the final instance of that recurrent DeLillo chiasmus whereby adults look to their children for guidance, rather than vice versa. (The Gladney family's death-defying trips are made to the same expressway where Wilder performs his feat.)

Notes to Chapter 9

1. Don DeLillo, *Mao II,* 54. Subsequent page references are given in the body of the text.

2. Those interested in DeLillo's life and opinions can look in Frank Lentricchia, *Introducing Don DeLillo,* especially "'An Outsider in This Society': An Interview with Don DeLillo," by Anthony DeCurtis (43–66).

3. See Lentricchia's "American Writer as Bad Citizen."

Notes to Chapter 10

1. George W. S. Trow's *My Pilgrim's Progress* speaks of this kind of processing with regard to three "caesuras," or massive nervous breakdowns, he sees the United States as having undergone in the twentieth century: World War I, World War II, and the "sixties." Because World War I was "the caesura . . . documented and processed by important literary minds, and the minds that agreed to process this material were immediately accepted as the cultural leaders of the time," it was the best integrated into our cultural life, whereas the other two were not (200). The general point I take from Trow's argument here is that a literary elite's function, to some degree a self-understood one, is to feed back the implications of major breaks in a culture, which further implies the elite's need for a crisis to which to respond.

2. Jacques Barzun wrote an article entitled "The Tenth Muse" in which he eulogized the late Clifton Fadiman, champion of middlebrow "bookchat" and tireless promoter of things artistic to the inartistic. He sees these popularization efforts without irony as part of a "mid-century crusade" to educate middle-class taste, whose loss he clearly mourns (80). So angered is he at those who dismissed work such as Fadiman's as middlebrow that he refuses even to name Fadiman critic Dwight Macdonald, for example, calling him instead "a writer for *Partisan Review,* whose name is now obscure and who has left no work of any moment," though he identifies the essay in which the unnamed critic attacks Fadiman as "Masscult and Midcult" so that nobody in the know could mistake whom he means to snub (77). I have more to say about Macdonald below, though his view of Fadiman may well have been too severe.

3. Book reviewer Jonathan Yardley, in a survey of the "State of the Art" of literature, puts the matter well: "What one must first understand about American literature is that it is un-American . . . because literature is something with which we as a nation are inherently uneasy. The first European settlers were . . . more inclined to action than reflection, . . . profit than . . . edification, and we have been the same ever since. We borrowed our language from the English, but we have little patience for polishing our prose as they do and none of their quaint affinity for bookishness. The excitement aroused by the Booker literary prize in England or the Prix Goncourt in France is unimaginable in this country" (1). Strangely, having admirably summed up the country's yawning indifference, nay hostility, toward all things highbrow, Yardley proceeds to forget what he has said in accounting for the sad state of the contemporary literary art, throwing essentially all the blame onto snooty authors who turn their backs on the rest of the country and gaze into their own navels. Yardley seems not to realize that if his description of the generality of the country is correct, the amazing thing is that serious writers endure in the United States at all.

4. It may be Yardley's obscure sense of competition with that other literature conduit known as the university that impels him to decry "the isolation of writing-school students (and teachers) from real-world America." He sees the campus as "a poor place to get any feel for life as most Americans live it," and the novels and stories resulting therefrom display no interest "in anything except the inner lives and private experiences of the author-surrogates who are its central characters" (3). This is a familiar and (within limits) apt critique, but one wonders whether professional-class Americans need to take up residence on a campus, or for that matter take up a pen, to be obsessed with themselves. Isn't this solipsism a trait of Americans in general, regardless of profession, at least in the current era? What Yardley objects to, without knowing it, may be how faithfully U.S. storytellers actually do represent their compatriots.

5. The famous writers of the so-called silent generation of the fifties in America are few. I can think only of Saul Bellow and Joseph Heller, and the latter's big book, *Catch 22* (1960) may disprove the rule, since its setting is the Second World War. In fact, it may be significant that in Yardley's estimation, apart from Bellow's *Adventures of Augie March* (1953), the most enduring work from that decade in American letters is *Lolita*, a *succès de scandale* penned by a Russian immigrant, and one that has virtually no aspirations to influence in what is usually thought of as the public sphere.

6. I recall in this connection one of the many anguished nineties debates over whether to continue the government's exiguous funding of the National Endowment for the Arts, which went forward in the seeming assumption that no performance artist in America went onstage without chocolate for the smearing. One of the Sunday morning talk shows mentioned the controversy and conducted a poll of the four people there present: all, liberal or conservative, were stoutly against any government money for the arts.

7. Macdonald's "Masscult & Midcult" essay, included in his *Against the American Grain,* suggests that the intermediate "step" between mass taste and high culture called middlebrow (or, as he shortens it, "Midcult") should be discouraged by devotees of artistic innovation. It is easy to see this argument as the most insolent arrogance, and I for one disagree with it: I do not incline to view any less than pure version of artistic endeavor as a positive roadblock to someone's capacity to appreciate the real thing and find Macdonald's version too Manichaean. What gets overlooked, though, is that even this seeming rejection of compromise is with a view to fostering the sort of "group culture" that produced the experimental ferment of high modernism: "there will always be happy accidents, because of the stubbornness of some isolated creator. But if we are to have more than this, it will be because our new public for High Culture becomes conscious of itself and begins to show some *esprit de corps,* insisting on higher standards and setting itself off—joyously, implacably—from most of its fellow citizens, not

only from the Masscult depths but also from the agreeable ooze of the Midcult swamp" (74). If he is an elitist, then, it is only in the interests of shoring up Eliot's "group culture" and nurturing thereby greater creative energy. Macdonald wants, in short, the sort of culture of informed aspiration that is assumed in Europe and the rest of the Anglo-Saxon world but not in the United States.

8. For what it is worth, the last novel I have read recently in the knowledge that it was an Oprah book club selection, Andre Dubus III's novel *House of Sand and Fog* (2000), was, I thought, quite literary enough. It did have one recognizably Oprahesque character, a female detective "in recovery" with whom one was clearly supposed to identify, but it also had the unlikely figure of an Iranian ex-member of the shah's private guard.

9. At least Oprah's capacity as a cultural authority did extend to the written word. The most melancholy reading in some time, despite (because of?) its studious pose of nonjudgmental benignity, is Michael Kammen's *American Culture, American Tastes,* which lists current American repositories of "cultural authority." For a start, there are essentially no writers: in the sixties there would at least have been a Norman Mailer, perhaps. But of the people who do get mentioned—Julia Child, Martha Stewart, and the like—Oprah Winfrey is perhaps the only one to have annexed the act of reading, if not writing, as part of her purview. (The lone luftmensch figure to have made the new "cut": Allan Bloom, of course [159–60].) More generally, though, Kammen does have a good point in claiming that increasingly in recent times cultural authority, which he calls "the capacity to bestow legitimacy or respectability upon a cultural custom or 'product,'" has been gradually supplanted by cultural power, which "involves the production, promotion, and dissemination of cultural artifacts" (133). This assessment of a milieu where the publicity apparatus of corporations, more than any guardians or cultivators of discrimination, is the engine of what people now think of as their culture seems to me depressingly accurate, though the good professor seems not depressed at all by it himself.

10. The *New York Observer* article entitled "When Oprah Stomped on Franzen, It Revealed a Vast Culture Split" by Gabriel Snyder details this pro-Oprah response, with comments such as this: "'When I ever even come close to voicing any sympathy [for Mr. Franzen], I am actually shouted down, . . .' said one New York editor. 'There seems to be a genuine siding in the literary community with Oprah. I don't think it's false.'" By contrast, though, a "New York book editor" who was asked "if anyone in the city actually respected Ms. Winfrey not as a sales rainmaker, but as a literary figure" replied: "'Not really. I think that's a fact—an uncomfortable fact, but a fact.'" Franzen's approach-avoidance problem seems to have been catching. Ironically, even Franzen's seemingly high-minded objection to appearing on Oprah Winfrey's broadcast may actually have arisen from concerns of demographic marketing: the article notes "Mr. Franzen's interview with Terry Gross on *Fresh Air,* where Mr. Franzen expressed concern that the Oprah selection may turn off male readers." But the greatest factor in the response, as always in this sphere of activity, may have been professional bitchiness. After all, no writer competes against Ms. Winfrey: "'Look, let me put it to you bluntly,' said an editor. 'The literary world runs on envy. The envy level in respect to Jonathan Franzen was already running at flood tide before *The Corrections* was selected by Oprah.'"

11. This analysis can be found in Huyssen's *After the Great Divide.*

12. I feel my own retrograde rhetoric even as I use the word *vulgarization,* which of course implies the sort of status hierarchy that has been, we are told, displaced under the regime of postmodernity and the media. John Seabrook's *Nobrow* defines the title word as existing in the new space of undifferentiated cultural signs, no one daring to be thought better, more authentic than any other. When his beloved *New Yorker* magazine is finally forced to give up its old building to join the Condé Nast publications on Times Square, Seabrook remarks, "To me, this was Nobrow—this building, here under my nose all along. This is what the world after

High-Low looks like. And it is all middle, I guess, though it doesn't look like the old middle [i.e., the world of middlebrow], because there's no more high and low to define it. . . . In Nobrow, everything becomes the same in the end. Times Square and SoHo become the same. The *New Yorker* and *Vanity Fair* [its new housemate] become the same. The Buzz abhors distinction." In the new building, Seabrook glumly glimpses "the exact midpoint at which culture and marketing converged" (211–13). So much for the place of Nobrow, although Seabrook is at pains to insist that every place (and no place) is that place, which I would call "plutopia." As for people who embody Nobrow, his interview with David Geffen says it all: "High Nobrow" (176–96).

13. Ironically, Franco Moretti's essay on mass culture in *Signs Taken for Wonders* entitled "From *The Waste Land* to the Artificial Paradise" (209–39), actually argues that utility is a concept that has been evacuated from that endeavor as well: "Mass culture's perennially uncertain and interminable semantics integrates with its fundamentally mytho-aesthetic character." He connects the "loss of all referential aim" in mass culture with "the proliferation of gadgets [which] has made it almost impossible to establish what is 'useful' and what is not, even in the field of everyday objects, let alone in the case of symbolic practices" (236). Insofar as this is true, it would be a melancholy fact for literature, which often puts forward its uselessness as a perverse sign of its sovereign indifference to the traffic of the world. Now, according to Moretti, the traffic is equally happy to be thought useless, or anyway to have an indeterminate use.

14. Gitlin has much of interest to say on the topic of the disposability of emotions in the media (see 41–42 and elsewhere). Defenders of the literary faith such as Sven Birkerts in his *Gutenberg Elegies* find as a result that much of their appeal must rest upon the very thing that media-fed masses claim they find least attractive about the literary: that it is time-consuming. Birkerts feels that art's identity as a "bride of silence and slow time" helps ensure that its emotions will be more authentic, less disposable, than those of TV.

15. One is caused to wonder idly what the master would have done when confronted with the prospect of appearing on TV. His biographer Leon Edel certainly did nothing to discourage Dick Cavett from having him on in the 1980s.

16. One lonely courageous exception is an article written by James Campbell. He points out that Franzen's own past words may have impelled him to act as he did. In 1996 Franzen wrote a piece for *Harper's* entitled "Perchance to Dream" which, as luck would have it, prophesied his own case. Says Campbell, "No doubt he recalled his own words of six years ago, that the evanescent glamour visited on the 'visible' author—'the money, the hype, the limo ride to a *Vogue* shoot'—was merely a consolation 'for no longer mattering to the culture.' . . . What seems to have taken almost everyone by surprise was that Franzen took his own part in this action seriously enough to stand by his word." One almost suspects Franzen of having courted this very result, confirming as it does his most dire analysis in his *Harper's* piece: that in a contest between a literary person and a TV celebrity over almost anything, the culture (very much including fellow literati) would plump unhesitatingly for the latter.

17. The middlebrow role of ambassadorship from literary to mass (and back) has a long and, on balance, glorious history, whose glories are revealed by Janice A. Radway's *A Feeling for Books* and by Rubin's *The Making of Middlebrow Culture*. The road to Oprah Station is well laid out in these two studies. As for Oprah herself as a tastemaker, Yardley gives her a backhanded compliment by in effect crediting Toni Morrison's mass-culture celebrity mainly to her: "With the possible exception of Toni Morrison, there is not a single American writer of literary fiction who could be called famous in the larger world of mass culture and celebrity— the way Fitzgerald was famous in the 1920s, Hemingway in the 1940s and 1950s—and her fame rests less on her work than on her Nobel Prize and promotion she has been given by Oprah Winfrey" (3).

18. John Ellis's *Visible Fictions* discusses the vital position of the segment and the series in chapter 7, "Broadcast TV as Cultural Form" (111–26). As the name might suggest, this chapter puts itself into polemical relation with Raymond Williams's pathbreaking book *Television: Technology and Cultural Form,* arguing that Williams's emphasis on flow of broadcasting overstates the importance of the *longue durée* of a given night's television viewing, as if it were comparable to the showing of a film: "His [Williams's] model is of cinema-style texts which appear in a context that reduces their separation one from another. In doing so, he underestimates the complexity of broadcast TV's particular commodity form, which has very little to do with the single text" (118). That commodity form indeed dictates the queer narrative space that TV, fictional or factual, tends to occupy as Ellis rehearses it. By the way, Ellis does not ascribe this segmentation of television primarily to advertising: "It is not only a characteristic of those TV channels that carry advertisements: it has also become the standard form of TV construction for the BBC as well" (119).

19. Ellis, 147. Ellis points out in this regard the curious fact that episodes of a series end "with a kind of coda in which the basic relations between characters are affirmed outside of any narrative context [the better to have] the effect of reaffirming the stasis from which the next episode will depart" (125). Ellis reminds us as well of our general experience in watching a series that seldom do the events within one episode even recall those of previous episodes, let alone build their stories explicitly on them.

20. This concern of broadcasters was actually appealed to earlier this year when researchers made much of a study that seemed to indicate that too much sex and violence in broadcast entertainment made viewers forget the messages of the commercials. Of course, this assumes that advertisers want us to consciously recall their messages, which may not be always be the case.

21. Alfred Hitchcock, quoted in Paul Virilio, *The Vision Machine,* 65.

22. I think some of this bite-size narrative approach is what George Trow assumes in his *Within the Context of No Context,* where he speaks of television as a particularly adept means of developing what he calls "ad hoc contexts," or moments that simulate a context or "sense of home" for the viewer (73–74). Trow senses that the units within which fictional and factual TV realities exist are too small, have too little temporal extension, to be seen as myths or even narratives. Hence perhaps his great dictum: "The work of television is to establish false contexts and to chronicle the unraveling of existing contexts; finally, to establish the context of no-context and to chronicle it" (82).

23. Ellis, 145.

24. Ibid., 128.

25. Ibid., 162.

26. There are of course times when the content breaks through, as on September 11. If it had not already been evident to people that a significant event had occurred, the fact that networks stopped selling things for many hours would in itself have been a powerful indicator of that significance.

27. Ellis records the frustration of being in a demonstration that is later televised: "the position to which you are recruited as TV viewer, one of sceptical non-involvement . . . subtly reinforces the detachment and isolation of the TV viewer, inviting dismissal of the event as less important than it considered itself to be" (166). On TV's relentless exploitation of a certain low level of irony, and even its use of the viewer's hostility toward it, the best analysis remains Mark Crispin Miller's essay "Big Brother Is You, Watching" (309–31), in his *Boxed In.* Musing on excessive irony—in a suitably ironic vein, of course—is seemingly everywhere. Typical is this passage from Arthur Phillips's novel *Prague,* in which a character named Tibor, a Hungarian who is taking an English-language class from one of the Americans central to the story,

gets off this summary of the United States in its crisis of no crisis: "'American culture lies fallow now. There is nothing living, only things waiting. And the earth gives off only a smell. This smell, not pleasant, is irony'" (55).

28. Williams evokes this strange status of TV as referring above all to itself when he insists that it is a system whose point is "transmission and reception as abstract processes, with little or no definition of preceding content" (25). In other words, the pipeline is far more important in the scheme of things than anything put through it. The sense we have that they will put almost anything on television, desperate as they are to keep filled the gaping maw, flows from this primary fact.

29. Trow for one sees a clear link between the domination of television, whose sole and all but announced purpose is to keep people in place to be sold things, and the decline in the appetite and now even the memory for anything serious. He defines it in the *Context* book as a "certain ability to transmit and receive and then to apply layers of affection and longing and doubt" (59). Trow seems to have intuited, in other words, what Williams analyzes at more length: that transmission and reception are functions that supervene any determinate content or purpose beyond themselves in the case of the mass media. Perhaps Trow's book could have been titled *Within the Context of No Content* and conveyed the same sense.

30. To boot, we have to remember that even Roger Straus had to "sell out" to the Georg von Holtzbrinck Publishing Group from Stuttgart, Germany. See the profile of Straus by Ian Parker called "Showboat." We are assured that nothing has really changed: "It's the takeover that never happened," says one of his friends (65). Be that as it may, it did happen, although the article implies that had his son agreed to succeed him it probably would not have.

31. Schiffrin points out that the U.S. book title output per annum stands now at about 70,000, adding cruelly that Britain, "which has one-fifth of America's population," publishes roughly the same number (7).

32. Schiffrin is again a worthy informant, especially chilling in one anecdote about an anti-censorship group called the Freedom to Read Committee formed by the American Association of Publishers, part of whose job was to shore up the public reputations of publishers, which had lowered as consciousness was raised about who was now running these concerns. Of particular worry were libel suits, which were increasingly being found for the plaintiff, often to a pricey tune. The staff from "one of New York's leading law firms" addressed one of the publishers' meetings, telling them that if lawyers could honestly tell jurors that these houses were "eager to publish books that expressed important ideas," some First Amendment cachet could be impressed upon them in their deliberations. "Looking at the forty or so of us who represented most of the major houses in New York, the lawyers asked, 'Can we assure jurors in the future that if an important book comes along you will publish it?' Not a hand was raised. No one seemed aware of the irony that the publishing industry's own anticensorship committee was itself part of the new market censorship." The attorneys, nonplussed, pressed the group that surely "publishers must occasionally take on a book pro bono. . . . 'Only inadvertently,' answered the chair of the group, bringing a wave of relieved laughter" (129–30). Among the things this laughter covered was the fact that the people currently running the nation's publishing houses had exhibited enough mercenary single-mindedness to shock even lawyers.

33. Trow's *My Pilgrim's Progress* treats this development in the passage from the social configuration of the United States at mid-century to the present. He divides the ethos of the ruling classes into the Roosevelt model, which tended still to dominate at mid-century, and that of the Vanderbilts: the former a noblesse oblige ethos and the latter Trow's model of wealth without responsibility, for which Ronald Reagan was a kind of annunciation angel. Indeed, Trow's epilogue is entitled "The Vanderbilts Won" (261).

34. See Thomas Frank, *One Market under God*, which defines "market populism" as a belief

in the legitimacy of "democracy and popular consent as revealed by the mediums of exchange" (179).

35. Frank argues that even the cultural studies movement within the university, from which he himself seems to hail, ends up collaborating with the forces of corporate dumbing down, for all its insistence on its leftist slant. The kind of egalitarianism they put forward, together with the reassuring stress on "audience agency" to avert any charge of manipulation, does not sound much different from the sort of arguments network executives make in defending the latest programs they send out to defile our living rooms, on the ever rarer occasions when they are required to defend them. See chapter 8 in *One Market under God,* "New Consensus for Old" (276–306).

36. Frank is especially good on the use of the French as villain here. Conveniently, the nation in question manages to be hated both for being impossibly highbrow and disdainful toward America and also for resisting the enlightenment of the so-called "American model" of capitalism shorn of all the "decency" elements that make France's welfare state such a drag on profitability. See *One Market under God,* 73–78. On a personal note, it does me good to see unsympathetic scrutiny of Roger Cohen's numerous tendentious stories on France for the *New York Times,* an egregious case of "reporting that seemed designed less to get at the essence of a country's politics than to spin a morality tale for readers back home" (78). By the way, Tony Judt in the *New York Review of Books* points out that one of the sturdiest pillars of that morality edifice, the allegedly lower productivity rate of the French as compared to the Americans, is not accurate. France had higher productivity last year in man-hours, the essential measurement, than did the United States, even though the U.S. per capita productivity outstripped that of France "in gross terms," because more Americans are forced to work, do so for longer hours, and contribute less in taxes.

37. Frank has so much on this phenomenon—the dot-com millionaire with the nose ring and the tattoos, the Republican congressman who lets it be known that Bono rocks his world—that I am tempted to cite his book passim. But I'm even more tempted to cite my favorite anecdote from his book despite its length, for it shows the Möbius strip that can result from the never-ending search for something authentic to attach to one's commodity. His chapter 7, "The Brand and the Intellectuals" (252–75), treats Frank's attendance at a couple of conferences of the growing field of "account planning," which gathers "ethnographic" data on how best to merchandise or "brand" a given product for a given demographic group. (Their enemy, of course, is Generation X's notorious "cynicism," by which they mean resistance to advertising.) One pair of planners for Nike, Pamela Scott and Diana Kapp, were among those with the task of retrieving Nike's tarnished 1997 reputation, sinking under tales of sweatshops and cultic suicide. The planners decided on a "sport as distant as possible from Nike's traditional advertising approach," settling on "women's basketball" as still seeming authentic. They "embarked on an ethnographic fact-finding tour" of various clubs across the South and elsewhere and shared the tapes of "unselfconscious laughter" and the "Dorothea Lange"–type pictures they acquired. But since "high school league rules forbade the agency to use an actual high school team," they then proceeded to invent "a replica team to reenact the love of sport" the women had seen on tour. This was done step-by-step, including a name ("the Charlestown Cougars"), time at basketball camp to build sisterhood, and so on: "we [in the conference audience] watched the intentionally low-budget-looking commercials that documented the Cougars' arduous, unsung way to fictitious championhood." Apparently many viewers fell for the commercials, "website hits and plaintive messages from real-life high school girls" figuring in the evidence. But, in the final turn of the "authenticity" screw, Scott and Kapp did not rejoice in their deceit. Rather, they chose to see their ads as not just about "Nike sales" but also about "raising consciousness" by building

"role models for young girls." This call to authenticity brought an ecstatic response from the account planners in attendance, according to Frank (270–72). A story such as this makes it impossible for the reader to tell where fooling others and kidding oneself take leave of each other, if anywhere. What one can conclude is that, for those in advertising, anyway, authenticity has nothing to do with telling the truth.

38. In this connection, Seabrook's book is instructive. His account of the new ways of culture introduced by the eighties and nineties has many items of consumption discussed, from tomatoes and T-shirts to furniture and recordings. Nowhere are books treated in any detail as an aspect of cultural life nowadays. It is as if "reading" had become the deciphering of hidden cues in the iconography of clothing or speech, rather than, well, reading. In a world where no brows are needed, evidently no reading glasses are required either.

39. Media critic and inveterate crank Neil Postman has once again gotten to the point with bleak precision: "Entertainment is the supra-ideology of all discourse on television. No matter what is depicted or from what point of view, the overarching presumption is that it is there for our amusement and pleasure. That is why even on news shows which provide us daily with fragments of tragedy and barbarism, we are urged by the newscasters to 'join them tomorrow.' What for? . . . We accept the newscasters' invitation because we know that the 'news' is not to be taken seriously, that it is all in fun, so to say" (87). If this attitude is true of news, how much truer must it be of fiction.

40. See Don DeLillo, "In the Ruins of the Future." DeLillo himself seems aware that parsing the reverberations of this unexampled event may be before the fact: "The writer wants to understand what this day has done to us. Is it too soon?" He goes on to imply that it probably isn't: "In its desertion of every basis for comparison, the event asserts its singularity. . . . The writer tries to give memory, tenderness, and meaning to all that howling space." The governing conceit of the DeLillo article, as the title would suggest, is that September 11 has altered America's customarily progressivist view of the future: "For many people, the event has changed the grain of the most routine moment. . . . This time we are trying to name the future, not in our normally hopeful way but guided by dread" (39). And who must guide us in this unfamiliar territory, yet to be mythicized? The writer. Thus do bad days for the routine stories of the culture sometimes result in renewed work for writers, in the recrafting of the nation's myths.

41. Still, DeLillo's capacity as prophet is not meager. A recent edition of the *New York Times* brings an article by Maureen Dowd called "Swastikas for Sweeps," discussing plans for a new TV miniseries on the young Adolf Hitler. The kitschy exploitation of the one European twentieth-century figure to make it into the masscult pantheon continues apace, as DeLillo warns us.

42. See Thomas Frank, "Dark Age," 274.

Bibliography

Adorno, Theodor. *Negative Dialectics.* Translated by E. B. Ashton. New York: Seabury Press, 1973.

Amis, Martin. *The Information.* London: HarperCollins, 1995.

Andreach, Robert. "Nathanael West's *Miss Lonelyhearts:* Between the Dead Pan and the Unborn Christ." In *Twentieth-Century Interpretations of "Miss Lonelyhearts,"* edited by Thomas H. Jackson, 49–60. Englewood Cliffs, N.J.: Prentice-Hall, 1971.

Anesko, Michael. *"Friction with the Market": Henry James and the Profession of Authorship.* New York: Oxford University Press, 1986.

Appel, Alfred Jr. *Nabokov's Dark Cinema.* New York: Oxford University Press, 1979.

Auden, W. H. "West's Disease." In *"The Dyer's Hand" and Other Essays,* 241–42, New York: Random House, 1962.

Bader, Julia. *The Crystal Land: Artifice in Nabokov's English Novels.* Berkeley: University of California Press, 1972.

Balzac, Honoré de. *Lost Illusions.* Translated by Herbert J. Hunt. Harmondsworth, England: Penguin, 1971.

Barnard, Rita. *The Great Depression and the Culture of Abundance: Kenneth Fearing, Nathanael West, and Mass Culture of the 1930s.* Cambridge: Cambridge University Press, 1995.

Barthes, Roland. *S/Z.* Translated by Richard Howard. New York: Hill and Wang, 1970.

Barzun, Jacques. "The Tenth Muse." *Harper's,* September 2001, 73–80.

Bataille, Georges. "The Sacred." In *Visions of Excess: Selected Writings, 1927–1939,* edited and translated by Allan Stoekl, 240–45. Minneapolis: University of Minnesota Press, 1985.

Baudrillard, Jean. *For a Critique of the Political Economy of the Sign.* Translated by Charles Levin. St. Louis: Telos Press, 1981.

Bell, Michael. "*Lolita* and Pure Art." *Nabokov's "Lolita,"* edited by Harold Bloom, 69–80. New York: Chelsea House, 1987.

Benjamin, Walter. "The Work of Art in the Age of Mechanical Reproduction." In *Illuminations,* edited by Hannah Arendt, translated by Harry Zohn, 217–51. York: Schocken, 1969.

Birkirts, Sven. *The Gutenberg Elegies: The Fate of Reading in an Electronic Age.* Boston: Faber and Faber, 1994.

Bloom, Harold, ed. *Thomas Pynchon.* New York: Chelsea House, 1986.

———. *Vladimir Nabokov.* New York: Chelsea House, 1987.

———. *Vladimir Nabokov's "Lolita."* New York : Chelsea House, 1987.

Boorstin, Daniel J. *The Image: or, What Happened to the American Dream.* New York: Harper and Row, 1964.

Bourdieu, Pierre. *The Rules of Art: Genesis and Structure of the Literary Field.* Translated by Susan Emanuel. Stanford, Calif.: Stanford University Press, 1996.

Boyd, Brian. *Vladimir Nabokov: The American Years.* Princeton, N.J.: Princeton University Press, 1991.

Branca, Cornel. "Don DeLillo's *White Noise:* The Natural Language of the Species." In *"White Noise": Text and Criticism,* edited by Joel Osteen, 456–79. New York: Penguin, 1998.

Brodeur, Paul. *Currents of Death: Power Lines, Computer Terminals, and the Attempt to Cover Up Their Threat to Your Health.* New York: Simon and Schuster, 1989.

Bruss, Elizabeth W. "Vladimir Nabokov: Illusions of Reality and the Reality of Illusions." In *Vladimir Nabokov,* edited by Harold Bloom, 27–64. New York: Chelsea House, 1987.

Campbell, Colin. *The Romantic Ethic and the Spirit of Modern Consumerism.* Oxford: Blackwell, 1987.

Campbell, James. "High Art in the Age of Oprah." *Boston Review* 27 (2002), no. 2. <bostonreview.mit.edu/BR27.2/campbell.html>

Chapman, Sara S. *Henry James's Portrait of the Writer as Hero.* Basingstoke, England: Macmillan, 1990.

Charvat, William. *The Profession of Authorship in America, 1800–1870.* Edited by Matthew J. Bruccoli. Columbus: Ohio State University Press, 1968.

Comerchero, Victor. *Nathanael West: The Ironic Prophet.* Syracuse, N.Y.: Syracuse University Press, 1964.

Connolly, Julian W. *Nabokov and His Fictions: New Perspectives.* Cambridge: Cambridge University Press, 1999.

Cornis-Pope, Marcel. *Narrative Innovation and Cultural Rewriting in the Cold War and After.* New York: Palgrave, 2001.

Cowart, David. *Thomas Pynchon: The Art of Allusion.* Carbondale: Southern Illinois University Press, 1980.

Crary, Jonathan. *Suspensions of Perception: Attention, Spectacle, and Modern Culture.* Cambridge, Mass.: MIT Press, 1999.

DeCurtis, Anthony. "'An Outsider in This Society': An Interview with Don DeLillo." In *Introducing Don DeLillo,* edited by Frank Lentricchia, 443–66. Durham, N.C.: Duke University Press, 1991.

DeLillo, Don. "In the Ruins of the Future." *Harpers,* December, 2001, 33–40.

———. *Mao II.* New York: Viking, 1991.

———. *White Noise.* New York: Viking Penguin, 1985.

Douglas, Ann. *Terrible Honesty: Mongrel Manhattan in the 1920s.* New York: Farrar, Straus, 1995.

Dowd, Maureen. "Swastikas for Sweeps." *New York Times,* July 17, 2002, A23.

Duvall, John N. "The (Super)marketplace of Images: Television as Unmediated Mediation in DeLillo's *White Noise.*" In *White Noise,* edited by Joel Osteen, 432–55. New York: Penguin, 1998.

Edel, Leon. *Life of Henry James: The Middle Years, 1882–1895.* New York: Avon, 1978.

———. *Life of Henry James: The Treacherous Years, 1895–1901.* New York: Avon, 1969.

Edenbaum, Robert I. "To Kill God and Build a Church." In *Twentieth-Century Interpretations of "Miss Lonelyhearts,"* edited by Thomas H. Jackson, 61–69. Englewood Cliffs, N.J.: Prentice-Hall, 1971.

Eisenstein, Elizabeth L. *The Printing Revolution in Early Modern Europe.* Cambridge: Cambridge University Press, 1983.

Eliot, T. S. *Notes towards the Definition of Culture.* London: Faber and Faber, 1948.

Ellis, John. *Visible Fictions: Cinema, Television, Video.* Rev. ed. London: Routledge, 1992.

Ewen, Stuart. *PR!* New York: Basic, 1996.

Ferraro, Thomas J. "Whole Families Shopping at Night!" In *Introducing Don DeLillo,* edited by Frank Lentricchia, 15–38. Durham, N.C.: Duke University Press, 1991.

Field, Andrew. *VN: The Life and Art of Vladimir Nabokov.* New York: Crown, 1986.

Fine, David, ed. *Los Angeles in Fiction.* Albuquerque: University of New Mexico Press, 1984.

Fiske, John. *Television Culture.* London: Methuen, 1987.

Flaubert, Gustave. *Oeuvres complètes.* 2 vols. Paris: Seuil, 1964.

Foster, John Burt Jr. "Poshlust, Culture Criticism, Adorno, and Malraux." In *Nabokov and His Fictions: New Perspectives,* edited by Julian W. Connolly, 216–35. Cambridge: Cambridge University Press, 1999.

Frank, Thomas. "Dark Age." In *Commodify Your Dissent,* edited by Thomas Frank and Matt Weiland, 255–74. New York: Norton, 1997.

———. *One Market under God: Extreme Capitalism, Market Populism, and the End of Economic Democracy.* New York: Doubleday, 2000.

Friedman, Jonathan. *Professions of Taste: Henry James, British Aestheticism, and Commodity Culture.* Stanford, Calif.: Stanford University Press, 1990.

Frosch, Thomas R. "Parody and Authenticity in *Lolita.*" In *Vladimir Nabokov,* edited by Harold Bloom, 127–42. New York: Chelsea House, 1987.

Frow, John. "Notes on *White Noise.*" *South Atlantic Quarterly* 89 (spring 1990): 413–29.

Fussell, Edwin. *The Catholic Side of Henry James.* Cambridge: Cambridge University Press, 1993.

Gehman, Richard B. Introduction to *Day of the Locust,* by Nathanael West. New York: New Directions, 1950.

"'A Gentle Chill, An Ambiguity': *The Crying of Lot 49.*" In *Critical Essays on Thomas Pynchon,* edited by Richard Pearce, 51–68. Boston: G.K. Hall, 1981).

Gilmore, Michael. *American Romanticism and the Marketplace.* Chicago: University of Chicago Press, 1985.

Gitlin, Todd. *Media Unlimited: How the Torrent of Images and Sounds Overwhelms Our Lives.* New York: Metropolitan, 2002.

Green, Martin. "Tolstoy and Nabokov: The Morality of *Lolita.*" In *Vladimir Nabokov's "Lolita,"* edited by Harold Bloom, 13–33. New York: Chelsea House, 1987.

Habegger, Alfred. *Henry James and the "Woman Business."* Cambridge: Cambridge University Press, 1989.

Habermas, Jürgen. *The Structural Transformation of the Public Sphere.* Translated by Thomas Burger. Cambridge, Mass.: MIT Press, 1989.

Henrickson, Bruce. "Functions of Women in the Art Tales of Henry James." In *Questioning the Master: Gender and Sexuality in Henry James's Writings,* edited by Peggy McCormack, 68–85. Newark: University of Delaware Press, 2000.

Hite, Molly. *Ideas of Order in the Novels of Thomas Pynchon.* Columbus: Ohio State University Press, 1983.

Horkheimer, Max, and Theodor Adorno. *The Dialectic of Enlightenment.* Translated by John Cumming. New York: Continuum, 1986.

Huyssen, Andreas. *After the Great Divide: Modernism, Mass Culture, Postmodernism.* Bloomington: Indiana University Press, 1986.

Hyman, Stanley Edgar. *Nathanael West.* Minneapolis: University of Minnesota Press, 1962.

Jackson, Thomas H., ed. *Twentieth-Century Interpretations of "Miss Lonelyhearts."* Englewood Cliffs, N.J.: Prentice-Hall, 1971.

Jacobson, Marcia. *Henry James and the Mass Market.* University: University of Alabama Press, 1983.

James, Henry. *The Complete Notebooks of Henry James.* Edited by Leon Edel and Lyall H. Powers. New York: Oxford University Press, 1987.

———. *The Complete Tales of Henry James.* Vol. 7. Edited by Leon Edel. London: Rupert Hart-Davis, 1963.

———. *The Complete Tales of Henry James.* Vol. 9. Edited by Leon Edel. London: Rupert Hart-Davis, 1964.

―――. *"The Figure in the Carpet" and Other Stories*. Edited by Frank Kermode. Harmondsworth, England: Penguin, 1986.

Jolly, Roslyn. *Henry James: History, Narrative, Fiction*. Oxford: Clarendon Press, 1993.

Judt, Tony. "Its Own Worst Enemy." *New York Review of Books*, August 15, 2002, 12–16.

Kammen, Michael. *American Culture, American Tastes*. New York: Knopf, 1999.

Kaplan, Fred. *Henry James: The Imagination of Genius*. New York: William Morrow, 1992.

Kappeler, Susanne. *Writing and Reading in Henry James*. London: Macmillan, 1980.

Kharpertian, Theodore D. *A Hand to Turn the Time: The Menippean Satires of Thomas Pynchon*. Rutherford, N.J.: Farleigh Dickinson, 1990.

Kim, Daniel Won-gu. "Shining Page." In *"The Finer Thread, the Tighter Weave": Essays on the Short Fiction of Henry James,* 105–16. West Lafayette, Ind.: Purdue University Press, 2001.

Leach, William. *Land of Desire: Merchants, Power, and the Rise of a New America*. New York: Pantheon, 1993.

Lears, T. J. Jackson. *No Place of Grace: Antimodernism and the Transformation of American Culture, 1880–1920*. New York: Pantheon, 1981.

LeClair, Tom. *In the Loop: Don DeLillo and the Systems Novel*. Chicago: University of Illinois Press, 1987.

Lentricchia, Frank. "American Writer as Bad Citizen." In *Introducing Don DeLillo*, edited by Frank Lentricchia, 1–6. Durham, N.C.: Duke University Press, 1991.

―――, ed. *Introducing Don DeLillo*. Durham, N.C.: Duke University Press, 1991.

Lewis, R. W. B. *The Jameses: A Family Narrative*. New York: Farrar, Straus, 1991.

Locklin, Gerald. "The Day of the Painter; the Death of the Cock." In *Los Angeles in Fiction,* edited by David Fine. Albuquerque: University of New Mexico Press, 1984.

Lyotard, Jean-François. *The Postmodern Condition: A Report on Knowledge*. Translated by Geoff Bennington. Minneapolis: University of Minnesota Press, 1984.

Macdonald, Dwight. *Against the American Grain: Essays on the Effects of Mass Culture*. New York: Random House, 1962.

Mackey, Louis. "Thomas Pynchon and the American Dream." *Pynchon Notes* 14 (February 1984): 7–22.

Madden, David, ed. *Nathanael West: The Cheaters and the Cheated*. Deland, Fla..: Everett/Edwards, 1973.

Martin, Henry-Jean. *The History and Power of Writing*. Translated by Lydia G. Cochrane. Chicago: University of Chicago Press, 1994.

Martin, Jay. *Nathanael West: The Art of His Life*. New York: Carroll and Graf, 1984.

―――. *Who Am I This Time? Uncovering the Fictive Personality*. New York: Norton, 1988.

Martin, Jay, ed. *Nathanael West: A Collection of Critical Essays*. Englewood Cliffs, N.J.: Prentice-Hall, 1971.

McCormack, Betty, ed. *Questioning the Master: Gender and Sexuality in Henry James's Writings*. Newark: University of Delaware Press, 2000.

McHale, Brian. *Constructing Postmodernism*. London: Routledge, 1992.

McKeon, Michael. *The Origins of the English Novel, 1600–1740*. Baltimore: Johns Hopkins University Press, 1987.

Mendelson, Edward. "The Sacred, the Profane, and *The Crying of Lot 49*." In *Pynchon: A Collection of Critical Essays,* edited by Edward Mendelson, 112–46. Englewood Cliffs, N.J.: Prentice-Hall, 1978.

Miller, Mark Crispin. *Boxed In: The Culture of TV*. Evanston, Ill.: Northwestern University Press, 1988.

Mitroff, Ian I., and Warren Bennis. *The Unreality Industry: The Deliberate Manufacturing of Falsehood and What It Is Doing to Our Lives*. New York: Oxford University Press, 1993.

Moretti, Franco. *Signs Taken for Wonders*. Translated by Susan Fischer et al. London: Verso, 1983.

Moynahan, Julian. *Vladimir Nabokov*. Minneapolis: University of Minnesota Press, 1971.

Mulvey, Laura. "Visual Pleasure and Narrative Cinema." *Screen* 16, no. 3 (fall 1975).

Nabokov, Vladimir. *The Annotated "Lolita."* Edited by Alfred Appel Jr. New York: McGraw Hill, 1970.

———. *Lolita*. New York: Vintage, 1989.

Ohmann, Richard. *Selling Culture: Magazines, Markets, and Class at the Turn of the Century*. New York: Verso, 1996.

Olsen, Lance. *"Lolita": A Janus Text*. New York: Twayne, 1995.

Ong, Walter J. *Rhetoric, Romance, and Technology*. Ithaca, N.Y.: Cornell University Press, 1971.

Osteen, Joel, ed. *"White Noise": Text and Criticism*. New York: Viking Penguin, 1998.

Page, Norman, ed. *Nabokov: The Critical Heritage*. London: Routledge and Kegan Paul, 1982.

Parker, Ian. "Showboat." *New Yorker*, April 8, 2002, 55–65.

Pearce, Richard, ed. *Critical Essays on Thomas Pynchon*. Boston: G. K. Hall, 1981.

Phillips, Arthur. *Prague*. New York: Random House, 2002.

Poovey, Mary. *The Proper Lady and the Woman Writer: Ideology as Style in the Works of Mary Wollstonecraft, Mary Shelley, and Jane Austen*. Chicago: University of Chicago Press, 1984.

Posnock, Ross. *The Trial of Curiosity: Henry James, William James, and the Challenge of Modernity*. New York: Oxford University Press, 1991.

Postman, Neil. *Amusing Ourselves to Death: Public Discourse in the Age of Show Business*. Harmondsworth, England: Penguin, 1985.

Profit, Marie-Claude. "The Rhetoric of Death in *The Crying of Lot 49*." *Pynchon Notes* 10 (October 1982): 18–36.

Prose, Francine. *Blue Angel*. New York: HarperCollins, 2000.

Pynchon, Thomas. *The Crying of Lot 49*. New York: Harper and Row, 1965.

Quilligan, Maureen. "Thomas Pynchon and the Language of Allegory." In *Critical Essays on Thomas Pynchon*, edited by Richard Pearce, 187–212. Boston: G. K. Hall, 1981.

Radway, Janice A. *A Feeling for Books: The Book-of-the-Month Club, Literary Taste, and Middle-Class Desire*. Chapel Hill: University of North Carolina Press, 1997.

Rampton, David. *Vladimir Nabokov*. Cambridge: Cambridge University Press, 1984.

Reid, Randall. *The Fiction of Nathanael West*. Chicago: University of Chicago Press, 1967.

Robinson, Douglas. *American Apocalypses: The Image of the End of the World in American Literature*. Baltimore: Johns Hopkins University Press, 1985.

Rorty, Richard. *Contingency, Irony, and Solidarity*. Cambridge: Cambridge University Press, 1989.

Rubin, Joan Shelley. *The Making of Middlebrow Culture*. Chapel Hill: University of North Carolina Press, 1992.

Saltzman, Arthur M. "The Figure in the Static: *White Noise*." In *"White Noise": Text and Criticism*, edited by Mark Osteen, 480–97. New York: Viking Penguin, 1998.

Schaub, Thomas. "'A Gentle Chill, and Ambiguity': The Crying of Lot 49." In *Critical Essays on Thomas Pynchon*, edited by Richard Pearce. Boston: G. K. Hall and Co., 1981.

Schiffrin, André. *The Business of Books*. London: Verso, 2000.

Seabrook, John. *Nobrow: The Culture of Marketing and the Marketing of Culture*. New York: Knopf, 2000.

Sennett, Richard. *The Fall of Public Man*. New York: Vintage, 1978.

Snyder, Gabriel. "When Oprah Stomped on Franzen, It Revealed a Vast Culture Split." *New York Observer,* November 5, 2001, 1.

Strychacz, Thomas. *Modernism, Mass Culture, and Professionalism.* Cambridge: Cambridge University Press, 1993.

Tanner, Tony. "*The Crying of Lot 49.*" In *Thomas Pynchon,* edited by Harold Bloom, 175–89. New York: Chelsea House, 1986.

Tekiner, Christina. "Time in *Lolita.*" *Modern Fiction Studies* 25 (autumn 1979): 463–69.

Todorov, Tvzetan. *The Poetics of Prose.* Translated by Richard Howard. Ithaca, N.Y.: Cornell University Press, 1977.

Torchiana, Donald T. "The Painter's Eye." In *Nathanael West: The Cheaters and the Cheated,* edited by David Madden, 249–82. DeLand, Fla.: Everett/Edwards, 1973.

Trilling, Lionel. "The Last Lover: Vladimir Nabokov's *Lolita.*" In *Vladimir Nabokov's "Lolita,"* edited by Harold Bloom, 5–11. New York: Chelsea House, 1987.

Trow, George W. S. *My Pilgrim's Progress: Media Studies, 1950–1997.* New York: Pantheon, 1999.

———. *Within the Context of No Context.* New York: Atlantic Monthly, 1997.

Veitch, Jonathan. *American Superrealism: Nathanael West and the Politics of Representation in the 1930s.* Madison: University of Wisconsin Press, 1997.

Virilio, Paul. *The Vision Machine.* Bloomington: Indiana University Press, 1994.

Volpe, Edmond L. "The Waste Land of Nathanael West." In *Twentieth-Century Interpretations of "Miss Lonelyhearts,"* edited by Thomas H. Jackson, 81–92. Englewood Cliffs, N.J.: Prentice-Hall, 1971.

Wells, Walter. *Tycoons and Locusts: A Regional Look at Hollywood Fiction of the 1930s.* Carbondale: Southern Illinois University Press, 1962.

West, Nathanael. *"Miss Lonelyhearts" and "The Day of the Locust."* New York: New Directions, 1969.

———. "Some Notes on *Miss L.*" In *Nathanael West: A Collection of Critical Essays,* edited by Jay Martin, 66–67. Englewood Cliffs, N.J.: Prentice-Hall, 1971.

White, Allon. *The Uses of Obscurity: The Fiction of Early Modernism.* London: Routledge and Kegan Paul, 1981.

White, Edmund. "Nabokov's Passion." In *Vladimir Nabokov,* edited by Harold Bloom, 209–22. New York: Chelsea House, 1987.

Williams, Raymond. *Television: Technology and Cultural Form.* New York: Schocken, 1975.

Wilson, Christopher P. *The Labor of Words: Literary Professionalism in the Progressive Era.* Athens: University of Georgia Press, 1985.

Woodmansee, Martha. *The Author, Art, and the Market: Rereading the History of Aesthetics.* New York: Columbia University Press, 1994.

Yardley, Jonathan. "State of the Art." *Washington Post Book World,* July 14–20, 2002, 1–3.

Zboray, Ronald J. "Antebellum Reading and the Ironies of Technological Innovation." In *Reading in America: Literature and Social History,* edited by Cathy Davidson, 180–200. Baltimore: Johns Hopkins University Press, 1989.

Index